CHRISTIAN PREACHERS

CHRISTIAN PREACHERS

NIGEL CLIFFORD

EVANGELICAL PRESS OF WALES

© Evangelical Press of Wales, 1994

First published 1994

ISBN 1 85049 114 3

Cover design by Digby Williams

Published by the Evangelical Press of Wales
Bryntirion, Bridgend, Mid Glam. CF31 4DX
Printed in Wales by D. Brown & Sons Ltd, Bridgend

CONTENTS

ILLUSTRATIONS

1
John Chrysostom
(c.347-407)

Chrysostom was the surname given to John by succeeding generations and means 'golden-mouthed'. This apt description draws attention to his peculiar talent, for he stood well above all the early church leaders as an eloquent preacher. Had he not become a Christian preacher he would have ranked among the finest Greek orators.

John was born in the city of Antioch in Syria in AD 347. His father, Secundus, was an officer in the Roman army, while his mother, Anthusa, was a devout Christian. His father died not long after his birth, leaving his mother a widow of twenty years. She never remarried but gave herself entirely to rearing her beloved son. Nothing else seemed to matter to her as long as he was well-cared. She gave him everything that could benefit him academically and spiritually, her devotion to him being not unlike that of Monica, Augustine's mother. Even his pagan teacher, Libanius, a famous professor of rhetoric, admired her virtues and remarked, 'Bless me! what wonderful women there are among the Christians.'

Originally he was trained to be an advocate at the courts of law. His education was the best available at the time and Libanius was much impressed by his intellectual ability and verbal proficiency. Of all his students Libanius considered John the best. As he lay dying, Libanius was asked who he would like to succeed him. 'John,' he replied, 'if only the Christians had not carried him away.'

Libanius had early tried to win Chrysostom to paganism by weaning him from his inherited Christianity. Owing to his mother's influence, and the spiritual instruction of Meletius, Bishop of Antioch at the time, John was kept from straying. For three years he was guided by Meletius in the study of the Christian faith, and then baptized and appointed a 'reader' in the church. This took place when he was twenty-three years of age. Though Libanius had failed to take

9

him from the church he did, however, succeed in developing his intellectual skills. He introduced John to the Greek classics, a study which fascinated him, and also had him memorize and recite large portions of them. In this way he was able to draw out the naturally reticent orator.

The prospects for Chrysostom as a legal advocate looked good. He possessed all the natural gifts to make a success of himself. At first he was 'a never-failing attendant at the courts of law, and passionately fond of the theatre', but his retiring disposition attracted him more to the cavern than the court. He increasingly desired to turn his back on his life as a lawyer, and dreamt of becoming a monk and leaving the city for the surrounding mountains and caves where all the truly devout monks lived. Had his mother not intervened he would have left his home for that hostile terrain. She pleaded with him not to leave her and deprive her of her sole comfort in life, and begged him not to make her a widow the second time. 'Wait at least till I die; perhaps I shall soon leave this world. When you have buried me and joined my ashes with those of your father, nothing will then prevent you from retiring into monastic life.'

For a time he continued to live at Antioch but the call to the hills became increasingly pressing. Eventually he gave in and sought the tranquillity of an ascetic life in a commune just a few miles from the city. Even before departing he had lived the life of an urban monk with his home as his sanctuary. He had maintained a strict diet, though his friends at court thought him odd. In his zeal he maintained a rigid silence to protect himself from slander. This gave the impression that he was an unsociable person. But nothing deterred him; even popular approval held little attraction for him.

The hardships of an ascetic life soon affected Chrysostom. After only a few years his health began to deteriorate and he was forced to return home to Antioch. But this monastic interlude in the hills was surely in God's providence, for during this time he had memorized huge portions of the Bible which helped prepare him for preaching.

In 381 at the age of 34 he was appointed a deacon in the church. This position allowed him to spend much of his time in writing. Later, in 386, he was ordained an elder or presbyter in the church by Flavian, successor to Miletius as bishop, an appointment which opened up a door to express his gift as a preacher.

When he preached his first sermon the congregation was electrified by his eloquence:

Some of those who were sitting rose from their seats, others were overcome with a kind of faintness, as if the preacher's mental force were sucking the life out of their bodies; and by the time the discourse came to an end, the great mass of that spellbound audience could only hold down their heads, and give vent to their emotions in tears. For a while at first, they looked at each other with glances of wondering delight, and clapped their hands in ecstasy; but the speaker, as if rather interrupted than gratified by these tokens of their admiration, rushed on and bore down their attempts at applause; and long before he was done, admiration gave way to such intense emotion, that they were no longer able to express their feelings in the customary form. In fact, the speaker was lost in the splendour and power of his speech. His hearers were past thinking of him, by the very force with which he turned their thoughts in upon themselves, and on the vital and almost visible truths with which he seized, filled, and mastered their minds. His person vanished, as it were, into a voice; and from the utter stillness that prevailed, it was like 'the voice of one crying in the wilderness,' and answered only by the sighing winds of the waste.

Preaching was central to the worship of the church in Antioch. There were no extras to embellish the service: no statues or music, just simple, unadulterated worship with the sermon as the focal point of it all. Unlike our services today, the preacher generally sat while the congregation stood. However, as Chrysostom warmed to his subject he would unconsciously rise to his feet as if carried away by a burst of emotion. If the preacher said anything striking the people would clap vigorously. Chrysostom, much to his credit, was often forced to reprove them for their excessive applause.

Although he was not the chief elder in the church, Chrysostom was undoubtedly its leading light. Flavian, the bishop, left the instruction of the church almost entirely in his hands. Seeing his great gifts, this wise old man took a back seat, allowing his young colleague a free hand to carry on the work.

And here in Antioch his work was cut out for him. Not only had he to contend with the enemies of the faith, he also was called upon to refute false views within the church, as well as rebuke lax and nominal Christians and, of course, establish the faithful. He preached

11

systematically, not from a script but spontaneously, and after much thought. His commentaries on Genesis, Psalms, the Gospels of Matthew and John, Acts, Paul's letters and Hebrews are series of sermons more than pure exegesis. He was a master of the art of preaching and these sermons, which were copied as they were delivered, reveal his distinctly practical bent. Though his sermons were soundly theological, his real strength was not in his theology but in his application of it. He had the ability to turn any text to some practical use, not by allegorizing, as the school of Origen taught, but by bringing out the literal, intended meaning. In this way he avoided the allegorical method, which tends to impose meaning on to the text instead of expounding it.

His preaching was not only practical but pointed. It was easy for some to take offence at his straight speaking. Whenever a Christian festival came around the church was always full of believers in name only. These were rather lax throughout the year and only attended the church at the festival services. One Easter Sunday he said to them:

> Today you are all filled with joy, and I alone am sad. For when I survey this Christian assembly, which may be compared to the great ocean, and contemplate the infinite resources of the Church, and then consider that the festival will no sooner have passed away than this multitude will vanish, I am sorely grieved that the Church, which hath begotten so many children, cannot rejoice in them at every celebration of divine service, but only on a festival. How great would be the spiritual exultation, how great the glory rendered to God, how great the benefit conferred on souls, could we behold at every performance of divine service the church and its enclosures thus crowded! Masters and pilots, when they traverse the deep, use their utmost endeavours to reach a haven; but we keep tossing on the open sea, overwhelmed by billows of earthly cares, haunting the forum and tribunals, but coming hither scarce once or twice in the year.

In his second year as presbyter there was a revolt in the city by an unruly element which threatened to bring upon its inhabitants the wrath of the Emperor, Theodosius. While the city continued to await its fate, Flavian the bishop took the initiative and went to Constantinople to plead with the Emperor on its behalf. Chrysostom was left in charge in his absence and called the people to prayer for the success of the Bishop's mission. He knew that the God of heaven controlled the hearts of kings and emperors alike. Fortunately, mercy was shown and the city was spared a terrible punishment which could well have followed.

This development gave Chrysostom an advantage over the people. The fear of impending doom quickly opened their ears to listen to the preacher. There was no longer a rejection of the message as the whole city seemed to be transformed. They clung to the gospel hope as the only thing worth having. The fruit of this panic situation remained for a long time after the danger had gone, which shows that what happened was not simply a reaction to a physical crisis, but real conversion.

For twelve years Chrysostom laboured in Antioch as preacher until his sudden call to the capital, Constantinople, in 398. This unsolicited call came at the command of Eutropius, a eunuch, who was the chief minister in the imperial court and possessed immense power. The move was probably motivated more by politics than principle, though Eutropius had previously heard Chrysostom and admired his eloquence.

To be Bishop of Constantinople held little real attraction for Chrysostom. Though others would have fought hard for it, he disdained it. This vacant seat had put the church into a furore. It was said that 'the whole ecclesiastical ant-hill was in motion; its industrious denizens rushing towards the tempting crumb which had come within their vision, and tumbling over each other in their eagerness to get at it'. But Chrysostom coveted peace more than power. His early days as a monk had left a great impression upon him. Above all, he feared the envy of his competitors. They craved high seats, long garments, important positions and human prestige. He foresaw that they would be constantly looking for ways and means of undermining him.

Reluctantly, he came to Constantinople. His departure from Antioch was very dramatic. Led secretly out of the city on some pretext, he was taken by the imperial officials post-haste by chariot from one city to the other. This unorthodox manner was employed to ensure that the people would not cause a commotion in the city because of his departure. It would not be wide of the mark to say that he was taken more as a prisoner than a presbyter or bishop to Constantinople.

His main concern on coming to this capital of the Eastern Roman

Empire arose from his knowledge of human nature. He knew that jealous eyes and greedy hands filled the imperial court. The separation of Church and State was often forgotten, or never considered, as court officials were sometimes appointed to positions of authority within the Church. Chrysostom possessed no ambitious tendencies but loved the simple things of life. At one time he even sold the precious utensils of the cathedral to ransom slaves. His daily life was free from all pomp and show. Though he could have lived sumptuously as Bishop of Constantinople, Chrysostom carried on his almost ascetic life within the episcopal palace. He preferred to give his money to the poor rather than hoard it away.

He set out to strengthen the Church within his new diocese, not only by refuting heresies such as Arianism (which teaches that Jesus is not the eternal Son of God), but also by giving positive scriptural teaching and applying it to the lives of his hearers in a most direct and fearless manner. His homilies on the lesser epistles of Paul belong to this period in Constantinople. As Bishop he was naturally involved in church politics, but he had also the time and energy to be concerned with the Gothic population in the city and its surrounding districts. He procured for them translations of portions of the Bible in their own language and engaged a Gothic presbyter to read and preach to them, and ordained and sent Gothic catechists and clergy to tribes on the banks of the Danube, as well as missionaries to tribes of nomadic Scythians.

Although Chrysostom's ministry was well-received at first, a gathering opposition soon made itself felt, chiefly from among many of the clergy whose lack of zeal and whose worldliness became highlighted by the untiring devotion and industry of their new bishop.

But his most bitter enemy was the Empress Eudoxia. She hated him. Not being accustomed to humble herself to anyone, as the most influential woman alive, her gnawing resentment towards Chrysostom was inflamed by a sermon he preached on the disorderliness of women. The Empress, thinking that some of the things he said were directed at her personally, took offence and complained to her husband, Arcadius. This was the beginning of the end for the outspoken bishop.

Another powerful enemy was the very man who had arranged his coming to Constantinople in the first place, Eutropius. He had systematically abused his position by accusing people as criminals and then taking their property and wealth for himself. In this way he had accumulated a vast fortune. He also had his own secret agents who informed him of anything he could use. Chrysostom, who had watched this development for many years, confronted him with his injustice and warned him of the consequence of his actions if he was found out. The haughty minister told him to see to his own affairs in the Church and leave his alone. When Eutropius finally overstretched himself, his descent was as quick as his ascent. Almost overnight, this despised man lost everything. The army of a Gothic general, Tribigild, was at the gate of the city threatening to sack it. The only thing which could appease him was the head of Eutropius. In an attempt to save himself Eutropius sought sanctuary in the cathedral. The enraged populace would have handed him over had not Chrysostom intervened. The following Sunday St Sophia's church was packed to capacity. The people had come out of curiosity to see what would become of the fallen minister. After listening to Chrysostom preach, the mass of people were broken down in tears. No longer was Eutropius a towering giant, threatening and fearsome, but a miserable little man, cowering and cringing for his very existence.

Chrysostom was quick to apply this opportunity to advantage. He used Eutropius as an example of the vanity of wealth and how quickly it can be lost:

> Where is the glory of this man? Where the halo of that light which surrounded him? Where the jubilee of the multitude who applauded him? Where the shouts with which he was received when he appeared in the theatre or at the racecourse? Gone— all gone! A sudden whirlwind has swept off the leaves and left the tree bare. The trunk stands forth naked and stricken to the roots. Where are all the friends who bowed down to him, who worshipped his greatness, and surrounded him with a cloud of incense? It was but a dream of the night; the morning has dawned, and the dream is dissolved. It has fled like a shadow; vanished like a vapour; burst like the empty bubble that it was! Oh, vanity of vanities, all is vanity.

Afterwards, Eutropius was given a reprieve with the forfeiture of all his goods and sent into permanent exile in Cyprus. However, like many in his position, he knew too much to stay alive and was later accused of using sacred horses on his chariot, a privilege enjoyed only by the Emperor, and was put to death.

Through this incident one of Chrysostom's most powerful enemies was defeated. However, the hatred of his arch-enemy, Eudoxia, remained undiluted. She was not prepared to let him go when the opportunity was afforded her to do him harm. Her pent-up hatred was about to be unleashed with particular cruelty.

Eudoxia found an ally in Theophilus, Bishop of Alexandria. Though he had ordained Chrysostom as Bishop of Constantinople, he had long cherished a dislike towards him. Together, they arranged his removal from office and banishment. Theophilus summoned a secret council of thirty-six bishops where Chrysostom was accused of treason and immorality. These trumped-up charges were enough to secure his downfall, especially as he refused to defend himself. When it became known that he had been banished for life the city was in uproar. They demanded the restoration of Chrysostom and were furious with Theophilus for his part in the whole affair. That night a huge earthquake shook the city. Eudoxia, terrified by what had happened, pleaded with the Emperor to bring Chrysostom back and appease God. When he returned, he was carried in triumph from the port through the city. But his victory was short-lived, for within a few months the evil Empress was again scheming.

Eudoxia, carried away with her position, erected a silver statue of herself outside the doors of St Sophia. This event was conducted with the normal revelry associated with such occasions, much to the disgust of the Bishop. When the day for the commemoration of John the Baptist's martyrdom came round, Chrysostom was particularly pointed in his allusions to similarities between his relationship with Eudoxia and that of John with Herodias. It was reported to her that he had said, 'Again Herodias is raging, again she is dancing, again she demands the head of John on a platter'. Whether or not it was true was immaterial; Eudoxia was incensed at it. She demanded of her husband that Chrysostom be exiled. This time the incarceration was more brutal than before. Soldiers entered the cathedral and dragged him off to prison during a baptismal service. Those in attendance were forced to flee for their lives. The city was again made dangerous for Chrysostom's supporters. Their houses were pillaged and they themselves were imprisoned.

In the year 404 Chrysostom left Constantinople for the last time. He was banished to Cucusus, a mountain village on the desolate northern frontiers of the empire, bordering Cilicia and Armenia. This cold and barren place intensified his suffering. He was no longer young, and age had brought with it its infirmities. But his resignation to his plight is shown in some 242 letters which have survived from that time, a correspondence which he kept up during the three years he was in exile in Cucusus. His main problem throughout this ordeal was not the severe cold but a sinking depression. His weakened constitution made him open to all kinds of despairing thoughts. But though the conflict was intense, he was never permanently defeated. He wrote to a friend: 'It is the nature of [divine] love not to be subdued by an accumulation of sufferings; but, like the flame, it forces its way through them all, and burns only with the greater intensity because of them.' And in a letter to his mother he describes his thoughts and spiritual condition in exile thus:

> I beg you to bear in mind that there is only one evil – sin. Power, reputation, glory among men, are all vanity. The way to heaven is through the deep sea of suffering. My intercourse with the holy Bishop of Cucusus has refreshed me not a little, so that I have become almost another man, and do not feel as if I were living in a strange place. I am encompassed by such a fulness of spiritual blessings, and my soul is so enriched and exalted, that I thank God without ceasing.

Meanwhile the Empress Eudoxia had died, but Chrysostom's enemies, disappointed with their attempts to quell his influence, persuaded Arcadius the Emperor to arrange to have him transferred even further afield. He was forbidden to write, and sent in 407 to Pityus on the Caucasus. This inhospitable place was considered the Siberia of its day. It was his last journey and should have taken three months on foot, but he never made it. As he and his guards passed through Pontus they came to a town called Comana where, it is said, he dreamt of his impending death. The following day, after walking only three miles, it became obvious to his guards that he was exhausted and could go no further. When they returned to Comana, he changed from his travelling clothes into his baptismal garments. These were white and reached down to the ground. He ordered bread and wine to be brought, consecrated them by Christ's own words and partook of his last communion in this world. Afterwards, he knelt down to pray and said, 'The Lord be praised for all things,' and peacefully died.

In an age fast moving towards a religious hierarchy, influenced more by power than prayer, Chrysostom remains a refreshing reminder of the power of true godliness. He was totally unaffected by worldly materialism or ecclesiastical grandeur, but lived a simple life according to his conscience.

But although he preferred the privacy of the closet to the publicity of the pulpit, it was as a truly great and eloquent preacher that he was known in his lifetime and to succeeding centuries. In Antioch, and later in Constantinople, he regularly addressed vast congregations, comprising all classes of people.

His was, no doubt, an eloquence that has rarely, if ever, been equalled. Florrid, ornate, impetuous and declamatory, it combined, at the same time, depth of thought, vivid conception, fertility of illustration, striking imagery, logically reasoned argument and profound learning . . . He would expose the latent excuses of the heart; lay bear the hypocrisy that lurked there; reveal to men secret sins and corrupt motives, of whose presence they were before almost unconscious, with the most marvellous power of mental dissection. Each one seemed to take the preacher's words as addressed especially to himself. (R.Wheler Bush, *St Chrysostom: His Life and Times*, p.111)

2
Augustine
(354-430)

Nobody before Luther has influenced the Church as much as Augustine. His writings were to become the bedrock of John Calvin's system. Strictly speaking Calvinism should be called Augustinianism, or better, Paulinism. Calvinism was not original to Calvin – he culled it from Paul and Augustine and gave it a more distinct profile.

Unlike our information on many other Church Fathers, that on Augustine is extremely detailed. His *Confessions,* written about AD 400, give a detailed account of what led him to become one valiant for the truth. He resisted the heresies and philosophies of his day to stand as *the* defender of the faith in the early Church, and his writings became its battering ram against their every stronghold. However, it is his spiritual pilgrimage and preaching which should concern us most.

His *Confessions*, directed to God and for his glory, reveal how his struggle to find inner peace ultimately led him back to a gospel that he had once openly ridiculed and rejected. His famous comment, 'Thou hast formed us for Thyself, and our hearts are restless till they find their rest in Thee', acts as a conclusion as well as an introduction to his testimony. To Augustine, it was the end of a long and winding road which he had trodden for many a weary year.

Augustine was born on 13 November 354, in Tagaste, Numidia, in Roman North Africa, of a mixed marriage. His father, Patricius, was an ill-tempered pagan, sometimes prone to drunkenness, but who nevertheless cared for his wife and family. His mother, Monica, was a Christian, born into and brought up in a Christian home. She stands out as a great Christian matriarch and her devotion, attachment and prayers for her wayward son are unquestioned.

Like most mixed marriages there was a conflict of interests, with Augustine standing in the midst of worldliness and godliness. Poor Monica had to endure opposition within the home, a trial which she bore meekly. Between Monica and her husband and mother-in-law, who lived with them, there was continual friction over her faith, but she was determined that Augustine would be brought up believing in the living God who gave his Son to redeem a sinful world. To this end she laboured and prayed continually, with the result that her husband and mother-in-law were also eventually won over to the gospel.

As a young teenager, Augustine was sent to Madaura, about six miles from his home, to study. There he rebelled against his teachers, and much preferred playing ball to preparing his lessons. All study became enforced, with threats and beatings. He did not mind studying Latin but hated anything Greek. It was not until later that he developed a thirst for knowledge.

Being away from home, Monica feared that her son would drift away from her instructions. While at home she had tried to instil her Christian beliefs into him, but it was many years before the seed would germinate and bear any fruit. Meanwhile, in Madaura, Augustine was learning more and more about the world. He attended the theatre, which was frowned upon by Christians, and studied the actors. Gradually, as the attraction of the world became stronger, he left behind him the childhood lessons of his mother.

When he eventually returned home at sixteen years of age, circumstances allowed Augustine to become idle. The changing fortunes of his parents meant he could not continue his education. By now, he was becoming independent and starting to assert himself. He did not like being subject to a petticoat government, and rebelled against it. As his father indulged him, so his mother's influence over him weakened. After hearing him speak, Patricius hoped that his son would one day become a great orator.

Not long after his return Augustine's father was converted. Monica was overjoyed. She had prayed for him ever since their marriage over sixteen years before. Sadly for her, no sooner had he made a profession of faith, than he became ill and died. Unfortunately, his influence over Augustine was pagan rather than Christian and the time was too short to be able to undo what he had already begun. The trend of Augustine's life had been set and it was too late to reverse it.

The resumption of his studies brought him to Carthage, the capital city of Roman North Africa, there to train for a career in law. This was made possible by the financial support of a rich relative,

Romanianus. Augustine was always grateful to him for his benevolence, though Augustine often wasted much of it. His life went from bad to worse when he took a concubine and became a father before his nineteenth birthday. He also continued attending the theatre and attracted much attention by his eloquence. Yet the applause could not deafen the cry within and the constant echo of his mother's voice and her early lessons.

About this time he was greatly influenced by Cicero's *Hortensius*, a treatise in praise of philosophy. As a result the development of the intellect now became the chief end of his existence. This new interest was due in part to the disappointment and dissatisfaction he felt in other things. Providentially it also inspired him to a renewed study of the Old Testament. He now longed for wisdom and craved the truth.

For all its virtues the *Hortensius* could not liberate him from sin. It lifted his horizons from the physical to the intellectual but fell far short of bringing him to salvation. All it succeeded in doing was to put another barrier in the way of faith. Instead of living on the lust of the flesh he lived on the lustre of the mind. He became proud of his abilities and his mind soon became his cage. He was trapped and yet the key lay within his grasp, if only he knew how to use it. What Paul once wrote to Timothy was just as applicable to Augustine, 'And that from childhood you have known the holy Scriptures, which are able to make you wise for salvation through faith which is in Christ Jesus' (2 Tim. 3:15).

In his search for truth he came into contact with the teachings of the Manichees, who taught that man is not responsible for his sin, but that it is due to the interference of the Power of Darkness. These teachings were to influence his life and thought for the next nine years. His zeal for these newly adopted ideas also touched the lives of others. His friend Alypius and benefactor Romanianus also embraced these teachings. At twenty, not wishing to burden his mother financially any longer, he left Carthage for Tagaste to open a new school.

Monica was far from pleased when she heard of her son's new creed. His second-rate marriage (as it was considered then), was bad enough, but his total abandonment of the Christian faith was more than she could bear. Instead of his living with her in Tagaste she

21

refused to allow him under her roof, and this must have been a particularly painful decision for her to make, considering her deep affection for him.

Not long afterwards Augustine left Tagaste and returned to Carthage to teach Rhetoric. Here his craving for human applause continued to escalate. He took prize after prize for his oratory and poetry in the theatre. He was also influenced by star-gazers and astrologers. For all this, he remained dissatisfied and restless with everything he tried. Even his interest in Manicheism began to wane after a few years. Age and experience had overcome the youthful ideologist. As a result, gone was that self-confidence of former years. While in this unstable condition Rome started to beckon him, and the thought of going to the centre of the empire began to appeal. Monica, who was again reconciled to him, opposed the idea. She followed him to the port and begged him not to go. Through his deceit he managed to escape from her, and left her mourning behind as he sailed from Carthage to Rome, where he opened a school of rhetoric.

However, if Monica could not follow him by sea she could at least follow him in her prayers. This remained her only recourse. Reason was out of the question. He was too much his own man to listen to her pleas. Now he was no longer within earshot but she had a God whose ear is ever open.

After a short spell in Rome he again had itching feet. He had been ill with a fever, even at the point of death, an illness which left him in a weakened condition. During this time he was brought to reconsider his state as eternity loomed before him. But soon after his recovery his fears were again forgotten. Later, he attributed his recovery to his mother's prayers. 'My mother knew nothing of this [his illness] yet was she praying for me in my absence; and thou, who art everywhere present, didst hearken to her where she was, and hadst mercy on me where I was, so far as to restore my bodily health, though my sacrilegious soul was still sick and mad.'

In 384, at the age of 30, he went to Milan, where he was received enthusiastically. Weary of the imperial city, he had successfully applied for the post of Professor of Rhetoric there. With his impeccable credentials, and after a public trial, he was given the position. Milan was destined to become the place of his conversion. He had heard of Ambrose, the famous Bishop of Milan, whose

22

reputation as a preacher was immense. It was this more than anything else that attracted Augustine. As a master of eloquence himself, he was curious to see how Ambrose performed in the pulpit. They had already met for a short time before his attendance at church, and their friendship deepened and developed as Augustine struggled to find the truth. His greatest fear was to die not knowing the truth. His mother also followed him to Milan to find out what was happening. There she found that his attitude towards the Scriptures had changed and that he was studying the apostle Paul's writings. His approach now was quite different. The arrogance of youth gave way to a more humble frame of mind. He was now earnest, almost desperate, in his search.

After some time he was told of Victorinus' conversion. He was a man very similar to Augustine, well-educated, a philosopher, and Professor of Rhetoric in Rome before becoming a Christian. One day, painfully aware of the chasm between his newly-found ideals and his conduct, Augustine went into his garden with his friend Alypius. Overcome with emotion he left Alypius to be alone. In some distress he cried repeatedly to God, 'How long, how long?' His period of waiting was almost over:

And lo, I heard a voice, as if it had been some boy or girl from a house not far off, uttering and often repeating in a sing-song manner, 'Take up and read. Take up and read.' And instantly, with changed countenance, I began to consider intently, whether children in some game of theirs were used to sing any such words; yet could I not find that I had ever heard the like. Then, stemming the course of my tears, I rose up, conceiving that I was required from heaven to read that chapter which the first opening of the book should lead me to . . .

Hastily therefore I went back thither, to where Alypius was sitting, for there I had laid the book of the Apostle, when I had risen from thence. I took it quickly into my hand, I opened it, and I read in silence from that chapter, on which first mine eyes were cast: *'Not in rioting and drunkenness, not in chambering and wantonness, not in strife and envying; but put ye on the Lord Christ, and make no provision for the flesh and its concupiscences.'* No further would I read, nor was there cause why I should; for instantly with the end of this sentence, as by a clear and constant light infused into my heart, the darkness of all former doubts was driven away. (*The Confessions of St Augustine*, Book 8, Ch.12)

This moving account he rehearsed to Alypius who had, strangely enough, also undergone a similar experience in the garden. They went into the house to tell his mother what had happened. Overwhelmed with the news, she praised God who had exceeded her earnest desires. Indeed now the moment of her triumph had come she found it hard to believe for sheer joy.

It was nearing the end of the summer of 386 when Augustine was converted, a few days before the end of his academic year. Not wanting to disrupt his students' studies, he continued teaching them for the remainder of the term, though he no longer believed what he taught. Afterwards, he immediately resigned his post because he could no longer pay lip-service to these deceits. The truth had finally set him free.

The stress and strain of those last few weeks had taken their toll. Augustine was weak and tired and desperately needed to relax and recuperate. A rich friend offered him the use of his country villa in Cassiacum, near Milan. It was exactly what Augustine needed. It was quiet and peaceful. His mother and friends accompanied him so that there was ample opportunity for discussion. There was a lot of chatter about his new-found faith, the past, the future, what he was to do seeing he no longer taught in Milan. Whatever lay before him he could go forward confidently, assured that God was with him and for him.

The following year he was baptized at Easter, confessing Christ as Saviour and Lord. He loved the meetings in Milan's cathedral and often wept as praise was sung to God. By the end of the year he was considering returning to Tagaste, in North Africa, with his little band of followers. It was a sad journey, with his mother, son, and a dear friend dying on the way. Upon their arrival, he immediately set up a Christian community on the estate that he had inherited from his father.

In the privacy of his home he was able to study quietly and steadily. Unknown to him, God had plans for him which were already in the making. For three years he continued to read and write in semi-monastic seclusion until his need was felt by the church in Hippo, near the modern Bona in Algeria. This unexpected development was the result of the insidious growth of heresy in that area. The ageing Bishop, Valerius, felt himself unequal to the task of stemming its flow and recommended that the church should seek a stronger, younger man. He proposed Augustine, a choice which was unanimously endorsed by the church. They had already benefited from his ministry for a short spell.

His move to Hippo was momentous. It struck at the very heart of the Church's enemies. A champion had come, able, skilled, eloquent in speech and pen. For several years he was content to work as co-presbyter until he succeeded to the bishopric after the death of his colleague in 395. Hippo was his only see. He never left it but continued to become North Africa's chief influence. Through his efforts Hippo became the launching pad of many a sound and solid preacher, for his home became the centre for training new preachers. It was a great boon for them simply to sit at his feet and hear the word of God preached. His sermons were far removed from what we may have expected:

> His sermons were biblical rambles: biblical, for they were exclusively concerned with the words of Scripture, with Christ and His Church, with Christian belief and behaviour; rambles, for they rarely fully explained any one text but passed quickly to many others drawn from all over the Bible, so that his talks were littered with hundreds of quotations. In this way his hearers acquired a knowledge of Scripture, for many could not read and very few possessed one of the bulky manuscripts of the Bible. He did not prepare the content of the messages in detail, nor keep to one subject, nor divide up his talks by clear headings, nor even tell Bible stories. His sermons were strictly spiritual, applying the word of God to the hearts of the people.

Whatever we may think of his method today, it attracted large congregations. Crowds endured extreme discomfort to worship in his church. He preached regularly, often as much as five consecutive days without a break, and sometimes twice a day. Before moving to Hippo he had demanded that he be allowed five days a week for the study of the Scriptures without being disturbed. Though it was agreed in principle it never worked in practice. Also he was often called upon to act as arbitrator between disagreeing Christians who otherwise would have had to take their case before the city judges, all un-believers.

As a preacher he was unrivalled in his day. He preached un-tiringly, with long series on the Psalms and the Gospel of John. Both the orthodox and heterodox went to hear him. At times the crowd would break out into spontaneous applause, ecstatic over his message. This may amaze our staid twentieth-century Christian but it was nothing unusual in his day. It was simply an expression of their appreciation. Yet for all their applause he remained unmoved. It was the effect of his preaching on their lives that was of most importance to him. To see people become believers and see lives transformed was his greatest delight. The gospel's impact was most evident when it was indelibly written in their hearts by the Holy Spirit.

It was common for some to take notes, not wanting to lose anything which might be useful later. Many more wept at the preacher's every strain. Even when he was weak through some illness, preaching seemed to revive him. His efforts to win the lost superseded and suspended the infirmities of his body. Towards the end of his life he even laid down rules and regulations for preachers in preparing their sermons.

One major controversy in which he was involved, and the one most associated with his name, was that of Pelagianism. This heresy was introduced by a British monk named Pelagius. If Augustine had done nothing more than to refute this heresy he would have done the Church a great service. Pelagius' doctrine undermined the whole fabric of biblical revelation concerning man's inherent sin through the fall of Adam in Eden. His main contention was that man had the ability, through the exertion of his own will, to save himself. Augustine knew that this was untrue. It did not only fly in the face of revealed truth but also contradicted human experience.

To summarize the difference, B.B.Warfield wrote that 'the central and formative principle of Pelagianism lies in the assumption of the plenary ability of man; his ability to do all that righteousness can demand – to work out not only his own salvation, but also his own perfection.' When Augustine prayed, 'Give what Thou commandest, and command what Thou wilt', he saw the inadequacy of man to do anything God demanded unless God first gave him the strength to do it.

In many ways he was the first to systematize theology. He wrote theological books on a variety of subjects. He had a vision of God's sovereignty in grace and history, infusing grace in the soul and permeating history by his plan. The idea which Augustine formulated, that none could be saved outside the Church, has been misapplied by the Roman Catholic Church. The Church to Roman Catholicism is first and foremost an institution, whereas to Augustine the Church, which is Christ's body, is spiritual, not material, and union with it is not by identification with an institution – as Roman Catholics would maintain – but by a living faith in Christ, brought about by grace. That Church is the one, ongoing Kingdom of God described in Augustine's *City of God*, whose permanence is guaranteed. The essence of his teaching and preaching stemmed from this all-embracing theology of a Sovereign Ruler of the universe.

His lifestyle was simple and frugal. He gave all his wealth away. Even the holy vessels in the church were melted down to buy captives their freedom. He believed people were more important than possessions. He was also hospitable and hated gossip and scandal. In all, time and the work of grace had transformed him into a generous and sympathetic man. His devotion to his people knew no bounds. When the Roman Empire was crumbling and the Vandals were at the gates intending to sack the city, he resolutely refused to leave Hippo. He was bishop, pastor and supporter of his flock.

As his health began to deteriorate his fear for the safety of his people increased accordingly. Many other places had already fallen before the Vandal hordes, some people sheltering in Hippo itself. He prayed that God would spare him the sight of seeing his adopted city destroyed and his beloved flock scattered. In his sick-room were hung David's penitential Psalms for him to read, and to remind him of his former sins. Throughout this period his anticipation of being with his Lord intensified. On 28 August 430 at the age of 75 Augustine died, leaving a collapsing empire only to be received into a kingdom which cannot be destroyed.

3
John Wycliffe
(c.1330-84)

John Wycliffe was the first true Reformer in England. There were others who had criticized the Church before because of its abuses, but no one had had the courage to grapple with its teaching. This had been generally held as inviolable for almost a thousand years. Though there was disquiet concerning many church practices there was general agreement about its doctrine. Heresy, as the Roman Church called it, was unknown in England before Wycliffe. Some Christian groups on the continent of Europe, such as the Waldensians, had challenged the Roman Church, but England had continued faithful to the Church.

When Wycliffe was born, possibly in 1326 but probably in 1330, there was a growing national awareness throughout Europe. England also was fast becoming proud of itself. This evolving nationalism helped to bring Wycliffe to the notice of King and Parliament. His outspoken attack against Rome in defence of the nation's independence gained for him the support of many powerful political leaders. Before this nobody belonging to the clergy had voiced any opposition to the power of Rome in England. They supported her claim to be its feudal lord with rights beyond that of the king. This inevitably led to friction between State and Church, with both claiming absolute sovereignty.

To understand this conflict one must go back to the signing of the Magna Carta on 15 June 1215. Before this, the reigning monarch, King John, had tried unsuccessfully to remove the Roman yoke from the neck of England. In response, Rome had forbidden all religious services, absolutions and baptisms to be performed until the King acknowledge her supremacy. Two years later John was ex-communicated and eventually was forced to hand the English crown over to Rome. In recognition of Rome's sovereignty the King agreed to pay 1000 marks per annum into Rome's coffers. This later provoked a

John Wycliffe

reaction from the English barons who insisted that the King, and not the Pope, was the true sovereign of England and that her people were free.

Before Wycliffe entered the national spotlight he had already been consecrated as a priest. Apart from his being brought up in the village of Wycliffe-upon-Tees in Yorkshire, where his family had its estates, little is known of his early childhood. About 1345 he went to Oxford where he began an outstanding academic career. If Oxford outstripped all the continental universities for academic excellence, including Paris, Wycliffe outstripped all the continental scholars. He became known as 'the Flower of Oxford,' which meant he was the most knowledgeable man in Europe at the time.

When the terrible disease known as the Black Death ravaged Europe and England in 1349-50, the population was drastically reduced. The fear of the plague created a concern within for his soul, and Wycliffe now studied the Bible with renewed interest. He read from the Latin version of the Bible, the Vulgate, which was the only version allowed by the Church. In this he preceded the Reformation teaching of *sola scriptura* (Scripture only). The Bible became the

29

central and controlling feature of his life. Like Calvin, he came to see that everything done within the Church must have a clear biblical warrant. This new concept inevitably made him realize that the Church of the Middle Ages did not fit the New Testament pattern.

With one fifth of the population employed by the Church either as nuns, friars or priests, there seemed very little chance of a radical transformation taking place within England. Nevertheless for all her seeming allegiance to Rome there were divisions and factions within her ranks. Friars and the regular clergy were age-old enemies; they were always bickering and backbiting at one another. There were always grounds for discontent and disagreement. When Wycliffe, a priest, attacked the clerical abuses of the monks, who were lazy and idle, he immediately gained the universal support of the friars. This alliance lasted only until he turned his attention to the abuses of the friars. These were considered the spiritual elite, the untouchables, but these mendicants, who should have lived on gifts of charity, had become wealthy landowners. Instead of living according to their vows of poverty they had become greedy and covetous. This attack naturally provoked a hostile response. They did not mind having the monks' dirty linen hung out, but their own was something else.

In order to continue his studies and lectures at Oxford, Wycliffe needed some form of financial support. This came in 1361 by way of a rich living in Fillingham, Lincolnshire. It was usual for aspiring scholars to receive such livings, otherwise few could afford the long, protracted studies necessary at Oxford. He was able to secure a licence of non-residence which allowed him to hold the position without actually remaining there. At the same time he successfully applied for the living in Aust, Bristol. Again, instead of moving there as its new prebend, he continued his studies and teaching at Oxford and employed someone else to perform his duties. This was a common practice at the time but one which he later condemned.

In 1365 he was chosen Warden of Canterbury Hall. When the appointment was contested it was sent to Rome for arbitration. He was still, as he described himself in 1366, 'a lowly and obedient son of the Church'. This disagreement dragged on for four years before a decision was reached, a decision which went against him. This was precipitated by his uncompromising support of the King against the Pope. The clash, over the payment of the 1000 marks, forced

Wycliffe to consider who actually ruled England. As he was increasingly becoming more of a patriot than a papist he endorsed the King's rights rather than the Pope's, something unheard-of before in a priest. There were major political factors which influenced Wycliffe's decision. England was at war with France, and at the time the papal court was based in Avignon in the south of France. The papal demands for the back payment of its annual 1000 marks would have substantially weakened England and possibly have been used to support France. With such considerations as these Wycliffe defended the regal rights of the King of England. If Rome frowned upon him, England favoured him. King, court and countrymen all began to hail him. He was suddenly elevated as England's voice on religion. But if he was a hero to the people, he was a traitor to the Pope; the whole body of religious institutions condemned him.

After becoming Bachelor of Divinity in 1369 and Doctor of Divinity in 1372, he was allowed to open his own Hall. As a Professor he helped support poor students; many came to him without any means of maintenance, but thirsty for knowledge. He found it hard to turn any away who had obvious natural ability.

He preached to his students in Latin and to the common people in English. He preached a series on the Ten Commandments in which he attacked the practice of buying forgiveness without repentance. Salvation, he pointed out, was not simply a matter of being absolved of one's sins by a priest, as Rome wrongly taught. It was not something which could be bought or sold on a religious market-stall. Some of his congregation must have become fidgety as they listened to all their hopes being dashed:

> Covet not thy neighbour's goods, despise him not, slander him not, scorn him not, belie him not, backbite him not; But many think if they give a penny to a pardoner, they shall be forgiven the breaking of all the commandments of God, and therefore they take no heed how they keep them. But I say to thee for certain, though thou have priests and friars to sing for thee, and though thou each day hear many masses, and found chanteries and colleges, and go on pilgrimages all thy life, and give all thy goods to pardoners: all this shall not bring thy soul to heaven.

If man cannot redeem himself, how then can he be saved?

> Have a remembrance of the goodness of God, how he made thee in his

31

own likeness; and how Jesus Christ, both God and man, died so painful a death upon the cross, to buy man's soul out of hell, even with his own heart's blood, and to bring it to the bliss of heaven.

The solution, he pointed out, was not found in man but in the God-man, Jesus Christ. Through his incarnation and crucifixion a way had been made possible. His death has atoned for sin and brought reconciliation between God and man. The terms laid down for man's redemption were beyond his own ability to pay, but through the intervention of Christ full payment had already been made.

While this rift between the King and Pope continued, those appointed to church offices, notably bishops, were chosen by the King and confirmed by the Pope. This action was a ploy by Rome to keep a foothold in England. To have opposed the King's selection would have deepened the divide and possibly resulted in a complete and irreconcilable separation. The Pope was too good a politician to allow this and waited quietly for a more favourable time. As he said, 'If the King of England had nominated an ass, I would have accepted him'. This compromise caused immense difficulties. The Pope continued his claim to many rich English benefices, a claim which sent shock waves through Parliament. Many felt that the Pope should have no say in any appointment, not even by way of confirming them, and should renounce all claims to these benefices in England. They maintained that it was the sole right of the Archbishop of Canterbury to endorse any induction.

To resolve their differences a commission was set up. It was sent to meet the Pope in Avignon, but instead met with him in Bruges in the summer of 1374. Wycliffe, along with three others, was sent as a commissioner. Apart from their discussions, it gave Wycliffe an opportunity to meet the Pope personally. No final settlement was reached when the delegation returned home. The impression left upon him was that of the corruption surrounding the Papal see. Apart from the double talk and deceit there was also intrigue. After returning from Bruges, one of the commissioners, Gilbert, the Bishop of Bangor, was quickly appointed as Bishop of Hereford. This appointment by the Pope was the very thing which they had gone to discuss with him. Little wonder they never got very far with a traitor in the camp.

After this encounter Wycliffe became even more outspoken

against the Roman system and declared that the Pope was the Antichrist. It is not surprising then to find him described as 'the Morning Star of the Reformation'. From now on there was no room for compromise: the Roman Church was seen as the enemy, and it was now a fight to the death.

At one time Wycliffe was promised a bishopric. Fortunately he was overlooked for someone else, which proved a blessing in disguise. Instead, he was appointed Rector of Lutterworth in 1374. Had he become Bishop of Lincoln he would have been distracted from his main task. His time would have been taken up more with administration than preaching and teaching. His studies also would have been drastically curtailed. All in all, a wise God was directing his steps.

Between his teaching in Oxford and preaching in Lutterworth the gospel was being spread abroad. He was considered by Rome to be the most dangerous man alive. There was need to deal with him, and Rome never shrank from such actions. Without warning he was called before a church tribunal and accused of heresy. He was summoned to St Paul's Cathedral in February 1377. His chief antagonist was Courtney, Bishop of London. He had virtually forced Sudbury, the Archbishop of Canterbury, into this action, much against his will.

It was a startling event. The cathedral was packed with bishops and people who had come to see the outcome. Prior to this, Wycliffe had been the people's champion, but public favour was soon to change. Instead of coming alone he came under the protection of the Earl of Lancaster, John of Gaunt, whom the people distrusted because they suspected him of coveting the crown. The meeting ended in turmoil with Lancaster and Wycliffe forced to leave the cathedral. Afterwards, Wycliffe returned to the peace of his beloved Oxford.

From there he continued his assault on the Church, but Rome retaliated. After the fiasco at St Paul's the Pope himself intervened, issuing five bulls or edicts against this turncoat priest. He could not allow himself to be seen as impotent regarding Wycliffe, since this might have given an opportunity to others of a similar persuasion to make public their opposition.

Wycliffe's position posed a real threat to the Roman see, especially when he began propagating the opinion that the Church's land and property was only held in trust, and could be confiscated at any time and given back to the people. This threatened the very life-blood of the Church. Its strength was in its monopoly on heaven, as it was custodian of the keys; this imprisoned men's consciences. Moreover, its power on earth was seen in its vast riches. Stripped of its wealth, the Church would lose much of its influence.

The papal edict demanded that Wycliffe be arrested. When it reached Oxford, the town leaders adamantly refused to enforce it. Eventually he was summoned to Lambeth Palace and charged again with heresy. This time there was no powerful political figure to protect him, but he remained unperturbed. Even earlier in St Paul's he had not trusted in the help of man but in the living God. He was alone, and yet not alone, for God was with him; without seeking help an unexpected protector arose. The Queen Mother sent a message to the Archbishop not to take any open action against Wycliffe, no matter what the outcome of the trial. This effectively tied the court's hands and everything else that followed became a farce.

He again returned to Oxford with the warning not to preach on any of their disputed points. It was now 1378, and Wycliffe began to realize that his time was fast running out. The great need of the hour was for others to spread his teaching. He began gathering a number of his most devoted followers around him and sent them to preach the gospel in the towns and villages of the land. However, his strength was beginning to give way and the following year he was close to death. To his opponents it seemed victory was drawing near. Church leaders came to see him, hoping he would recant before dying. When they suggested that death was imminent and that he should consider his condition he retorted, 'I shall not die, but live, and again declare the evil deeds of the friars.'

When he recovered, much to the dismay of the Church, Wycliffe began to think of the long term. What would happen after his death? Besides his travelling preachers, he saw that the only way to promote the truth was for everyone to have a Bible, written in his own language and intelligible to the commoner. This was the beginning of the first English Bible. He believed that everyone had the right to read the Bible for himself, that it was not the inherent right of the Church to be the only interpreter of God's Word. This had inevitably led to abuses when the Church had foisted its opinions and interpretations of the Bible on to the people.

This new project reached its culmination before Wycliffe died. There were many difficulties in its production, not least the fact that nobody understood the original Hebrew and Greek. Their only recourse was to use the Latin version, the Vulgate. How much Wycliffe actually translated himself remains in dispute, but the work was successfully carried out by 1382, much to his great delight and satisfaction. Until it was completed Wycliffe encouraged his preachers to teach the people to memorize portions of Scripture. If they could not hold God's Word in their hands they could store it in their hearts. It was of the highest importance that the common folk should have the Word of God, even if it was only in a limited way.

After his recovery the storm with Rome had still not blown over. In fact he was heading towards another major dispute. The heart of the Roman Church's teaching lies in its doctrine of transubstantiation, the belief that in the mass, the bread and wine are actually changed into the body and blood of Christ, and that he is again being sacrificed upon the altar at the hands of the priest every time the mass is celebrated. When Wycliffe started to spread his belief that he no longer accepted this, he was striking at Rome's jugular vein. It was not surprising to find that even his former friends were becoming startled. John of Gaunt rushed to Oxford in an attempt to restrain him from declaring it, but was unsuccessful. From being a political asset he now became a political liability. His shift of emphasis from the political to the more ecclesiastical aspects of the faith left Wycliffe in an isolated position.

When Courtney, Bishop of London, succeeded Sudbury as Archbishop of Canterbury, things looked ominous for Wycliffe and the Lollards (the name given to his supporters and preachers). Once he had received his charge from the Pope there was no stopping Courtney. He was a born persecutor, an ardent supporter of Rome, and a violent enemy of the Lollards. He immediately called for a synod to deal with the growing influence of heresy. A list was drawn up of heretics and heresies; topping the list was Wycliffe. He had led the revolt; he must therefore be first to pay for it.

As the synod sat deliberating at Blackfriars, London, a massive earthquake shook the city. This unexpected earth tremor struck fear into the hearts of the clerics. They thought it was a sure sign of God's displeasure. Courtney pacified them by saying, 'Know you not that

35

the noxious vapours which catch fire in the bosom of the earth, and give rise to these phenomena which alarm you, lose all their force when they burst forth? Well, in like manner, by rejecting the wicked from our community, we shall put an end to the convulsions of the church.' Wycliffe and his followers preferred the synod's first conclusion and capitalized on it by telling the people it was of God.

When the Bishop of Lincoln, under Courtney's orders, demanded that Oxford hand Wycliffe over, he was met with marked resistance. This support of Wycliffe against the Church lasted only a short time. Many of his first supporters, for various and personal reasons, recanted. Wycliffe himself was banished from Oxford and left in retreat to Lutterworth, where he had remained throughout the fray. Instead of destroying the movement it only succeeded in advancing it; he became more influential. Many of the students in Oxford, seeing that it was no longer a place for free thought, left for Lutterworth.

Wycliffe sending out his preachers

They formed a new school of the prophets around their declining master. He was also given more opportunity to study and write and preach. By his example and teaching they were taught the importance of true biblical preaching: to give a practical interpretation and relevance to Scripture, which had for centuries been hidden under every kind of allegorical interpretation possible. He told his eager pupils:

> To the people the Gospel must be preached as God commands. The truth must be proclaimed to them even though they receive it unwittingly. Not comedies or tragedies, not fables or droll stories, but simply and solely the Law of the Lord as Christ and the Apostles delivered it: for in the Law, that is the Gospel, is hidden the life which is able to quicken the church. The Lord's Word is the food which sustains it. He who preaches to the people without reading and explaining to them the Gospel, gives them a meal without bread. Those pseudo prelates set aside the Gospel. If they mention the Gospel at all, they do not preach it in full.

These new preachers went out preaching wherever they could; every opportunity was used to share the good news. Their sincerity won them general support as the people heard them gladly. They were recognizable by their simple dress. They wore no sandals, only a coarse garb, and carried a long stick. Yet for all their simplicity they were impressive preachers. 'Like their master,' wrote one opponent, 'they too were eloquent . . . mighty in words, they exceeded all men in making speeches'.

When he was summoned to appear before the Pope in Rome, Wycliffe was disabled by a stroke. After this his activities were confined to Lutterworth. Here he preached, wrote and prepared the next generation to carry on the work. Towards the end of 1384, he suffered his third stroke. On the last Sunday of the year as he was about to dispense the Lord's Supper, he was struck down. His friends carried him home where he died quietly in bed on 31 December.

What Wycliffe did was to light a torch for others to carry on after him. When, in May 1415, his grave was desecrated and his bones exhumed and burnt, his ashes were sprinkled into the river Swift. This indeed portrays the lasting effect of his ministry. As one so graphically wrote: 'The little river conveyed Wycliffe's remains into the Avon, Avon into the Severn, Severn into the narrow seas, they into the main ocean. And thus the ashes of Wycliffe are the emblem of his doctrine, which now is dispersed all the world over.'

4
Hugh Latimer
(1485-1555)

During the sixteenth century the pace of change in England in reforming the beliefs of the Roman Catholic Church on the basis of the Bible was much slower than in the rest of Protestant Europe. The Reformation battle continued to rage for years without a decisive victory to either the Protestants or Roman Catholics. This was often due to the changing fortunes of Henry VIII. His continued conflict with Rome over his wife, Catherine of Aragon, drove a wedge between himself and Pope Clement VII. He wanted his marriage disannulled, an expedient which could only be granted by the Pope, who refused. The headstrong king, who was once declared by the Church of Rome 'the Defender of the Faith', was eventually forced to take things into his own hands. He was not a man to be humiliated by some foreigner, even if that foreigner was thought to be Christ's vicar on earth. His patience, which was never great, soon ran out and he sought other means of getting rid of Catherine.

Throughout Henry's turbulent life, Reformers like Latimer had to tread carefully. The king's lack of patience could often end literally with someone's head on the block. The king himself often appeared a mass of contradictions. He was easily swayed, depending on his circumstances and courtships. Sometimes he favoured the Catholics, then the Reformers. However, although he made himself head of the Church of England, at heart Henry remained a Catholic throughout his life.

Latimer was born in 1485 near the small village of Thurcaston, Leicestershire, twelve miles from Lutterworth. His father, a staunch supporter of the monarchy, once helped Henry VII to secure his crown in the battle at Blackheath, during the Perkin Warbeck rebellion. As his father prepared to go on his horse to Blackheath Field, Hugh helped by buckling the harness. This farmer's son was educated in the country schools and later sent to Cambridge where he received his Master's degree in 1514. At first he was an ardent Roman Catholic. 'I was then', he said, 'as obstinate a papist as any in England.' His religious zeal won him the right to carry the university cross through Cambridge for seven successive years. This was considered a great honour.

Roman Catholicism was the only religion Latimer had ever known. He had heard of the Lollards, their preaching and suffering, but had been protected from their teachings by his father. Any doctrine which did not conform to the Church's standards was considered heresy, and heretics were burnt. He used to ridicule George Stafford, one of the university lecturers, because he taught directly from the Bible. He often attended his lectures simply to put Stafford off. He also intimidated many of the other students by his presence. He was a typical Roman priest, zealous for the Church but ignorant of the truth.

After becoming a Bachelor of Divinity in 1524, when he was approaching forty, he was expected to give a lecture before the university. His theme was 'Philip Melancthon and his Doctrines'. He attacked the great German Reformer's teaching and defended Roman dogma. He also used this opportunity to warn his congregation about meetings held in the White Horse Inn where a group of fellow students met to read and to study the Bible. These were led by the tiny figure of Thomas Bilney. Bilney was as keen and zealous for Bible reading and teaching as Latimer was for his rites and rituals. 'Little Bilney', as he was known, was present when Latimer vociferated against them, but in the applause which followed, Bilney decided to try and win this Roman zealot to the Reformation cause.

Latimer returned to his rooms in the full flush of his achievement, being hailed as the champion of the Catholics. Yet Bilney had other hopes for him. He followed Latimer home and knocked on his door. When Latimer opened it he was surprised to see Bilney standing there. Bilney immediately took the initiative. 'For the love of God, be pleased to hear my confession,' he said. The young priest thought that he had regained this erring brother by his lecture. Little did the fox realize he was being pursued by the lamb!

As a priest Latimer had heard countless confessions; but Bilney had not come for absolution but confrontation. He was as harmless as a dove but as wise as a serpent. He knew only too well that by

Hugh Latimer

debating their differences he could never get Latimer to listen to reason or revelation. It was by hiding the hook long enough under the guise of his confession that he hoped to catch him unawares. Bilney told him plainly of the anguish he had felt, of his own efforts to secure peace in his heart, and of how he had found forgiveness of sin only when he had trusted in Christ.

Before he realized it, Latimer found himself confronted with the gospel in all its simplicity. He was rooted to the ground, conviction growing by the moment. Before Bilney had finished, Latimer was a changed man. He once said in a sermon, 'I learnt more by this confession than before in many years. From that time forward I began to smell the word of God, and forsook the school doctors and such fooleries.' After his conversion Latimer was viewed with suspicion. From being the university's cross-bearer for several years he now took up the true cross of Christ. He became a sufferer for righteousness' sake.

His conversion was a notable victory for the Reformation. His colours had been changed and hoisted for all to see. Instead of preaching tradition, he preached the gospel. Bilney became his bosom friend, and they could be seen walking together up 'Heretics Hill' discussing points of theology. He now became an associate of that despised group of students who frequented the White Horse. This inn acted as a gathering place for all those who received nothing from the priests' ministrations and yet loved the truth.

At first Latimer was unclear on some aspects of Roman Catholic dogma. For instance, for years after his conversion he continued to believe in the doctrine of transubstantiation, the belief that the bread and wine in the sacrament of the Lord's Supper turns into the very substance of the body and blood of Christ. His theological progress was slow compared with the European Reformers, who seemed to grasp the essentials of the gospel far more quickly than their British counterparts.

However, although Latimer was not the best English theologian of his day, he was undoubtedly the best preacher. He preached in Latin to the scholars and in English to the peasants. In the sixteenth century he was one of the first to see that England had been starved of the gospel under Rome and was now in desperate need. To redress the balance, preaching became the prime instrument in this Reformer's offensive. The gospel was no mere debating point for academics, but life and death for the masses. As a farmer's son he could speak to the common people in a language they were able to understand. He used natural, homely illustrations to prove his points. It has been said that 'What Tyndale was to do for England by his pen, Latimer was to do by his preaching.'

When the Bishop of Ely, Nicholas West, tried to catch him preaching heresy toward the end of 1525, Latimer proved more than a match for him. The Bishop entered the church while Latimer was preaching. Latimer immediately stopped and courteously waited for the Bishop and his retinue to be seated before resuming. However instead of carrying on from where he had left off he quickly changed his theme. His new sermon was taken from Hebrews 9:11, 'But Christ came as high priest of the good things to come.' He preached on the spiritual and ministerial responsibilities of priests and especially bishops. Some of the things he said must have given offence to West, for they were hard-hitting truths, which few observed conscientiously.

Afterwards the Bishop thanked him for this timely reminder of what was expected of him. However it was all sham, for he was scheming on how best to trap Latimer. Whereas the Bishop used slyness to catch him, Latimer used shrewdness in response. West asked Latimer to help him. He wanted Latimer to write an article denouncing the German Reformer, Martin Luther. Latimer immediately saw through his ploy and declined, pleading that he was not competent for such a task since he was not familiar with the teaching of Luther. He reminded the Bishop that it was not permitted to read Luther's writings. As far as the sermon that day was concerned, Latimer insisted, 'Sure I am that I have preached before you this day no man's doctrine, but only the doctrine of God out of the scriptures.'

The Bishop of Ely was not a man to be made a fool. He responded by suspending Latimer's preaching licence. This meant that he could not preach anywhere in the Bishop's diocese or in the university itself. This harsh treatment was a heavy cross for him to bear. But relief was on its way. It came from an area which was free from the control of the Bishop. After hearing what had happened, the Augustinian Prior in Cambridge, Robert Barnes, arranged for Latimer to preach in his chapel pulpit on Christmas Eve, much to the annoyance of West.

It was not long before Latimer's enemies drew him to the attention of the Pope's representative in England, Cardinal Wolsey, a man who hated all Reformers and was merciless in dealing with heretics. Latimer was summoned to appear before him charged with heresy. After questioning him on Luther's doctrine Wolsey was pleased to find that Latimer had never read him. On the contrary, his reading had been confined to the early Fathers and medieval schoolmen. Latimer, quick to see his chance, brought up the incident of the Bishop of Ely's attendance at his service and its outcome. He rehearsed everything that had taken place between himself and West, and assured the Cardinal that he had said nothing more. Wolsey was so impressed by Latimer that he gave him his own personal licence which allowed Latimer to preach anywhere in England.

Latimer returned to Cambridge victorious. With his preacher's licence restored he now had liberty to preach again. His influence in Cambridge continued to grow as the students flocked to hear him.

Between Stafford's lectures and his preaching, the minds and lives of many were being changed. His practical sermons explained how people should live before God.

Nevertheless not everything went well for the Reformers. Little Bilney was brought before Wolsey and forced to recant. Bareheaded, he was made to walk around St Paul's, London, with a bundle of sticks on his shoulder, indicating that he would be burned at the stake if he should wander again. When he was reunited with his friends in Cambridge, Bilney was inconsolable. His sense of guilt for denying his faith lay heavily upon his heart. Latimer never forgot this painful event.

After Wolsey fell from the King's favour, dying in 1530, some began attacking Latimer's right to preach. But he remained adamant. His licence had been restored to him while Wolsey was fully entitled to grant it. About the same time he caused a stir in Cambridge with his famous 'Sermons on the Card'. It was a popular pastime with the people at Christmas to play cards. Latimer, taking the initiative, based a series of sermons around a set of playing cards and how best to play them. He emphasized the law and its demands and how easy it was to abuse it. He pointed out the need to be 'practical' as well as 'professing' Christians.

Latimer's opponents laboured to no avail. His influence was growing and he was in favour with the King. Henry had heard of his preaching and influence in Cambridge and wanted to hear him. Latimer was invited to preach before the court in London at Lent in March 1530, and Henry was delighted. Latimer was then, along with several others, appointed to make a list of the best religious books available. At the same time he was made one of the King's chaplains.

After spending some time at court he found it fruitless ground for the gospel. He then began to think of new avenues of service. He did not pine for the applause of court or yearn to walk with the high and mighty. He found more kinship with the commoner than the court official. Owing to some influential friends at court he was given the living of West Kington, near Chippenham in Wiltshire. Thus in January 1531 he found himself rector of a small country parish. His pulpit was no longer in the heart of learning as in Cambridge or in the heart of the legislature as in London, but in the heart of a lonely rural area. There were no longer any academics or aristocracy in his congregation, but unlettered people. These found his preaching simple and profitable.

Yet even in this quiet setting his preaching could not go unnoticed. He was England's best-known preacher and the people wanted to hear him, though the priests feared him. He was considered a heretic and they were afraid he might infect his hearers with the same disease. For all their efforts the priests were unable to contain his influence as the people continued coming to hear him. Only the prejudiced could not benefit from his preaching. The unbiased were generally impressed with him, as another Reformer wrote, 'None, except the stiff-necked and uncircumcized in heart, went away from it without being affected with high detestation of sin, and moved unto all godliness and virtue.'

While he was living at West Kington other Reformers were being persecuted. This assault was led by Bishop Stokeley of London and supported by Sir Thomas More, the Chancellor. Though it was unconstitutional, the King turned a blind eye to it. For a long time Stokeley had desired to have Latimer brought before him but had failed in his attempts. While he was in Wiltshire he was outside his jurisdiction, but during a visit to London in 1531, Latimer was induced to preach. Much of his sermon was directed against the clergy in general and the Bishop of London in particular. Stokeley was furious. Again, Latimer was able to escape the Bishop's clutches because of Henry VIII's kind regard for him.

Stokeley, never a man to forget an insult, worked hard to bring Latimer to task over his teaching. By stealth and manipulation he was finally able to summon Latimer before him. At the beginning of 1532, Latimer stood accused of heresy before a church tribunal in London. After he had been questioned on several points of doctrine the Bishop and his followers were unable to condemn him. As the trial dragged on, new issues were raised until Latimer was ordered either to recant or be excommunicated. At first he refused. After being excommunicated from the Church he awaited his fate at Lambeth. The next few days were torturous. His life hung in the balance as a compromised solution was being discussed behind the scenes. What was finally agreed between Latimer's friends and foes is uncertain. The result was that Latimer recanted and was received back into the Church. It has been suggested that Henry himself had intervened and requested Latimer to obey the bishops. This event has been described as 'the darkest page in Latimer's history.'

In August of the same year, Warham, Archbishop of Canterbury, died. This left the King in a predicament. He wanted an end to his marriage with Catherine of Aragon so that he could marry Anne Boleyn. He knew that he needed an immediate successor to Warham, but Henry wanted a man who could be trusted to be the King's man and not the Pope's man. He appointed Thomas Cranmer who was then living abroad. He was summoned to appear before the king but due to the stormy weather his arrival was delayed until the following January. His accession to the see of Canterbury brought a new spiritual climate to the land, a ray of light after a very dark and dismal time. Cranmer was the first truly Protestant Reformer to become Archbishop of Canterbury.

Soon after his appointment took effect Cranmer began looking for support in the synod of clergy of his province. Several vacant bishoprics needed to be filled. In August 1535 Latimer was given the royal assent to become Bishop of Worcester. This meant not only the strengthening of Cranmer's hand but of the whole Reformation cause in England. Latimer, however, was always happiest in his role as a preacher and never really liked being an administrator. He craved neither position nor prosperity. All he wanted to do was to promote the gospel.

As Bishop he found some of his duties rather unwelcome and burdensome. When the monasteries came under review by a royal commission, Latimer was surprised to find how far they had deviated from their vows of celibacy and asceticism. Corruption and deception were found on a massive scale. The report read, 'We have discovered not seven, but more than seven hundred thousand deadly sins. Here are the confessions of the monks and nuns subscribed with their own hands . . . The monasteries are so full of iniquity that they ought to fall down under such a weight. If there be here and there any innocent cloisters, they are so few in number that they cannot save the others.' This 'Black Book', as it was called, is thought to have been destroyed during the five-year reign of 'Bloody Mary', the Catholic daughter of Henry and Catherine.

When many of the monasteries were closed in 1536, most of the deposed friars were given pensions to live on. For those horrified by their closure, Latimer had a word for them. He described what a real religious house consisted of:

> Look at that man and woman living together piously, tranquilly, in the fear of God, keeping His Word and active in the duties of their calling: they form a religious house, one that is truly acceptable to God. Pure religion consists not in wearing a hood, but in visiting the fatherless and the widows, and keeping ourselves unspotted from the world. What has hitherto been called a religious life was an irreligious life; yea, rather hypocrisy. (Douglas C. Wood, *Such a Candle*, p.95)

With Cranmer in Lambeth and Latimer in Worcester things began to appear more favourable for the Reformation cause, but then in the middle of 1539 'the Whip of Six Strings' or 'the Bloody Statute' was given royal assent. This set the Reformation movement back several years. It comprised six main articles:

1. The real presence of Christ in the sacrament.
2. The denial of the cup to the laity.
3. The celibacy of the clergy.
4. The obligation of monastic vows.
5. The benefit of private masses.
6. Auricular [told privately in the ear] confession.

These were in essence a re-establishment of Romanism within the Church of England. Needless to say, Cranmer and Latimer were unable to accept them all, even though some remnants of their old faith, like transubstantiation, still remained. They refused to endorse them. The King had given his assent to them on 28 June 1539. On 1 July, Latimer resigned his bishopric.

The King was incensed at Latimer's action and ordered him to be put in custody in London. Cranmer fared better than his friend. Henry, not from any generous motive, still kept him as Archbishop. There were good political as well as personal reasons for doing this. Poor Latimer was kept in seclusion and forbidden to preach for eight years and was placed in the last year of Henry's reign in the Tower of London.

When the King died on 28 January 1547, a new era dawned for the Reformers. Edward, his young son, by his third wife Jane Seymour, wholeheartedly supported the Reformation. He was not quite ten years old when he ascended the throne. With the accession of Edward, Latimer was set free. His period of silence and his term in the Tower felt long but was fruitful. He was given an opportunity to crystallize many of his ill-digested thoughts as more of his Romanism was abandoned.

Latimer by this time was in his sixties but the next seven-year period was to become Latimer's most fruitful. He regularly preached before the boy king at court, though his ministry was not confined to the ruling classes. It was said that 'No one of the Reformers probably sowed the seeds of sound Protestant doctrine so widely and effectually among the middle and lower classes as Latimer.' The reason why Latimer was more successful than other Reformers in preaching to all classes was because of his grasp on the emphasis of the New Testament on preaching: 'it pleased God through the foolishness of the message preached to save those who believe' (1 Corinthians 1:21). To Latimer preaching was central.

> His emphasis on [preaching] was unique among English Reformers but it elevated Latimer to a place above his fellow Reformers. They had seen the life-giving power of the Scriptures but failed to take it to its logical conclusion: 'Faith comes from what is heard, and what is heard comes by the preaching of Christ.' The place that baptism occupied in the church still confused the other Reformers and many ascribed to it the same regenerating power that Rome does. But this was not the case with Latimer: 'By the Word of the living God, by the Word of God preached and opened — thus cometh our new birth.' (Douglas Wood, *Such a Candle*, p.151)

Sadly for the Reformers Edward died on 6 July 1553, and we can only imagine what could have happened had he lived. This event dramatically affected the Reformation in England. 'Bloody Mary' succeeded Edward to the throne. She was the daughter of Catherine of Aragon and a staunch Catholic. This new development brought the Reformers into great danger, for the Catholics rallied around the new Queen and many of the Reformers found themselves in prison. There were to be two hundred and eighty-five deaths before Mary's reign of terror came to an end.

When Latimer was summoned to appear before the Lord Chancellor he was encouraged to flee to the continent. Knowing the effect this would have upon other Protestants he refused to run. Instead, he made his way to the council meeting. As he passed Smithfield, the place where martyrs were burnt, he said, 'Smithfield has long groaned for me'. He had already considered what lay ahead of him.

Latimer, along with Cranmer, Nicholas Ridley and John Bradford, was placed in the Tower with Elizabeth, Mary's half-sister. They were there several months before being sent to Oxford to face the best of Rome's theologians. In the ensuing debates the question of the mass, Rome's 'acid test of orthodoxy', came up for discussion. Inflexibility to accept the mass meant certain excommunication as heretics. As all three by this time denied transubstantiation they were all condemned to burn as heretics.

On 16 October 1555, Latimer and Ridley were taken from their cells to face the flames. After the statutory sermon against heretics neither man was allowed to speak. As the faggots were lit, Latimer encouraged his friend and brother in the faith, 'Be of good comfort, Master Ridley, and play the man. We shall this day light such a candle, by God's grace, in England, as I trust shall never be put out.'

5

Martin Luther

(1483-1546)

Martin Luther, more than anyone else, changed the religious face of Europe. Though there were others who had disagreed with the Roman Catholic Church nobody made such an impact as this Augustinian monk. The monolithic structure of the Church, which had remained intact for over a millennium, was suddenly shaken and shattered within a few short years.

The Reformation was a rediscovery of a lost gospel, a fresh realization that man is saved by faith alone, through grace alone. It came about by Luther's move away from medieval scholasticism, the theology and philosophy taught in the universities or 'schools' of the Middle Ages, into a more penetrating analysis of the Bible. Under the light granted him from heaven he came to see things which had for centuries been hidden, and as in the case of John Hus, if they did begin to surface they were soon sunk by persecution and consumed in fire. For this reason there was need for someone of Luther's calibre to champion the cause of God and the gospel, to stand firm against the pressures of Church and State. Even in the face of death he could say defiantly, 'Here I stand; God help me. I cannot do otherwise.'

Martin Luther was born on 10 November 1483 in Eisleben, in the electorate of Saxony, Germany. His father, Hans Luther, had risen to the middle classes from a poor background. If Hans was ambitious for himself he was even more so for his son. He hoped that some day Martin would become his provider when, through age or infirmity, he would be unable to fend for himself.

As a boy Martin was often severely punished for minor mis-demeanours. This was nothing unusual but was the standard practice of the day. He was bright and intelligent and his parents had great hopes for him, but things were to change through one dramatic event. He had entered the University of Erfurt in 1501, and once, when he was returning there after visiting his parents, lightning narrowly missed him. This unexpected encounter with death threw him to the ground and struck fear into his heart. Momentarily, wrath and vengeance seemed to echo from heaven. In a fit of fear he cried out to his father's patron saint, 'St Anne help me! I will become a monk.' This hasty vow, made in a panic situation, bound his conscience. From then on the cowl was to be his new attire. His reason for making this vow was the general belief that those in holy orders were far more likely to evade hell than those outside. It was the fear of hell, not the attraction of heaven, that caused him to take the oath.

Martin Luther

Learning of his intention to become a monk, his father bitterly opposed it. Even at his first mass, Hans could hardly conceal his resentment. When Martin approached him hoping to receive some encouraging words, his father reproached him. 'You learned scholar,' he said, 'have you never read in the Bible that you should honour your father and your mother? And here you have left me and your mother to look after ourselves in our old age.'

Luther joined an Augustinian monastery in Erfurt, known for its strictness. For twelve long years he was a zealous monk, and looking back he believed that owing to his severe and austere attitude as a monk his health had been permanently impaired. He was so keen to follow everything religious that nothing was left undone. Yet where conscience holds sway over a person seeking a salvation by works, there can be no real comfort. The problem is that there is always something more that can be done, more prayer, more fasting, more vigils. Soon the question arises, how much has to be done in order to be saved? As there is no adequate answer to the question there is no adequate solution to the problem. The person is then left with a troubled mind. Luther continued to lack peace within. His struggle to find it was to last several more years before he came really to understand the gospel. What makes salvation by works so frustrating is that the more conscientious a person is, the more peace seems to evade him. 'Who knows whether these things please God?' Luther said. 'The more I sweated it out like this, the less peace and quiet I experienced.'

His connection with Wittenberg began in 1508, when he went there, a young man of 24, to lecture on theology for a year in its newly established university. By then he had received his doctorate and was becoming increasingly known as an academic. In 1511 he returned to Wittenberg where he was to remain for the next thirty-five years until his death in 1546. Wittenberg was to become the command centre of the Reformation. It was here the young monk was to challenge the might of Rome and its dogma.

After returning to Wittenberg the next five years were to see a marked change in Luther's theological outlook. His study of Greek and Hebrew opened up the Bible in a way he did not foresee. His lectures covered the book of Psalms and Paul's Letters to the Romans and Galatians. The more he studied, the brighter the light became. Eventually his grasp of the gospel became clearer as the medieval veil was removed. Instead of going to the Schoolmen, the teachers of philosophy and theology of the medieval European universities, he now went to his Bible. Here he found all that a sinner needed to be just before God. His study of Augustine also helped to clarify some points and confirm others.

Before he came to a lasting peace with God a huge struggle had

51

to be fought within. He had exhausted and exasperated his confessor, Iohann von Staupitz, with his confessions, which sometimes lasted as long as six hours. Compelled to read his Bible because of his work he came to a completely new understanding of the meaning of God's justice. Whereas once it had brought terror, now it brought peace:

> I greatly longed to understand Paul's Epistle to the Romans and nothing stood in the way but that one expression, 'the justice of God', because I took it to mean that justice whereby God is just and deals justly in punishing the unjust . . . Night and day I pondered until I saw the connection between the justice of God and the statement that 'the just shall live by his faith'. Then I grasped that the justice of God is that righteousness by which through grace and sheer mercy God justifies us through faith. Thereupon I felt myself to be reborn and to have gone through open doors into paradise. The whole of Scripture took on a new meaning, and whereas before the 'justice of God' had filled me with hate, now it became to me inexpressibly sweet in greater love. This passage of Paul became to me a gate to heaven . . .

Nailing the ninety-five 'theses' to the door of the Castle church in Wittenberg

After seeing through the veneer of Roman hypocrisy he became increasingly intolerant of unbiblical practices such as the sale of indulgences or grants of pardon for sins. It was this more than anything which ignited the Reformation fire and set the whole of Europe ablaze. To suggest that Rome possessed a treasury of merit from which it could dispense indulgences, as and when it wanted, was repugnant to him. This treasury was supposed to contain the accumulated merit of Christ and the excess merit of the saints, and this merit was sold to anyone who had money to buy it. When John Tetzel, a Dominican monk, came to Germany selling indulgences it provoked such a hostile response from Luther that he challenged Rome with his famous ninety-five 'theses' or points for debate nailed to the door of the Castle Church in Wittenberg, the usual place for academic notices. This took place in October 1517, on the eve of All Saints' Day, and judged by its consequences it was a historic event. He had begun his attack on the Roman Church in earnest.

This attack on the Church caused an immediate response in Rome. Early in 1518 the Dominican monks, coming to the defence of one of their brothers, accused Luther of heresy. He had already been warned to guard his words, but the impetuous monk was undeterred by these threats. Unwilling to be brought to heel, Luther was summoned to appear in Rome within sixty days. It was an ominous sign and one intended to instil anxiety. Fortunately, he had a friend in Spalatin, chaplain to the Elector of Saxony. Spalatin convinced the Elector that if a court was to be held it should be heard on German soil and not in Rome.

A meeting was arranged to be held in Augsburg. In September Luther, along with another friar, set off for his first direct confrontation with Roman totalitarianism. He was interviewed and questioned on his views by Cardinal Cajetan, one of Rome's most famous scholars. When they parted the outcome remained indecisive. The cunning Cardinal, for all his education, could not unhinge or humble the unrepentant wanderer. As far as Luther was concerned he saw nothing in his views which needed revision. He then returned to Wittenberg to resume his lectures.

But a rogue spirit could not be allowed to run free within the Church and he had to be silenced. He had singlehandedly caused more embarrassment to Rome than any other living person. For years the Church had accepted criticism against the immoral practices of its clergy, but Luther had gone beyond this. He had struck at the very vitals of the Church by attacking the Pope and priests alike. Within two short weeks of his nailing his ninety-five theses to the church door, they were in print. That new invention, the printing press, allowed a phenomenal upsurge in the amount of material that could be circulated compared with what was previously available. They were sold throughout Germany and found a ready acceptance with the people. Added to this, a general anti-clerical feeling was already abroad which helped to promote Luther's views.

As time passed, Luther went from strength to strength. He saw that sound faith must be based solely on the Bible. No tradition, no philosophy, could compensate for its loss. 'Scripture alone' soon became the clarion call of the whole Reformation. Throughout this time Luther was gaining support from ordinary people. Though the people barely understood his theology they supported him personally. They knew that here was a genuine man fighting for a cause in which he believed. From within the Church itself his main support came from the younger friars. The old conservatives remained loyal to their first love and opposed him.

In an attempt to scupper this growing movement, the Pope issued his bull against Luther. He was ordered to submit to the Church and make a formal and public recantation. He responded by burning the edict amidst a huge gathering in Wittenberg on 10 December 1520. As he threw it into the bonfire which was lit to burn other Roman rubbish, he shouted, 'Because you have condemned the truth of God, He also condemns you today to the fire, Amen.'

Things were seemingly getting out of hand when Luther was summoned to appear before a diet or conference in the city of Worms. Here a cluster of state and church dignitaries had assembled to discuss his position. Some of his friends felt it was a summons to his death and not to defend his faith. If this was the case, Luther faced it with unusual courage. When the summons came the court had already been in session since 27 January 1521. He was ordered to attend by the Emperor Charles V himself in mid-March. He was promised a safe conduct to and from the Diet of Worms. He arrived there on 16 April, undeterred by what confronted him.

Like his master before him, Luther was branded a seditious fellow.

His actions were misconstrued for political as well as religious reasons. He was accused of being a 'revolutionary'. This slur upon his character may well have been a ploy to influence the Emperor's judgment. Yet despite all the threats and innuendoes, Luther made a triumphant entry into Worms. 'Unless I am held back by force,' he wrote, 'or Caesar revokes his invitation, I will enter Worms under the banner of Christ against the gates of hell.' Though he knew his danger he was confident. 'I have had my Palm Sunday,' he said. 'I wonder whether this pomp is merely a temptation or whether it is also the sign of impending passion.'

When he came before the Diet, he was faced with some of the most powerful men alive. For this cloistered monk to have entered such an august arena may well have daunted his spirit. He was unaccustomed to addressing the high and mighty of this world. He was more suited to the working classes than the upper classes. When he was asked if he affirmed his own works and words, he asked for some time to reconsider. This unusual act must have taken the court by surprise, not least Eck, his appointed examiner.

The following day Luther came forward exuding a new confidence. That night's vigil of prayer had obvious benefits. This day was to become the summit of his life, a day which will live in the annals of history, when one man alone resisted the might of Church and State. Those who were present must have been stunned almost into silence by the force of his expressions:

> Since then Your Majesty and your lordships desire a simple reply, I will answer without horns and without teeth. Unless I am convinced by Scripture and plain reason – I do not accept the authority of popes and councils, for they have contradicted each other – my conscience is captive to the Word of God. I cannot and will not recant anything, for to go against conscience is neither right nor safe. God help me. Amen. (Roland H. Bainton, *Here I Stand,* p.144)

Such boldness must have irritated Eck, the Roman representative who had felt that Luther had wavered the day before when he had asked for time to reconsider. In one fell swoop, all hope that he would retract what he had written was gone. He was a man set free by the truth and made captive to his conscience.

When he finally left Worms, he must have been relieved to be still in one piece, but on his way to Wittenberg he was seized by armed guards. These were not, as some thought, sent by his enemies: the whole exercise was staged for his protection. He was taken to Wartburg Castle, in the territory of the Elector Frederick of Saxony, his protector. Too many people would have liked him to have met with a fatal accident or even be brutally murdered. It was rumoured that he had been found with a knife in his back. This alarmed many of his followers; one wrote, 'O God, if Luther is dead, who will henceforth expound to us the gospel?'

This forced confinement, from May 1521 to March 1522, was not much to his liking. Though he felt himself inactive he kept himself very busy. 'I can tell you,' he wrote, 'in this idle solitude there are a thousand battles with Satan.' For all this, he wrote there many of his books and was able in ten weeks to write a German translation of the whole New Testament. Some achievement for someone living in 'idle solitude'!

If Luther himself was for a time removed from spearheading the Reformation, his writings continued to carry it forward. They were sold almost as soon as they came off the press. This helped to consolidate the work. The people were now being gripped not so much by a common movement but by a spiritual dynamism hitherto unknown in Germany.

It was almost a year before he was back in circulation. After his unusual detour, he finally reached Wittenberg on 8 March 1522. He came trusting in God's protection. His aim was to transform the Church by bringing it into conformity with God's Word, and this was to be done through preaching and teaching, not by force of arms. He separated himself from anything which created disorder or anarchy. It was not the overthrow of Rome by violence that he wanted. He was convinced that the Word of God alone possessed its own innate power to carry this out effectively:

> I will preach the Word, will declare it, will write it. But I will never force or press anyone with violence, for faith can only be willingly, unconstrainedly nourished . . . I have done nothing; the Word everything. If I had so wished, I might have deluged Germany with blood; yea, I might have started such a game at Worms that the Emperor himself would not have been secure. I have only let the Word act.

Luther recognized two branches of divine authority, State and Church. They were ordained for the social and spiritual welfare of ordinary people. It was the State's responsibility to protect the liberty of the Church and the Church's responsibility to support the authority of the State. This seemed clear to him. It was never his intention to create social unrest, but rather a spiritual revolution.

Within the confines of the Church he saw the Word of God as central. For years, even centuries, Rome had allowed it to recede further and further into the background. What the Reformation did was to bring it back to its rightful place. For Luther, the whole life and health of the Church depended upon its attitude to the Scriptures. What took place in Wittenberg was a revival of the truth of God as embodied in the Word of God. According to Luther:

> The Church does not make the Word of God, but she is made by the Word of God. For while the Word of God flourishes, all things flourish and go well in the Church – and that is the reason that at this day the Church is not only withered away into luxury and pomp but is almost wholly destroyed. It is because the Word of God is disregarded, and the laws of men and the artful inventions of Rome are taught. (V.H.H.Green, *Luther and the Reformation*, p.140)

Whenever the Word of God has this kind of support and belief within the Church and among its leaders there must be a healthy outlook and prospect for its future. The vehicle for its transmission was its preachers and teachers appointed by the Church. These were recognized by their gifts and knowledge. They were not to be thought of in the same way as the traditional priests, as an elite group over and above and distinct from all others. A new understanding of the Scriptures had brought a new concept of the true nature of a biblical priesthood. It was not restricted to the few but was extended to all, a gift to every believer. Those appointed to the ministry of the Word were to confirm believers in their faith.

To reinforce this new perception of the truth, former priests and nuns, who had taken an oath of celibacy, were permitted to marry. Many of them were glad to be able to cast off this intolerable yoke. They sometimes married each other almost to reaffirm their new found liberty. Luther himself took a wife. Not that he had had any previous intention to marry; he thought that he would always remain single, even though he wholeheartedly agreed with the principle. He had become caretaker of nine escaped nuns who had been brought to Wittenberg. He was expected either to find them employment or husbands. The first eight were soon suitably settled. This left only one remaining, Katherine von Bora. She was twenty-six, Luther forty-two. A possible suitor was found but met with her disapproval. To emphasize her dislike of him she said that she would rather marry a professor at Wittenberg, or even Luther himself, than marry him. Within a short time Luther married his Kate on 27 June 1525. It was a happy union as she reorganized his life and cared for him.

Though he met other Reformers to discuss points of doctrine, Luther's main occupation in Wittenberg was preaching. He was not an organizer but a preacher. His expository lectures run into numerous volumes. He was systematic in his approach, expounding book after book, and much of the Old Testament was covered. But his great love was that resurrected doctrine of justification by faith, embodied chiefly in Paul's epistles to the Romans and Galatians. It had a powerful effect upon him, so that his preaching automatically tended to flow in this direction, no matter where he was preaching.

The church held many preaching services throughout the week, too many for one man to cater for. This meant that several others were appointed to maintain continuity. Luther sometimes preached several times on a Sunday and throughout the week. His position made him a kind of father figure to some of the younger men. They often sought his advice on preaching. His own lucid and simple style made him intelligible to the most common of his hearers.

One discouraged preacher came to him complaining about the shortness of his sermons and their apparent worthlessness. Luther rebuked and encouraged him:

> If Peter and Paul were here, they would scold you because you wish right off to be as accomplished as they. Do your best. If you cannot preach an hour, then half an hour or a quarter of an hour. Do not try to imitate other people. Centre on the shortest and simplest points, which are the very heart of the matter, and leave the rest to God. Look solely to his honour and not to applause. Pray that God will give you a mouth and to your audience ears. I can tell you preaching is not a work of man. Although I am old and experienced, I am afraid every time I have to preach. You

will most certainly find out three things: first, you will have prepared your sermon as diligently as you know how, and it will slip through your fingers as water; second, you may abandon your outline and God will give you grace. You will preach your very best. The audience will be pleased, but you won't. And thirdly, when you have been unable in advance to pull anything together, you will preach acceptably both to your hearers and to yourself. So pray to God and leave all the rest to him.

With an ever-increasing number of aspiring preachers it was necessary to lay down some ground rules for their selection. They were not all adequately suited or qualified. Luther looked for natural as well as supernatural endowments. If he advised preachers 'to pray to God and leave all the rest to him', he did not wish to imply that native ability was not important. It was assumed that this was present before that advice was given. As always, Luther's directives were clear and to the point, and included counsel on the use of language, voice, memory – and on knowing when to stop!

Towards the end of his life he suffered terribly from ill health. He was worn down by continual labour. The effects of the ongoing campaign had taken their toll. He felt his age creeping up on him and everything was becoming a toil. He also experienced long bouts of severe depression. Life for him had lost its pleasure. Yet throughout, he never lost sight of God or his gospel which he had so fervently sought to reassert. It was his first and last great stronghold in the midst of a turbulent and changing world.

Writing to his friend, Jacob Probst, he said: 'Old, decrepit, bereft of energy, weary, cold, and now one-eyed I had hoped that now at least peace would be vouchsafed to me as to a dead man. And yet, as if I had never done anything, never spoken, written, achieved anything, I must still be overwhelmed with such toils. But Christ is all in all, both to do and to finish, blessed for ever!'

When death finally came of a heart attack on 17 February 1546, he was on his last preaching tour. He happened to be at Eisleben where he was born, where he preached to large congregations in full churches. It was a fitting epitaph to the life and ministry of this great Reformer.

6
John Calvin
(1509-64)

'John Calvin', wrote William Cunningham, 'was by far the greatest of the Reformers with respect to the talents he possessed, the influence he exerted, and the services he rendered in the establishment and diffusion of important truth.'

In many ways it is strange to find Jean Cauvin, to give him his French name, placed in this position. From his background and temperament he would have preferred living in obscurity to being at the centre of controversy. His natural inclinations disposed him towards becoming a 'man of letters' rather than a 'man of the Word'. It was the quiet retreat of his study which held out the greatest attraction for him. He feared contention and shunned the limelight. However owing to a seemingly incidental visit to Geneva the whole direction of his life was dramatically changed.

Born on 10 July 1509 in Noyon, about sixty miles north-east of Paris, in Picardy, not far from its famous cathedral, Calvin was brought up as a gentleman. His ambitious father, who was an astute financier, ascended the social ladder by his skill. He had come from a typical working class family but had succeeded in entering the ranks of the upper middle classes to become one of the citizens of Noyon in 1497. This was a highly regarded and prestigious position and increased his influence with others.

Almost from birth John's father began to prepare him for the Roman Catholic priesthood. The Church was a powerful institution and offered many lucrative positions, everything a good father could wish for his son. He was extremely ambitious for himself and the family name. He had visions of it being ranged with those of the renowned. It would, but not in quite the way he anticipated.

When he was a boy John's devout mother used to take him on religious pilgrimages. However, for his father the Church was more a means to an end than an end in itself. It offered security and huge financial benefits. With the right contacts there were golden opport-unities for an aspiring young priest. His father, who was himself in the employ of the Bishop of Noyon, secured for him a benefice from the cathedral and a shared chaplaincy. This meant that before his twelfth birthday John was financially independent.

As a student he surpassed all his peers intellectually and was in a class of his own. His quick intelligence and excellent memory secured for him a place of pre-eminence among his contemporaries. His early friends belonged to the gentry. He studied with the children of the wealthy and powerful Montmor family, and along with them he was taught and groomed for future usefulness.

John Calvin

Together they went to Paris to study at the College de la Marche. When John left home he was still only fourteen years old. His devotion to study coupled with his intelligence enabled him to rise in leaps and bounds academically. He was a serious student of sombre appearance, with the result that some of his colleagues began calling him 'The Accusative Case'. At La Marche he learnt Latin, which was considered 'the door-keeper to all the other sciences'. Afterwards, he went on to further study at Montaigu, a college specifically designed for theological students. This was an educational monastery for future priests. As an institution, it imposed a hard regime, and became noted for its cruel beatings with the birch and its poor food.

But then, for some unknown reason, his father suddenly re-directed his studies away from theology to law. From what is known of him it seems certain that he was financially motivated. With the rise of Lutheranism in Germany and the development of other Reformed groups in Europe, the now fractured Roman Church did not seem such a sound proposition as it had originally. He was a man of discernment who sensed the winds of change. Calvin himself wrote: 'Even while I was a boy my father had destined me for the study of theology; then, later, as he considered that the knowledge of law commonly enriched those who followed it, this hope made him straightway change his mind.'

Theodore Beza, Calvin's first biographer and successor, refers to Calvin's own changing views. He had recently come into contact with the new teaching spreading throughout Europe. His opinions and ideas were being challenged and his thoughts were in a state of flux. It would have been sheer hypocrisy for him to have entered the priesthood without some definite faith.

From Paris he came to Orleans to study law under the most celebrated French lawyer of the day, Pierre de l'Estoile. Again he excelled in his studies and was often asked to stand in for absent lecturers. He was often placed over other students and acted more as a tutor than a fellow student. When he came to leave Orleans he was offered a doctorate because of his assistance to the college. Whether or not he accepted it remains uncertain. His last academic port of call was in Bourges where he was probably converted. This took place towards the end of 1529 or early 1530. The circumstances sur-rounding it are hazy. All that can be said with any degree of certainty is what Calvin himself wrote: 'Although I was so obstinately given to the superstitions of the papacy, that it was extremely difficult to drag me from the depths of the mire, yet by a sudden conversion He tamed my heart and made it teachable, this heart which for its age was excessively hardened in such matters.'

The effect of this change can be seen in his rapid rise as a teacher of the Reformed faith. It stirred and inspired him with an enthusiasm hitherto unknown:

> Having thus received some taste and knowledge of true godliness, I was immediately inflamed with so intense a desire to make progress therein, that although I did not altogether leave off other studies, I yet pursued them with less ardour. I was quite surprised to find that before a year had elapsed, all who had any desire after purer doctrine were continually coming to me to learn . . . I then began to seek some secluded corner where I might be withdrawn from the public view; but so far from being able to accomplish the object of my desire, all my retreats were like public schools. In short, whilst my own great object was to live in seclusion without being known, God . . . never permitted me to rest in any place, until, in spite of my natural disposition, he brought me forth to public notice.

God, the dispenser of every good gift, never allows them to be hidden, but finds ample use for them in the advancement of his kingdom. If there was one thing Calvin had learnt during these preparatory years, it was how to think. With Latin at his fingertips, and a thorough knowledge of Hebrew and Greek, plus the benefit of a lawyer's precision, Calvin had every qualification to make him a theologian of great clarity of thought and expressive ability.

His conversion and the start of his preaching ministry took place almost at the same time. The first mention of him preaching was at Bourges. Perhaps, like Saul of Tarsus, his conversion was in a blaze of glory and he could not wait to tell others what the Lord had done for him (Acts 9:20). It is obvious from what has already been quoted that he was an immediate success. As a teacher he was of the first magnitude. He also lectured on rhetoric in the local Augustinian monastery where it is said that 'he often preached in the stone pulpit which still stands in their ancient church.'

For the next few years Calvin was continually on the move. He spent time at Orleans, Noyon and Paris. One major event during this time was the publication of his first and only secular book. This was a revised edition and interpretation of Seneca's *De Clementia* in 1532. However his desire for academic recognition was not wholly quenched by his conversion. He had a living to make, now that his future looked uncertain.

Towards the end of 1533, Nicolas Cop, rector of the College de Navarre, a Reformer and possible Lutheran, came to address the college. His attack upon the existing *status quo* in the Church resulted in him having to make a hasty exit from Paris. Beza maintains that Calvin had written the script for Cop. Calvin was quickly implicated in the affair and he too had to flee from Paris. For the next year he was a fugitive, preaching in the villages. Eventually he came to rest in Claix where he spent several months in seclusion, and where he began a small introduction to Christian doctrine which over the years grew to be his monumental work, *The Institutes of the Christian Religion.*

The *Institutes* was to embody his theological thought. It went through several stages, culminating in its final form in 1559. Though additions were made, its essence never changed. His theology from first to last remained the same. Its first printing took place in 1536, though it was probably finished before the close of 1535. It was a remarkable achievement, considering Calvin had not yet reached the age of twenty-seven.

His connection with Geneva began soon after this event. After more than a year in Basle, and Ferrara in Italy, and following a short stay in Paris, he was forced to leave France altogether because of increased hostilities. On his way to the German city of Strasbourg, a city which had officially accepted Protestantism, Calvin, with a small group of friends and family, spent a night in a Geneva inn. It was here that he first met his life-long friend Guillaume Farel. It was a historic and dramatic scene:

> Wherever else I had gone, I had taken care to conceal that I was the author of [the *Institutio*]; and I had resolved to continue in the same privacy and obscurity, until at length Guillaume Farel detained me at Geneva, not so much by counsel and exhortation, as by a dreadful curse, which I felt to be as if God had from heaven laid his mighty hand upon me to arrest me. As the most direct road to Strasbourg, to which I then intended to retire, was shut up by the wars, I had resolved to pass quickly by Geneva . . . Farel, who burned with an extraordinary zeal to advance the gospel, immediately strained every nerve to detain me. And after learning that my heart was set upon devoting myself to private studies, for which I wished to keep myself free from other pursuits, and finding

that he gained nothing by entreaties, he proceeded to utter the imprecation that God would curse my retirement and the tranquillity of the
studies which I sought, if I should withdraw and refuse to help, when the
necessity was so urgent. By this imprecation I was so terror-struck, that I
gave up the journey I had undertaken . . . (T.H.L. Parker, *John Calvin*,
pp. 52-53)

Farel's intervention was to have major consequences not only for
Calvin himself but for Geneva, Europe and the world. Farel could not
bear to think of him going anywhere else other than Geneva. His own
contribution to the transformation of Geneva had been great, but there
was need to consolidate the work. Calvin, he felt, could give it that
missing ingredient which neither he nor the other preachers could – a
structured system of theology.

When Calvin came to this republican city, it had about ten
thousand inhabitants (not much more than a large village by modern
standards). Only a year before, Geneva had been won by the evangelicals for the gospel when the city voted to live by its standards.
Calvin came at first as a simple reader of theology; his title was
simply 'lecturer in holy Scripture'. He refused to take any public
office though he was soon elected to the pastorate. He put preaching
and the Bible above everything. They were central to his whole
thinking as a pastor-preacher.

As he set about reorganizing the church, several proposals were
put before the city council for endorsement. Except for one they were
all passed. The church was now taking on another shape since the
Roman mould had finally been shattered, but there were still factions
in the city who were decidedly hostile toward Calvin. With the
growing threat of France annexing Geneva from Switzerland, rum-
ours were spread suggesting he and Farel were French spies. This
malicious taint stuck to him for the next twenty years. It was a
ridiculous suggestion, but one taken seriously by some. Eventually,
things became intolerable and he and Farel were expelled from the
city.

After leaving Geneva in 1538 the exiles went first to Bern, then
on to Basle where they settled. Soon, others hearing of this began to
show an interest in the author of the *Institutes*. The leading lights in
Strasbourg, Bucer and Capito, asked him to come there as pastor to

the French Church, a company mostly of French refugees driven out of France by persecution, and also to lecture in theology. After meeting them Calvin decided not to go because the offer was limited to himself and did not include Farel. Bucer, taking a page out of Farel's book, cursed him for refusing God's call. Again, Calvin responded to this somewhat irregular method and accepted the call.

His situation in Strasbourg was a comparatively easy one. There were between four and five hundred people in the church there. He had his problems but they were nothing like those in Geneva. Here he was among his own people. It was a real home from home. 'I have my own share of contests and wrestlings where I am,' he wrote, 'and most arduous they are. But they do not overwhelm me; they merely keep me training.'

One problem which continually vexed him in Strasbourg was a shortage of money. These French immigrants were poor, and therefore he had to supplement his income by giving private lectures and doing some legal work. Apart from this things went on quite well and he was fairly happy with his lot. He had also married, had two step-children, and still found time to work on his new, revised edition of the *Institutes*, which was published in 1539.

The ejection of Calvin and Farel from Geneva did not bring about a lasting peace to the city. Within two years developments had overtaken them and several seemingly insurmountable difficulties faced the city's council. During this critical time they came to realize their mistake in sending Calvin away. His ecclesiastical and social reforms would have given the city a measure of stability. Instead, he was settled in Strasbourg with little chance of returning. After consultation the council decided to send a delegation to Strasbourg inviting him to return. Calvin greeted the proposal with horror. The wounds of his former encounter had only just healed and the thought of returning to Geneva terrified him. 'Rather,' he wrote, 'would I submit to death a hundred times than to that cross on which I had to perish daily a thousand times over.' To Farel he wrote, 'Whenever I call to mind the wretchedness of my life there, how can it be but that my very soul must shudder at any proposal for my return.'

Yet for all his fear, return he did. The cross which he so much dreaded he was prepared to retake if God so desired. His thoughts were that God had not led him away from this work. On the contrary, he was forced to leave it because of his enemies. Was it, therefore, right to refuse a summons to resume the work?

When Calvin entered Geneva in October 1540 it was as a returning hero accompanied by his entourage. Immediately by his preaching he began restructuring the church. Given the warm reception he had on his return he was able to make several changes both within the church and society. Several ecclesiastical ordinances soon became law. However he was not without his enemies. The Libertines continued to oppose his narrowness. They preferred the old city with its brothels and prostitutes to the new morality inspired by Calvin. They posed a constant threat to his reforms and remained his obstinate antagonists until 1555. Then, due to some political insurrection, their influence and power was finally destroyed.

Throughout the fifteen years preceeding the final defeat of the Libertines, Calvin had concentrated all his efforts on preaching and teaching. His approach to preaching can be seen in his first sermon after returning to Geneva. He was so consistently systematic that he took up where he had left off! To him, the heart of the Reformation movement was its preaching. The extent of his preaching and the importance he gave to it can be measured by the frequency with which sermons were preached in Geneva throughout the week. And these sermons were not mere ten minute slots in the service, for someone to explain a few words from the Bible. The sermon was the hub of the service around which everything else turned.

Calvin preached twice on Sunday and every day of the week on alternate weeks. On Sundays, he generally preached on the New Testament and on weekdays on the Old Testament. His sermons were always expository and applicatory. There was nothing of hanging sermons on suitable texts. Preaching was considered as nothing less than the voice of God speaking, and its importance could not be minimized. It was one of Calvin's three constituent marks of a true church, the other two being the proper administration of the sacraments and discipline. It was the latter of these which tended to stir up most opposition. As he preached, his sermons were taken down in shorthand, written out later into books, and borrowed by the people. His systematic method meant that he missed nothing. Every topic had to be dealt with in order. His productiveness and the volume of his sermons can be seen in his commentaries. These reveal how he presented his material from the pulpit. They were not written addresses but preached directly from his Hebrew and Greek Bibles.

The reason for Calvin's strong emphasis upon preaching was because it is God's means of sanctifying his Church. Through it he instructs and corrects his people. Calvin's preaching was pastoral as well as intellectual, and the thrust of his sermons was always in that direction. Preaching and teaching were of supreme importance.

However, before Geneva became 'Calvin's Geneva', there was a long uphill battle to be fought. Calvin did not always get his own way on everything, but often suffered defeat at the hands of his antagonists. But when they looked to have struck a final death blow, God turned their wisdom to folly. They made several ill-advised, political manoeuvres which resulted in their total overthrow. Some were executed, while others were forced to flee the city. The day had now dawned when Geneva was to become what Jerusalem was in the Old Testament, 'the joy of the whole earth'.

For Calvin the spiritual and moral struggle had ended in triumph. He was now able to realize his vision of a truly Reformed Church. It was the heyday of Geneva and the Reformation. To those visiting or living in Geneva, it was incomparably the best living example of godliness affecting society ever seen. The Scottish Reformer, John Knox, who lived there for a time wrote: 'Here exists the most perfect school of Christ which has been since the days of the Apostles on earth. Christ is preached everywhere . . . yet nowhere did I find that morals and faith have been improved more sincerely than here.' And to the exiled Bishop of Ossory, John Bale, Geneva was a sanctuary: 'Is it not wonderful that Spaniards, Italians, Scots, Englishmen, Frenchmen, Germans, disagreeing in manners, speech and apparel, sheep and wolves, bulls and bears, being coupled with the only yoke of Christ, should live so lovingly and friendly?'

Within the church in Geneva there was a happy, joyful people. One of the things Calvin introduced into the service was the singing of psalms, something which he had also done in Strasbourg. He found it both stimulating and exhilarating in worship, a means of drawing him nearer to God. Another major development he introduced in Geneva was its college. If he had a concern for the spiritual welfare of his congregation he also had a concern for that of Europe. The greatest need of the hour was for a more faithful and well-informed ministry. The Church was not simply to live for today but to prepare for tomorrow. By 1559, a site had been chosen and a college erected with Theodore Beza as its first Rector. At the same time, a heated dispute erupted between the faculty of Lausanne and its council in Bern, with the result that they resigned *en bloc*. These, at Calvin's request, migrated to Geneva and took charge of the new college. Before his death in 1564, over a hundred preachers were sent out from Geneva to churches all over Europe. It was the capstone of his work and marked the tenacity and achievement of Geneva's great Reformer.

It is sometimes thought that Calvin was a dry academic, harsh and autocratic, but nothing could be further from the truth. He did, as did all writers of his day, use highly charged and emotive language in disputes. He could also become very irritable and impatient, and speak abruptly to people (for which he afterwards repented). Yet at heart, he was a timid, withdrawn man who enjoyed the company and fellowship of friends. When the opposition was intense he was known to say that 'he could not live without friendship.'

To those Genevans who knew him best, he was much loved. Towards the end of his life he was carried to the city hall, where he spoke to the council members for the last time and in such a way that all were moved. The council's clerk recorded that, 'He talked with exceeding breathing difficulties and with such marvellous graciousness that the gentlemen were hardly able to hold back their tears.'

For a long time before his death, Calvin had been plagued with ill health. His complaints were many and varied. On Christmas Day 1559, as he was awarded citizenship in Geneva, he preached so powerfully that afterwards he vomited blood. Unknown to him his fragile constitution had contracted tuberculosis. It was a slow death. With immense difficulty he continued to preach and lecture right to the very last. As his time drew near he wrote to Farel: 'Since it is God's will that you should outlive me, remember our friendship. It was useful to God's Church and its fruits await us in heaven. I do not want you to tire yourself on my account. I draw my breath with difficulty and expect each moment to breathe my last. It is enough that I live and die for Christ, who is to all his followers a gain in life and in death.' Calvin died on 27 May 1564.

7
John Knox
(c.1514-72)

One of the most unusual pictures that history records of John Knox is of him acting as a bodyguard to George Wishart. For five weeks, as Wishart preached throughout Lothian, in Scotland, Knox carried a two-handed sword. Needless to say, they were traumatic days.

This picture of Knox does little justice to his true character. He was far more suited to wielding the sword of the Spirit than a sword of steel. The Scottish Reformation which took place under him came about by the Word of God which is 'living, and powerful, and sharper than any two-edged sword, piercing even to the division of soul and spirit, and of joints and marrow, and is a discerner of the thoughts and intents of the heart' (Hebrews 4:12).

Knox was born some time between 1513 and 1515, probably in Haddington, in Lothian, about seventeen miles from Edinburgh. His father was a yeoman without importance or influence. He was an astute man and helped forward his sons' careers, setting one up in business and sending another, John, to school. When he came to St Andrews, Fife, Reformed theology was beginning to infiltrate the university there and the advance of Protestantism was well under way. By the end of March 1543, John was either already converted or very nearly so.

George Wishart's influence on Knox cannot be minimized. Not long after Knox's conversion, he had taken a post as a private tutor, but Wishart's preaching prompted him to take a more public and militant stand for the gospel. Wishart's assumed complicity in a conspiracy to assassinate Cardinal Beaton, the Roman emissary, meant that he was a wanted man. This was the reason why he needed the protection of a bodyguard and why Knox became so intimately involved with him for those five weeks before eventually leaving him. Within five hours of their separation Wishart was caught and handed over to Beaton. On March 1 he was tried, found guilty, and sentenced to death. Wishart's death shook Knox. Had he remained with him only a few hours more, he too could have suffered the same fate as his friend. He felt immediately that the mantle of this fiery preacher had fallen upon him. His opposition to Beaton and the Roman Church intensified.

Until this time Knox had enjoyed relative obscurity as a teacher. Now that he had shown his colours, he too was under threat. It was only a matter of time before he would become the object not only of Rome's invective, but also of her attack. After leaving the security of the household of the Laird, whose children he taught, Knox spent some time going from place to place hounded by Archbishop Hamilton's men. Finally he came to St Andrews where a number of the gentry, along with their supporters, were holding the castle of the hated Cardinal Beaton, whom they had killed. These became known as the Castilians. When he entered the castle with three pupils who had accompanied him, it was prepared to repel an armed invasion.

The garrison had been significantly strengthened to ward off a military strike by the enemy.

For a while Knox continued to instruct his pupils. Later he was invited to become assistant pastor to John Rough among these Castilians. Until now he had never preached publicly, and quickly refused the offer. His excuse was that 'he could not run where God had not called him.' Nevertheless, it was decided by some that he would be formally called and appointed to the office of preacher. After Rough had preached one Sunday on the election of ministers, he turned to Knox and repeated the call with the wholehearted support of the congregation. Knox, taken by surprise, gave no response but broke down in tears. He left the church not knowing what to do. He would either have to accept the offer or leave the city. Aligning himself with these in such a public manner meant he would invariably be courting a martyr's crown. Suddenly, Knox was thrown into a bout of deep depression.

When Knox came to preach his first sermon it confirmed the church's decision and his call to the ministry. He took as his text Daniel 7:24-25. After his attack upon Rome he challenged anyone present who wished to discuss the sermon further to meet him afterwards. The general feeling was that 'while other preachers lopped off the branches, Knox struck at the very roots of papistry'.

This action brought Knox into extreme danger. When the Castilians were finally forced to surrender in August 1547 to the French supporters of Mary Stuart, he was numbered among them. They were sent to France where he was sentenced to life on the French galleys as an oarsman. Due to the intervention of the English, this lasted only nineteen months, but it was a severe penalty. The other galley slaves were godless criminals, and the treatment he received at the hands of his captors was very harsh. Once he came very close to death, which must have appeared a glorious prospect compared with his immediate situation; but he survived.

During this time of captivity his faith was strengthened, his character formed, and his prayer life developed. His galley often sailed with a French flotilla up the English Channel to Scotland. On one of these visits, as they came within sight of St Andrews, his sickness was at its worst. His friends, fearing for his life, asked if he knew what port they were approaching. As he looked around and saw the church's steeple he said, 'Yes: I know it well, for I see the steeple of that place where God first in public opened my mouth to his glory, and I am fully persuaded, how weak that ever I now appear, that I shall not depart this life, till that my tongue shall glorify his godly name in the same place.'

To Knox, this time of suffering was for Christ's sake. There was no room for complaint. It was a token of God's love, a time of chastening. The apparently paradoxical statement that God chastens those whom he loves (Hebrews 12:6) was of great encouragement to him throughout his confinement.

When his release came at last there was no possibility of his returning to Scotland. Instead, he went to England where Archbishop Cranmer was encouraging continental theologians to come and live. Knox came to England in early 1549. This was the heyday of England's Reformation. With the death of Henry VIII in 1547 and the accession to the throne of his son Edward VI, Protestantism was thriving.

Soon after his arrival he was appointed a minister of the church in Berwick, and then of Newcastle in the North of England. His close proximity to Scotland caused several problems. Because of the fractious conditions across the border, many of the Scots were migrating south. With Knox so close at hand and under the protection of the English monarch, these migrants gravitated to him, causing the Scottish contingent in that area to multiply. He was a fellow countryman and never tried to conceal it. He also understood them and sympathized with their plight, but it was his preaching first and foremost that drew them.

This time of comparative tranquillity enabled him to regain his physical strength and develop his thoughts. As things took shape in his mind and his ideas crystallized, he became a full-blooded Reformer. His whole-hearted attachment to the Reformers on the continent of Europe, as opposed to the English Reformers, often brought him into conflict with the latter. They were partial, rather than total Reformers; there were remnants of the old religion which they wanted to keep. As the English Reformers, led by Cranmer, were laying the bedrock of Anglicanism, Knox and his company were becoming more and more disenchanted with them. He had suffered too much to give way to a partial reformation. To him, it must be all or nothing.

About five weeks before the second Edwardian Prayer Book of 1552 was published, Knox made a scathing attack before the King on the question of kneeling to receive the sacrament of the Lord's Supper, something Cranmer held dearly. Knox said it was idolatrous, a worshipping of the consecrated bread and wine, and he advised his congregation in Newcastle to refuse to do it. Though Cranmer finally won the day, he had to make concessions. He was forced to insert what was called by the anti-kneeling party the 'Black Rubric'. This was a note attached to the finished Prayer Book, stating that kneeling before the elements in the communion service was not an act of worshipping those elements. However, Knox was still not totally happy with this arrangement.

Owing to the enmity of the Duke of Northumberland, Knox came further south. After the Duke had found him unsupportive in furthering his political intrigues he soon had him removed. Knox's growing influence in the north meant he was becoming dangerous and needed curbing. The only way to do this was to separate him from his flock. Afterwards, he was offered the bishopric of Rochester but refused it. One reason for his rejection was his fear of a Roman Catholic resurgence. Eventually he was appointed to All Hallows in London, under the control of Bishop Nicholas Ridley.

His fears of a resurgence of Roman Catholic power were not unfounded. When the young Protestant king, Edward VI, died on 6 July 1553, the question of who would succeed him became critical. Before his death, wishing to divert the crown from the head of his sister Mary, he made plans to have Lady Jane Grey crowned. However, Mary made short shrift of her opponents after Edward's death. She was able to scupper their plans and rid herself of most of her worst enemies at the same time. In 1553 she became Queen. This promised ill for the Reformers. Mary was a rigid Roman Catholic and it was not long before she started to turn England Romeward again.

With this change of events in England, Knox left the country. In February 1554 he was in France heading for Switzerland. By March, he was in Geneva. After the final overthrow of the Libertines in the city, Geneva had become everything he could have wished for in a Christian community. Life was ordered and regulated by the Word of God. Here he found the realization of what at home had been only an ideal.

When Mary married Philip of Spain, England's fate looked sealed. Against the combined military might of Spain and England, who could stand? This union became a clarion call for other Protestants to leave England for the comparative safety of the continent. Many of these exiles began an English colony in Frankfurt, Germany and invited Knox to become their pastor. His immediate response was to refuse, which he would have done had not Calvin intervened. He encouraged Knox to accept it, and by November he was in Frankfurt.

When Knox arrived, he found himself in the midst of a heated controversy over the use of the second Book of Common Prayer. He had been called as pastor by those who wanted to reform it without compromise. They remembered how much he had opposed certain aspects of it while in England and felt he was the perfect man to champion their cause. His opposition to the Prayer Book had also become more resolute since leaving England. When some new members, led by Richard Cox, tried to force it upon the established members in Frankfurt, Knox immediately opposed them. These had recently joined the church, turning the minority into the majority. They were also adamant about the structure of the church. It was to have an 'English' face not a Continental one. They gave no room for compromise, but insisted upon an unmodified Prayer Book.

The inflexible Anglicans went even further. Now that they held the reins of power, they prohibited Knox from preaching. This impassioned debate resulted in Knox being forced to leave Frankfurt altogether. The city council, tired of these internal squabbles, began pressurizing the parties into agreement. When a meeting was convened to resolve their differences, Knox refused to accept its conclusion – the reintroduction of the Prayer Book. His opponents reported him to the council who expelled him from the city. When he returned to Geneva, Calvin fully supported him in his stance.

Soon after his return Knox was on the move again, this time to Scotland. While he was away a number of his Frankfurt congregation came to Geneva. These, along with several other English exiles already living there, formed a new church. It was the first real Puritan church. This was structured on the Reformed pattern, with preaching at its heart. They appointed two men as acting ministers in Knox's absence. To them he was still their pastor. When he returned in September 1556, after spending nearly a year in Scotland, he brought with him his new wife, Marjory Bowes, his mother-in-law, and several others.

In Geneva he continued pastoring the new English congregation, and it was there that he published his *First Blast of the Trumpet against the Monstrous Regiment of Women*. This was an attack upon the national rule of women. 'Bloody Mary' still ruled over England, while 'Mary, Queen of Scots,' ruled in Scotland. For Knox, this was an unnatural situation and the chief cause of strife in both kingdoms. When Elizabeth I ascended the throne of England, Knox had to modify some of his statements while courting English support for the Protestants in Scotland.

When Mary Tudor died on 17 November 1558, it meant that the English Protestants in Europe could return to their own land. This allowed the English-speaking church in Geneva to be transplanted to its home soil. After their migration, Knox was left alone in Geneva and decided to return to Scotland. While waiting in Dieppe for clearance to travel through England to Scotland, he helped in the English refugee church there. His preaching was so effective that many were added to the church, even of the gentry.

Meanwhile, a year or so before his arrival in Scotland, Mary of Guise, the mother of Mary, Queen of Scots, had persuaded the Scottish parliament to hand the Scottish crown over to the French. To secure this she had led them to believe it would be advantageous for them that her daughter be allowed to marry Francis, heir apparent to the French throne, and that Scotland should be annexed to France. At first, she was quite friendly towards Protestant preachers and allowed them freedom to preach almost anywhere, but once her scheme had run its course and its end had been achieved, she began to oppose them. When they failed to turn up for a meeting to discuss church affairs in Scotland because of political reasons, she declared them rebels.

The response of the Scottish nobles, lairds and burgesses who were Protestant and anti-French was immediate. They agreed to protect the preachers and unite together in a covenant to 'establish the most blessed Word of God and His congregation' – from which they were nicknamed 'The Lords of the Congregation'.

On 2 May 1559 Knox arrived back in Scotland. From here on, it is said, Knox was becoming the moral and spiritual, if not the political leader of the reformed movement. His presence and preaching made him an inspiration to others. When Knox went to St Andrews and preached at the parish church on Christ's cleansing of the temple, it was with such telling effect that they agreed 'to remove all monuments of idolatry, which also they did with expedition, including the images in the Cathedral . . . As to Scotland's future, he was confident. In a letter written at this time he said:

> The long thirst of my wretched heart is satisfied in abundance, that is above my expectation for now forty days and more, has my God used my tongue in my native country, to the manifestation of his glory . . . The thirst of the poor people, as well as of the nobility here, is wondrous great which puts me in comfort that Christ Jesus shall triumph for a space here, in the North and extreme parts of the earth.

This unexpected support, which surprised even Mary of Guise, plus several military skirmishes which drove her out of Perth, forced her to make concessions to the Lords of the Congregation. This compromise, in fact, was simply a playing for time, but it suited both parties for the time being. The following months saw an escalation in political intrigue. While Mary looked to France for support, the Protestants turned to England. Before the end of 1559, in December, Mary was spurred on to renew her attempts to put down the Congregation by an additional nine hundred French soldiers recently despatched from France. As the Protestants were being forced to retreat and Mary looked to be winning the battle, she gloated, 'Where is now John Knox's God?'

Her celebrations, however, were short-lived. Elizabeth I had also moved quickly and had sent help to the beleaguered Protestants. By the time a treaty was agreed in July 1560 between the Scots, the French and the English, Mary of Guise was dead.

Throughout this time the Reformation had gradually been gaining momentum. Knox had been called to the church of St Giles in Edinburgh on 7 July 1559, after the first settlement between Mary and the Lords of the Congregation. Churches were also sprouting up throughout the land under his strenuous preaching. Even when fever struck he pushed himself to the limit to attract popular support for the gospel. By August 1560, the Scottish Reformation had reached its peak, in principle if not in practice. Scotland was legally declared a

Protestant country by an Act of Parliament, and an official National Church was to be established along Calvinistic lines.

In the last thirteen years of his life, from 1559 on, Knox was to do his greatest work. He soon became a national hero and Scotland's best-known Reformer. Everything prior to this was preparatory. The struggles of the past were precursors to those of the future. His presence alone in Scotland helped fortify the Reformed movement.

Throughout these flurried years, as Scotland was brought to the brink of civil war on several occasions, Knox carried the Reformation steadily forward. It was his preaching more than anything else that struck terror into his enemies. Dr Martyn Lloyd-Jones once said of him:

> His great characteristic as a preacher was vehemency . . . John Knox was a powerful preacher, with the result that he was a most influential preacher. The effect of his preaching upon Edward VI was quite remarkable; and that was not only true of Edward VI but of many others also. It is traditional to refer to the effect of his preaching on Mary, Queen of Scots. He could make her weep; not under conviction but in anger. She was afraid of him, and she said she was more afraid of his prayers and his preaching than of many regiments of English soldiers . . . Many times did one sermon delivered by Knox change the whole situation. When the Lords and others were alarmed, and frightened, and ready to give in, Knox would go up into a pulpit and preach a sermon; and the entire situation was transformed. (Westminster Conference Paper, 1972, pp.99f)

With the introduction of a National Reformed Church in 1560, Knox along with the other church leaders set about organizing it. No doubt his experience in Geneva helped to formulate the Church along those lines. The Reformed theology which he had absorbed there became the hallmark of his and their preaching. The sovereignty of God held everything else together. He was the King who ruled and held sway over the hearts of men and women alike. These leaders felt that their greatest need was for additional preachers. To help achieve this, superintendents were established to supervise their increase. These were not permanent bishops but temporary overseers of this work.

While all these momentous events were taking place in Scotland,

Mary, Queen of Scots was living in France with her husband. When he died in early December, the question of her return became an issue. She was told that on no account was she to reinstate the mass in Scotland, but her first Sunday in Scotland was spent in a private mass. Knox responded by thundering out a warning against her use of it. At this point he saw the issue far more clearly than the politicians, who thought he was being too extreme. He felt this was the thin end of the wedge which threatened the whole process of reform in Scotland, and he was right. Her private use of the mass proved to be a continual cause of tension within the realm for years to come. Nevertheless Knox had the measure of the woman. After their first meeting he could record, 'if there be not in her a proud mind, a crafty wit, and an indurate [callous] heart against God and his truth, my judgment faileth me.'

From Mary's point of view Knox stood as the main bulwark against the reintroduction of Romanism into Scotland. The art of intrigue, learnt at the French Court, was not wasted on her. She was subtle and devious and used her charm and wit to muster support. However Knox saw through her. There was also an underground Roman Catholic movement which she helped promote. In short, she was prepared to do anything to bring Scotland back to Roman Catholicism.

Soon after her marriage to Lord Darnley in July 1565, a marriage which she contracted in order to strengthen her claim to the English throne, Mary thought that Scotland's time to return to the Roman fold had finally come. But she was grossly mistaken. After bearing their son James, she developed a growing antipathy towards her husband. This culminated in his murder by the Earl of Bothwell, her lover. This incident finally proved her undoing. Her infatuation for the young Earl, coupled with his lust for power, caused them to make one fatal mistake. He forcibly carried her off to Dunbar Castle and married her. This brought upon them the ire of both Roman Catholics and Protestants alike. In the ensuing events they were forced to flee. Eventually, Mary surrendered to her pursuers and in 1567 was forced to abdicate the throne in favour of her infant son James, while she herself was imprisoned in Lochleven Castle. This effectively ended Mary's influence in Scotland, though her struggle to regain power continued for some time afterwards.

When Knox returned to Scotland after a short time in England, he demanded the death penalty for the disgraced Queen on the grounds of adultery and murder, but was unsuccessful. He also preached at the young King's coronation, while the Earl of Moray became Regent. For Knox, this meant victory for the Reformation. The Reformed faith became the official religion of Scotland both legally and financially. For him, personally, it meant a change of role. He was happy to leave the political arena to concentrate on what was nearest to his heart, the strengthening of the emerging Reformed churches.

Knox himself continued in St Giles to be what he had always wanted to be, the minister of a parish. For years he had had, by conviction and providence, to act as an Old Testament prophet, standing between God and the nation. Like Elijah, he had almost single-handedly torn down the altars of false worship and idolatry and restored true worship. Through his preaching Scotland had been purged of the Roman Catholic mass, but owing to the strain of these difficult years, Knox had become old before his time. His influence in the General Assembly of the Scottish Church also decreased as the years passed. He suffered a stroke and had to walk with a stick. Yet to the people he ever remained *the* Reformer of Scotland. 'God', they said, 'has made him both the first planter, and also the chief waterer of His Kirk among us.'

When he was forced to leave Edinburgh in 1571 through Mary's last-ditch attempt to seize control of the country, he came to St Andrews. After resting for a few weeks he began preaching again. James Melville, who heard him, wrote that he became 'so active and vigorous, that he made me so to quake and tremble that I could not hold a pen to write.' Mary was defeated, the danger subsided, and he returned to Edinburgh.

As his end drew near, Knox felt the weariness of life. His last public act was on 9 November 1572, when he preached at an induction service, praying fervently for God's blessing upon the incumbent and the church. Two days later he was taken ill. He lingered on for a few weeks before dying on 24 November. Before he died, he asked for a reading 'where he had first cast his anchor', the seventeenth chapter of John.

Those who visited him in his last days were summoned by him. His successor, elders, and deacons crowded around the dying man's bed. His final testimony to them was a reflection on his whole ministry – misunderstood, misrepresented, but not mistaken:

> The time is approaching which I have long thirsted for, wherein I shall be released from all my cares, and be with my Saviour Christ forever. And now, God is my witness, whom I serve with my spirit in the Gospel of his Son, that I have taught nothing but the true and sincere word of God; and that the end that I proposed in my ministry, was, to instruct the ignorant, to confirm the weak, to comfort their consciences who were humbled under the sense of their sins, and borne down with the threatenings of God's judgments. I am not ignorant that many have, and do blame my too great rigour and severity; but, God knows, that in my heart, I never hated those against whom I thundered God's judgments, I did only hate their sins, and laboured according to my power to gain them to Christ. (John Gillies, *Historical Collections*, pp. 61-62)

As they laid him to rest, the new Regent, the Earl of Moray, declared, 'Here lies one who never feared the face of man.'

8

Robert Bruce

(1554-1631)

Robert Bruce was an outspoken defender of the faith. When crown and mitre set themselves against him to quieten him he remained faithful. What was once prophesied of his Master was re-enacted in him. 'Why do the nations rage, and the people plot a vain thing? The kings of the earth set themselves, and the rulers take counsel together, against the Lord and against his Anointed' (Psalm 2:1-2).

Bruce lived at a time when the rule of the Stuarts was at its most powerful. Not only did they demand absolute monarchical sway over the land but they wanted it over the Church also. A church commission, established by James VI of Scotland, had effectively become his lackey. Its members were simply the executors of his will within the Church and carried out his every whim.

Bruce, on the other hand, possessed an inflexible and indomitable spirit. He could not accept the King's rule over his conscience as well as his body. He considered his conscience the sole domain of His Majesty in heaven (as he often described the Lord Jesus Christ). Keeping a clear conscience was his first aim throughout life, even when it meant his expulsion from the realm. For him, there was no room for compromise. If he had not been the man he was he could well have ascended to the most influential political or ecclesiastical seat in the land.

If there is some uncertainty about the time and place of his birth (probably in 1554 at Airth Castle, near the mouth of the Forth), there is no uncertainty about the time and place of his conversion. After a very long and painful experience of conviction of sin he finally found peace through faith in Christ in his father's castle in Airth, on 31 August 1581. The burden of his sin was so intense that he could later write, 'I was so fearfully and extremely tormented that I would have been content to have been cast into a cauldron of hot melted lead, to have had my soul relieved of that insupportable weight.'

A convicting conscience remained the terror of his life. To Bruce, it was the greatest affliction anyone could experience. It was the fear of violating his conscience that effectively controlled his every movement. Physical pain or suffering could not compare with the misery of conscience' accusing finger: 'to him hell consists chiefly in a conscience unappeased.'

His father, Alexander Bruce, Laird of Airth, intended him to become a lawyer. But he felt the call to the ministry weigh more heavily upon him. As early as 1571, when he was about to take his Bachelor's degree at the University of St Andrews, he felt a constraint to enter the ministry. Ten years were to pass before this was finally realized. In the meantime, he took his Master's degree at St Andrews and then went on to further study in Europe, the heart of medieval scholarship.

Between the dates of his call to the ministry in 1571 and his conversion in 1581 there is a ten-year gap. These years, he considered, were years of resistance to the clear will of God. For this reason his conscience often tormented him. In his old age he recalled, 'I was first called to my grace, before I obeyed my calling to the ministry: He made me first a Christian before He made me a minister. I resisted long my calling to the ministry: ten years at least I never leaped on horseback nor alighted, but with a justly accusing conscience.'

It may prove difficult to reconcile his statements about his calling to the ministry and his calling to salvation. This need not be the case. In God's providence his call to the ministry would eventually entail a call to salvation, for in order to function effectively as a minister of God one must be converted. Bruce persisted in this resistance until he finally gave in to God both in grace and ministry.

His college background at St Andrews may help to unravel this mystery. He attended St Salvador's, the old conservative college. This expressed the natural preference shown by his parents, especially his mother, for their traditional religion. She belonged to a strong, dogmatic Roman Catholic family. As such, there was no possibility that Bruce would have been allowed to attend the more radical, Reformed college of St Leonard's.

During that time the ageing Scottish Reformer, John Knox, came to St Andrews and preached a series of sermons on the book of

Daniel. His stay lasted from July 1571 to August 1572. The power of Knox's preaching told on the students. James Melville, a contemporary of Bruce's at St Andrews and a lifelong friend, wrote, 'I had my pen and my little book, and took away such things as I could comprehend. In the opening of his text he was moderate in the space of an half hour; but when he entered to application he made me so to grew [quake] and tremble that I could not hold a pen to write.' Bruce may well have felt the force of his preaching and teaching, but because of his inbred prejudice he resisted the overwhelming convictions of his mind and floundered for the next ten years.

After leaving St Andrews, he went to study law in Louvain, Belgium. Again, this was a centre for anti-reformation feeling. When he eventually returned to Scotland his future was assured. Born into the right family, he possessed all the right connections to thrust him forward into the highest legal council in the land, the College of Justice. However instead of rising to prominence in the legal profession, he rose on that first day of September 1581, to become a great Reformation light in Scotland. That night, his conviction finally came to a head and he was wonderfully converted.

After this conversion experience he immediately set his course for the ministry, much to the displeasure of his mother. She demanded that before she would consent to this he must lose his right to the estate of Kinnaird and several other possessions, which he willingly did. (These were later restored to him by his kind and benevolent father.)

Another two years were to pass before he began his theological course. This may have been due to his aggrieved mother who violently opposed it. In 1583 he went to St Mary's, commonly called the New College, which was attached to St Andrews University. Here he began his theological course under the guidance of Andrew Melville, uncle of James Melville. Andrew Melville, another impassioned Reformer, was a student of Knox and possessed something of his spirit. Melville once told the King:

There are two kings and two kingdoms in Scotland: there is King James, the lord of this commonwealth, and there is Christ Jesus, the King of the Church, whose subject James the Sixth is, and of whose Kingdom he is not a King, nor a lord, nor a head, but a member. We will yield to you your place, and give you all due obedience, but again I say, you are not the Head of the Church; you cannot give us that eternal life which we seek for even in this world, and you cannot deprive us of it. (John Macleod, *Scottish Theology*, p. 46)

When Bruce came to New College as a post-graduate student he was twenty-nine years of age. Though he was much older than his fellow students he was extremely bashful about preaching. At first, he refused even to speak to the students at their meetings. Eventually, he began speaking to a few of them alone in his apartments. Afterwards, he was induced to give them a series of addresses on the Letter to the Hebrews. These acted as a launching pad for his future ministry which was to make such an indelible impression on the minds of the Scottish people in general and the people of Edinburgh in particular. When he began preaching in St Andrews the city folk flocked to hear him. They abandoned King James VI's Archbishop for this impressive new preacher who gave them solid food and not husks.

Bruce, following in the tradition of Knox and Melville, had an intrepid spirit. It was inevitable that he would eventually fall out with the King. When the King interrupted his sermon to speak to his courtiers for the third successive time, Bruce rebuked him, 'It is said to have been an expression of the wisest of kings, "When the lion roars, all the beasts of the field are quiet": the Lion of the Tribe of Judah is now roaring in the voice of His Gospel, and it becomes all the petty kings of the earth be silent.'

Andrew Melville, a shrewd scholar and judge of men, realized Bruce's potential and nominated him to succeed the deceased Knox in St Giles, Edinburgh. Bruce, reticent as ever, was finally coaxed into letting his name go forward, though he very much doubted his suitability. He preached in his usual way and when the vote was taken it was virtually unanimous that he should become their next minister. This call brought him to the most influential pulpit in Scotland. At first he refused, preferring to go back to St Andrews where he had already received a previous call. Even the added weight of Andrew and James Melville failed to dissuade him. He was stubbornly fixed on going back to St Andrews. As he was returning, a delegation was sent from Edinburgh to press him to reconsider his position, which he did reluctantly.

The main reason for his initial rejection of St Giles was because he had no desire to preach before the court, which often attended the church. He knew that sooner or later he and the court would disagree and so it would be best left alone. His return to Edinburgh was more like a prisoner than a recruit. He felt forced into accepting and wrote, 'Loath was I to go: they threatened me with authority. So I advised with my God, and thought it meet to obey.' Afterwards, when St Andrews tried to reclaim him, he was more adamant about staying than he had been against coming. For the next twelve years he was the standard-bearer of the Reformation in that great city of Edinburgh.

At first, his relationship with the young King was more than cordial. When James went in pursuit of his Danish bride, Anne, who was just sixteen years of age, Bruce was left as one of the King's trustees over his kingdom. Scotland never knew a more peaceful or happy time in her history. While the King was away he wrote several letters to Bruce applauding him for his faithful stewardship. His training as a lawyer stood him in good stead for the activities of state. These letters were often used later to good effect on the older more domineering monarch. He sometimes reminded the King of his earlier attachment to him, calling him 'our right trusty and well-beloved counsellor', and saying that he was 'worth the quarter of his country', and reckoned himself 'beholden while he lived', for the services he had rendered him and would 'never forget the same.' It was Bruce who anointed the young Queen's head with oil at her coronation.

It seems that as Bruce's popularity with the people grew the King's regard for him dwindled, especially when Bruce began contradicting some of the King's plans. James did not so much fear but envy him. Bruce was so well established in the people's affections that it irritated the King. Though there was no one more loyal in all Scotland, James's innate despotic tendencies would not allow Bruce to live in peace. The rift between monarch and minister persisted until James's death. Throughout his life, he persisted in maliciously hounding Bruce. Yet it was not simply a personal vendetta the King was pursuing – it was just as political as it was personal. James's religious preferences lay with episcopacy, not presbytery. Bishops were always willing vassals of the King to do his bidding. He even coined the adage, 'No Bishop, No King.' Through subtle manipulation of events he sought to assert and advance episcopacy over a people who hated it. Bruce, not hoodwinked by his ploys, stood as a bulwark against him.

Edinburgh was the political and spiritual capital of Scotland, and Bruce's coming had had a gripping effect upon its people. Every class was affected. James Melville wrote in his diary, 'The godly for his powerful and most moving doctrine loved him; the worldly for his parentage and place reverenced him, and the enemies for both stood in awe of him.' It was this assertive power the King wanted to curb.

His preaching regularly attracted huge congregations. There were often more than a thousand people present at his services, and those who heard him were deeply moved. One descriptive writer said, 'He made always an earthquake upon his hearers, and rarely preached but to a weeping auditory.' John Livingstone, no mean preacher himself, wrote, 'No man since the apostles' time spake with such power.' This is high praise indeed, considering he came in the wake of John Knox. But unlike Knox, whose voice thundered, Bruce's was comparatively mellow.

If his ministry presented something of the grandeur of God, it also presented something of the grace of God. Though God is high, he condescends to the weakness of men. He takes no pleasure in seeing his children stumbling fearfully through life. Rather, he gives such an inner sense of acceptance that they know his love, peace and joy. They know the salve of the blood of Christ. If life is precarious, God is in it. The Puritan's pilgrim concept was just as real to Bruce. As he travels on his voyage, he needs to know his position is assured. This alone gives confidence in life and death:

> Whosoever has God to be a God to him, do him injury who please, prince or people, God will revenge it . . . I tell thee, the heart that may heartily say it [that 'God is a God to me'] . . . that heart has set the whole felicity of it on God only, that heart makes God to be the armour of it, to be the storehouse out of which it will seek provision. It converses perpetually with God, and depends ever upon His providence; it counts the presence of God in bondage to be liberty; in poverty it counts the presence of God to be riches; in sickness it counts the presence of God to be health. Now he that may say, 'God is a God to me,' if he have to do with help, will not run to man, but to God, and will depend upon the help of God. (D.C.MacNicol, *Robert Bruce*, p.202)

When a comparison is made between the King's initial attitude towards Bruce and his later antagonism, it simply underlines the man's fickleness. The King, a coward at heart, was always devising schemes behind the scene. Since Bruce resolutely opposed and exposed these schemes, several major disputes developed between them which ended in Bruce's banishment to France in 1600. Though some friends at court managed to get him a reprieve, it lasted only a year. Bruce's problem was that he was becoming increasingly suspicious of the King and distrusted him. He saw him manipulate everything to his advantage. Finally the King, wishing to silence Bruce and restrict his influence, had him banished.

The cause of his expulsion was a case of conscience. The young Earl of Gowrie and his brother were killed under suspicious circumstances and then accused of treason. The Earl, a rising light for the Reformation cause in Scotland, was said to have made an attempt on the King's life in his castle. The King, who was on a hunting trip, claimed that he was lured to the Earl's residence by a fictitious story of an unusual pot of gold which some stranger had left there the previous night. When the King, alone with his host, was attacked, he and an aide, who had come to his rescue, killed both the Earl and his brother in the fray.

Unable to accept this account, Bruce felt that the King's hand was somehow more deeply involved than at first appeared. The story lacked credibility and he found it impossible to remove all suspicion from the King. When he, along with four other ministers in Edinburgh, were ordered to declare the King's innocence from their pulpits and pronounce the Earl a traitor, they refused. Though the others were later persuaded, Bruce remained adamant. He was prepared to acknowledge the King's innocence and that the deaths were not intentional, but he could not bring himself to believe that Gowrie was a traitor.

In this, Bruce probably went too far. Even when the court found the King innocent of all complicity in their deaths, Bruce was not convinced. Perhaps his strong attachment to the young earl may have clouded his judgment in the matter. But his conscience would not allow him to vindicate the King. This stubborn attitude persisted even after his restoration from France. Though he was prepared to acquiesce in the court's judgment of Gowrie, he refused to go throughout Scotland's pulpits publicly denouncing him.

Bruce had been such a thorn in his side that the King absolutely refused to allow him to preach again in St Giles. Consequently, in 1603, at the time of King James VI's ascent to the English throne as

James I, Bruce was forced to leave Edinburgh and his flock. This event proved counter-productive, for instead of curtailing his influence it only succeeded in enlarging it. His preaching opportunities were increased and for the next two years he regularly preached in many of the country churches as well as out of doors. Still his activities did not go unnoticed. The King, still smarting over the Gowrie affair, used this situation to place him under internal exile. He was ordered to Inverness in the North of Scotland. This may appear a comparatively minor sentence today but his biographer points out that in those days it was like sending someone in Russia to Siberia. This was his first internal exile and lasted for eight years.

In 1613 he was allowed home to Kinnaird. His time in the North had been difficult – once someone had tried to shoot him. Yet even there his influence continued to grow. He was allowed to preach, and preaching was his strength. When he arrived at Kinnaird he was glad to be home. The 'wild north', as he called it, was not the place for him.

Between his first and second exile his wife died. Since he was banned from entering Edinburgh she had carried out all his business affairs there for him. Now that she was gone there was no one else to do it. This meant that he was forced to sneak into the city for thirty-six hours to arrange some important financial matters. Unfortunately, he was caught and imprisoned in the Castle of Edinburgh for five months. Afterwards, the King again sent him to Inverness. The King wrote to his deputies in Edinburgh, 'We will have no more popish pilgrimages to Kinnaird, he shall go to Inverness.'

Bruce's second exile was more severe than the first. He was now, in 1622, close on seventy years of age and the journey seemed much farther. He also had no personal comforters. His wife, who had accompanied him on his first exile, was no longer with him. He was now entirely alone and dreaded the thought. Yet he managed to find comfort in his God. It seems that the Lord was with him in an exceptional way. He had peace within which was to him the greatest of all blessings. As he was on the point of mounting his horse to leave he was suddenly transfixed for a time. When he was asked what occupied him so, he replied, 'I was receiving my commission from my Master to go to Inverness, and He gave it me Himself, before I set my foot in the stirrup, and thither I go to sow a seed in Inverness that shall not be rooted out for many ages.'

At such times, Bruce enjoyed more of heaven than he did of earth. His inner comforts remained the strength of his soul. After his arrival in Inverness his influence continued unabated. Though at first he was faced by tremendous opposition and hatred, he survived to arouse the attention of the clannish chiefs to the gospel. These warring and bloodthirsty leaders were attracted to his preaching and were converted. There was a great change wrought among them which, apart from the gospel, would not have been possible. The ageing Bruce was like an Apostle to the North. Great multitudes from Ross and Sutherland and other places in the north crowded to Inverness every Sabbath to hear him.

When King James died in early 1625, his son Charles I, not wishing to carry on the feud between his father and Bruce, allowed him to return home. The aged preacher maintained to the last that he was the only lawful living minister of Edinburgh. All the others had been thrust upon the people by coercion and not conviction. Sadly, he never returned to his pulpit. His ban from Edinburgh remained in force until his death.

Though he was forbidden to preach in Edinburgh his ministry elsewhere remained highly successful. He preached in country houses, and churches where he was invited, and in open-air meetings when great concourses of people gathered. Indeed, he became one of the founders of Scotland's huge outdoor communion services. People responded to the trumpet call of his ministry and these meetings began to take deep root in the hearts of the Scottish people. They were times of refreshing, times of blessing, times when God drew near to his people.

Bruce had been the greatest torch-bearer of that generation. He had taken it from the hand of John Knox and passed it on to Alexander Henderson, the next great leader of the Reformation cause. Henderson had been a firm supporter of episcopacy until he was dramatically converted under Bruce's ministry.

When Bruce became a Christian it was a matter of conscience. He knew that he was a sinner and that the gospel was true. The only thing he found that could appease his accusing conscience was the blood of Christ. It was his only peace and consolation. After feeling its power there was nowhere else to go and nothing else to trust. The Bible became his law and his conscience his judge.

His end was sudden. There was nothing to show that his life was drawing to a close. The morning of his death he rose and ate a good breakfast. As he was musing, he called to his youngest daughter Martha, who lived with him, 'Hold, daughter, hold; my Master calleth me.' Then he asked for the large family Bible. It was opened at the eighth chapter of Romans. But he was unable to read it due to his failing sight. He began quoting it from memory until he came to the last two verses: 'For I am persuaded that neither death nor life, nor angels nor principalities, nor powers, nor things present nor things to come, nor height, nor depth, nor any other created thing, shall be able to separate us from the love of God which is in Christ Jesus our Lord.' 'Set my finger on these words,' he said. 'God be with you, my children. I have breakfasted with you, and shall sup with my Lord Jesus this night. I die believing in these words.'

Robert Bruce died on 27 July 1631, a man at peace with God and himself.

9
Walter Cradock
(c.1610-59)

Walter Cradock was one of the most outstanding leaders of the Welsh Puritan movement in the seventeenth century. Forced to leave the established church, he became co-founder of the first Dissenting church in Wales. Along with William Wroth, whom he assisted, he established a church in Llanfaches, Gwent. This differed from every other form of church government in Britain and followed the New England pattern in colonial America, a kind of compromise between Presbyterianism and Independency. This church has been described as 'the Antioch church of the Gentiles to the Christians of South Wales.'

It soon became a centre for great spiritual activity. William Erbury said of it:

> For I will speak the truth without partiality. There were not more spiritual and suffering saints in any part of English ground than were in Wales; so self-denying and dying to the world – yea, so wise-hearted and knowing Christians: let all the English counties about them testify, and tell how many saints from Somerset, Gloucestershire, Herefordshire, Radnorshire, Glamorganshire, &c., came in multitudes to Llanvaches. What light and labour in the Spirit was there! – how heavenly-minded! – what holy language among them! – what watching! – what prayers night and day, in the way they went, in the work they did, at their plough; everywhere in private that spirit of prayer and pureness of heart appeared. (Thomas Rees, *History of Protestant Nonconformity,* p. 40)

This was the shape of the church created by its founders. It was spiritually alive and active, with obvious evidence of the Holy Spirit's activity to all but the prejudiced.

Walter Cradock was born probably in 1610, in Trefela, Llangwm in Gwent, or the old Monmouthshire. He belonged to a comparatively wealthy family. When he inherited the family estate it realized £601 a year in income. This must have given Cradock an appreciable sense of independence. After coming to St Mary's Church, Cardiff, as curate to William Erbury, he was soon in trouble with the authorities. The intolerance of William Laud, the Archbishop of Canterbury, and the crackdown on Puritanism were rife. When he came under the eye of the Bishop of Llandaff it was because of his refusal to read publicly the Book of Sports, a directive which authorized the playing of particular games on Sundays. The Bishop was incensed by this inflexible upstart. True to the establishment he took things in hand to deal with Cradock and revoked his preachers' licence. He notified Archbishop Laud, who in turn, notified the King of his action.

> The bishop of Llandaff certifies that this last year he visited in person and found William Erbury, vicar of St Mary's Cardiff and Walter Cradock his curate have been very disobedient to your majesty's instructions, and have preached very schismatically and dangerously to the people. That for this he has given the vicar a judicial admonition, and will further proceed, if he do not submit. And for his curate being a bold ignorant young fellow, he hath suspended him, and taken away his licence to serve the cure. (Noel Gibbard, *Walter Cradock 'A New Testament Saint'*, p. 4)

Ejected thus from his curacy, Cradock in 1634 went to Wrexham in North Wales to become curate to Robert Lloyd. However he was soon hounded from here also, not by the church this time but by a local brewer. Cradock's preaching had such an effect upon the people that the brewer's profits were drastically cut. Along with other interested parties, he applied a great deal of pressure on the gentry until Cradock was finally forced to leave. His preaching in Wrexham attracted huge early-morning congregations. Morgan Llwyd, the mystic Puritan, and Vavasor Powell, a prominent preacher and author, were both converted under his ministry. Edmund Jones wrote:

> Instead of reading the Morning Prayers, as the manner before was, he expounded the Scriptures with such heavenly fire and plainness as greatly affected the people, so that when the bells would toll at six o'clock in the morning, the people would presently flock from town and country to hear him, and fill that large church. And by both his preaching and expounding a great reformation followed, which had not followed upon the reading of the Common Prayer, and many sinners were turned

to the Lord. (Thomas Rees, *History of Protestant Nonconformity in Wales,* p. 47)

Though his stay in Wrexham was short-lived, memory of him was enduring. For the next one hundred years those who were seriously religious were reproached as 'Cradockians'. Obviously, he had left an influence which took over a century to erase.

From here he fled to Shrewsbury where he spent some time with his friend Richard Symonds. It was here that he met the young Richard Baxter who recognized in Cradock the evidences of true godliness. Pursued by the Bishop's agents he again had to leave, this time to Llanfair Waterdine and Brampton Bryan, on the border of the counties of Hereford and Radnor. This was the home of Sir Robert Harley, a strong supporter of Puritanism. For the next few years Harley was his patron and in Brampton Bryan he lived in comparative peace, while preaching throughout the neighbouring Welsh shires.

Again his preaching was effective with many instances of conversion. One remarkable example of his influence as a preacher is seen in the conversion of his chief antagonist, Morgan Howell. Howell used to mimic Cradock's preaching for the amusement of his friends. If he was unable to preach indoors Cradock would go outside. Howell, learning that Cradock was about to hold an open-air meeting, arranged a football match to be played in the same place and at the same time as the service. As he was about to kick the ball, Howell slipped and fell, spraining his ankle. Immobilized by his fall he was forced to hear Cradock preach and was converted. Afterwards whenever Cradock was preaching in that area he always lodged at the home of Morgan Howell. This spiritual child of Cradock became a gospel teacher himself and founded the first church of believers in his locality.

Cradock returned to Wales in 1639, to join William Wroth at Llanfaches to found the first Independent church in Wales. It was an historic event. However the joy of that day was short-lived. In 1642, just before the Civil War broke out, Wroth died. Cradock, his natural successor, took up the leadership of the sapling church.

At the beginning of the war, Wales, predominantly Royalist, soon became a dangerous place for supporters of the Parliament. Cradock, like many others, was forced to flee from Wales and came first to

Bristol, and when that city fell to the Royalists, went to London. Here, he ministered at All Hallows Church in Lombard Street. Though he had left the Principality of Wales he could not forget it. His concern for Wales remained as fervent as ever. And the need for Welsh-speaking preachers was also much upon his heart.

During his absence those remaining Dissenters who were unable to leave Wales suffered extremely. A huge wave of persecution engulfed them. Husbands became the victims of violence, while wives and children were terrorized. There was no escaping what was happening and their only recourse was in God. By faith they were able not only to withstand the onslaught but to advance against the odds. Instead of being quenched, the gospel fire, by means of ordinary, uneducated and unordained men, continued to burn in Wales. A sermon of Cradock shows the profound effect these stalwarts had had on the people.

> I use not to tell stories but let me tell this one thing. Since I have been from you of late I have observed, and seen, in the mountains of Wales, the most glorious work that I ever saw in England, unless it were in London. The gospel is run over the mountains between Brecknockshire and Monmouthshire, as the fire in the thatch. And who should do this? They have no ministers; but some of the wisest say that there are about *eight hundred* godly people there, and they go from one to another. They have no ministers, it is true; if they had, they would honour them, and bless God for them. And shall we rail at such, and say they are tub-preachers and were never at the University? Let us all fall down and honour God: what if God will honour himself that way? They are filled with good news, and they tell it to others; and therefore vex not at them, and say . . . Oh, such a man, he was never a Master of Arts, he was never at the University, and he takes upon himself to preach; – when it may be he hath more of God in him than I, and a hundred that have all this. (Thomas Rees, *History of Protestant Nonconformity in Wales,* pp. 67-68)

For all these encouraging signs the burden for Wales remained with him. The crying need was for preachers, experienced men, who could bring the gospel to the masses in a language they could understand. In a sermon before Parliament in 1646, Cradock pleaded for his beloved country.

Oh, let not poor Wales continue sighing, famishing, mourning, and bleeding, while you have your days of feasting, rejoicing, thanksgiving, and praising God. Oh, how loathe I am to mention it to you! Is it not a sad case, that in thirteen counties there should not be above thirteen (God grant there be more! I know not so many) conscientious ministers, who in these times expressed themselves firmly and constantly faithful to the Parliament, and formerly preached profitably in the Welsh language twice every Lord's day? Yet, praised be our God, some few there are, though I myself am unworthy to be reckoned amongst them, who are ready and willing to spend and be spent for the glory of God and the good of the country. (Thomas Rees, p.68)

It was not long before Cradock was on his way back to Wales. His sermon, preached on 21 July, met with an immediate response. Soon, along with Henry Walter and Richard Symonds, Cradock was appointed an itinerant preacher to South Wales. They were to be supported from the coffers of the dioceses of St David's and Llandaff. Towards the end of October these three were instructed to make their way, at the earliest convenience, to their new posts. Later, the church in All Hallows sent another six preachers to aid them in Wales. Cradock's efforts to win his fellow countrymen met with huge success. Many were converted as the preaching began to take effect.

For Cradock, the only way to consolidate the work was for the people to possess their own Bibles. So few Welsh Bibles were readily available and these were so cumbersome that a more portable Bible was felt necessary. Along with Vavasor Powell, Cradock arranged for a much smaller New Testament in Welsh to be printed in 1647. This new development would inevitably give greater access to the Word of God and lead to a deeper impression being left on the hearts and minds of his congregations.

The high esteem accredited to Cradock resulted in his becoming one of twenty Commissioners in Wales. These were given executive powers to grant preachers' licences. As long as five of them were in agreement over a person's ability and piety they could endorse his right to preach. This meant, in effect, that those who had previously been able to enter the ministry without adequate qualifications would be screened out. The ministry would therefore become more exclusive and protected, with a better quality of man leading the churches.

Cradock was a very liberal-minded man. The evangelical faith was more important to him than any one branch of Evangelicalism. His scruples were on primary, not secondary issues. What was important was whether or not a person believed and accepted the whole gospel. Working out the finer points, such as church order, were not unimportant but not so important as to blur what united them. It grieved him to see brethren at war with one another. Speaking on the differences that existed between Presbyterians and Congregationalists he said, 'Every little difference and dissent makes not a new religion, being between brethren, and for a thing so small, why should there be strife among us?' His fight was for the centre ground of the gospel not for fringe issues, those secondary matters which at times seemed to channel Christians' minds and energies away from essentials. The result of this was to make the Church introspective and breed internal squabbling among believers. It was this clear vision of what was crucial which freed Cradock from becoming too narrow-minded in his view of church life and structure.

It also gave him a greater insight into the true nature of a life in union with God, the heart of all true religion. It was Cradock's concern for the maintenance of spiritual life and vitality which led Richard Baxter and others to attack him as an antinomian (that is, one tending to disregard God's law and excuse sin). His emphasis on the spirit of the law over against the letter of the law led to this misunderstanding. Seeing the danger of a legalistic mentality taking possession of a person, Cradock stressed the need not to lose sight of the Christian's freedom from the law as a means of salvation. Puritanism, as a whole, was in danger of destroying itself by its own self-imposed rules. His great fear was that too much stress on self-examination could enfeeble the life of the Christian so that he became governed more by the maxims of men than the Spirit of God. This same stumbling block was placed before the Galatian church, the error which Paul attacked. Cradock had a clear insight into the difference between the Old Testament dispensation and that of the New.

Unfortunately, this charge of antinomianism was laid against him more often after his death, when he was unable to defend himself. In reality, Cradock saw that some were putting more stress on their sanctification than they should for their peace of mind. He emphatically declared that justification (that is, faith in Christ alone for salvation) was to be their only stay. No matter how good or bad they were, it could not materially affect their justification. As he said:

> Your justification doth not lie, or is not built upon anything that is in you, or that is done by you, or that you may hope to do hereafter; you are not justified by your own personal good, or unjustified by your own personal evils, you are not one jot the more just when you have done all the good you can in the world, and you are not one jot less just when you have committed all the weaknesses, and fallen into all the frailties that a saint can fall into. (Noel Gibbard, *Walter Cradock 'A New Testament Saint',* pp. 9-10)

The point Cradock wanted to make was that if the Christian's joy rested upon what he did, then every little failure would result in a sense of guilt, doubt and misery. Instead of being cheered up he would be cast down. To avoid this the Christian needed to grasp the whole concept of justification.

It seems indefensible to condemn Cradock as an antinomian. He maintained a balanced view of the doctrines of justification and sanctification (progressive holiness). Obviously, there are dangers involved in such a bold defence of justification. Weaker-minded people could misunderstand it to mean that a person can live just as they liked after conversion, to think of it as a kind of licence to sin with impunity. But Cradock was as practical as he was theological. To abuse the doctrine of justification, as some did, met with his denunciation. 'Cradock', wrote Thomas Richards, 'especially denounces men who are, "puffed up with spiritual pride, flying too high above the Gospel", making the doctrine of justification a pretence for "swagger, and even looseness and wantonness."'

Though Cradock was highly critical of some people he possessed a remarkable spirit of love. He always aimed to speak the truth in love and believed that all malice and deceit should be something unheard-of among Christians. This generous spirit was displayed both in his attitude towards lay preachers and other people. Since he had concern for their souls at heart, he used every means possible to bring the gospel home to them. Simplicity and illustrations to keep the people awake became the hallmarks of his ministry. He considered book-learning helpful to sharpen the preacher's own natural powers, but the study of men was just as important as the study of books. It was learning about the heart by experience and not just by textbook that was essential. There was also the need to depend upon the Holy Spirit in the act of preaching as well as in preparation of the sermon. This all told in his own ministry and many were converted under his preaching.

In 1659, Cradock died prematurely, leaving behind a glowing testimony of how he lived and walked with God. The effect of his ministry reached into the next century. Someone once said as late as 1740, 'that many of the Dissenters talked much of Walter Cradock.' To summarize his life's work no better tribute could be paid to him than that given by the author of *A Winding Sheet for Mr Baxter's Dead:*

> For Mr Cradock (however despised by Mr Baxter) was a man of very quick and pregnant natural Parts (which it is true) his many avocations too much kept him from cultivating and improving a man that had a wonderful faculty of coming down and bringing the things of God to the meanest of his Auditors; and a man for whose very successful labours the mountains of Wales praise Almighty goodness, who sent many to Heaven, where he himself also (I doubt not) is, and where we leave him out of reach of Detraction and Calumny. (Noel Gibbard, *Walter Cradock 'A New Testament Saint',* p.15)

10
William Perkins
(1558-1602)

Few Evangelicals today know anything about William Perkins. Yet he stood at the threshold of the Puritan awakening and was considered one of the ablest preachers of his day. The author of Richard Sibbes' *Memoir,* who was a contemporary of Perkins, spoke of 'Perkins' seraphic yet pungent ministry', and that he was a 'renowned preacher of righteousness.' It has also been said of him that

> he stood at the fountain head of Puritanism's new and vigorous development in the last decades of the sixteenth century. Perkins' great ministry at Cambridge resulted in his becoming mentor of an army of young men who developed his expository and pastoral emphases. (Peter Lewis, *The Genius of Puritanism,* p.16b)

Perkins' life stretched almost from the beginning to the end of the reign of Queen Elizabeth I (1559-1603). It was comparatively short yet extensively useful. A life's work must be measured not in terms of its quantity of years but by its quality of service. His usefulness as a preacher can be seen in the lasting effect his ministry had in Cambridge. His life, though a brief 44 years, was remembered and cherished by a rising generation of preachers. When Thomas Goodwin went to Cambridge, as a twelve year old boy in 1613, he mentions the profound effect Perkins' ministry still retained there. 'The Town', he wrote, 'was then filled with the discourse of the Power of Mr. Perkins' Ministry, still fresh in Men's Memories'. Though he had been dead for over ten years, the people of Cambridge still could not forget the way in which he had preached to them.

The influence of Perkins was not confined to the university town of Cambridge but extended throughout the nation and later the continent. His mark upon England may be assessed by the number of times his works were published. In this he outstripped all the best

European authors and theologians. Even Calvin, whose *Institutes* were virtually always in the press, was left far behind. His literary achievements kept the printers of Cambridge busy, as edition after edition rolled off the press. Many of these were translated into several European languages. One editor in 1604, commenting on his commentary on Galatians, said that it was as good as Luther's.

Perkins was born in Marston Jabbet, Warwickshire, in 1558. He came to Cambridge to study in Christ's College in 1577 where he received his BA in 1581 and MA in 1584. Before the end of 1584 he was appointed 'lecturer' at Great St Andrews. This allowed him the opportunity of preaching regularly. The role of lecturer focused attention on preaching as opposed to ceremony. This new office of lecturer evolved from the issue of vestments then raging in the Church of England. For those who wished to preach but not wear what were considered Romanized vestments 'lecturing' provided a solution.

Perkins' life had not always been characterized by godliness and holy living. As a young man he was notorious for his intemperance. He was addicted to drink and spent much of his time at the tavern. It was only when he overheard a woman say to her fractious child, 'Hold your tongue, or I will give you to drunken Perkins yonder,' that he seriously considered his state. This sobering remark was the beginning of that great change which was to alter the whole course of his life.

After his conversion he became concerned for the souls of others, especially the prisoners in the castle prison. He asked if he could preach to them. Every Sunday the jailor led the prisoners out in chains to hear Master Perkins preach. Soon many of the townspeople also began to attend these services. The power of his preaching was quickly felt as he impressed upon all the need for repentance toward God and faith in the Lord Jesus Christ. On one occasion, a condemned convict who was about to be hanged, descended from the scaffold to speak to him about salvation and was converted on the spot. Instead of frequenting the taverns, as he had previously done, Perkins now spent his time reading and praying. He possessed such a retentive and assimilative mind that he made huge theological strides. His wasted years were soon replaced with solid learning. He made such rapid progress in his studies that he became the greatest theologian of that age. This was one reason why his writings met with such widespread approval and continued to make such a lasting impression after his death.

Towards the end of the sixteenth century when so-called religious radicals were being repressed by the state, Perkins also came under scrutiny and was questioned about Puritanism. But he avoided all political and controversial issues. In this way he was able to maintain his Cambridge ministry unmolested. Even his printed works armost devoid of discussion concerning the ecclesiastical issues of the day and reveal a mind more occupied with the question of salvation than

Old Cambridge

church order. This raises the question whether or not Perkins was strictly speaking a 'Puritan'? Undoubtedly, he never saw himself in this way. Even the term 'Puritan' was derisory in his day. He once defended some conscientious believers by saying that those who 'keep purity of heart in a good conscience' should not be 'branded with vile terms' – such as 'puritan'. When he married in 1595, he was forced to resign his Fellowship in Christ's College. His prestige can be seen in the doleful note it provoked in some members of the faculty. Samuel Ward wrote, 'Good Lord, grant that now after Mr. Perkins departure there follow no ruin to the College.'

If his influence at College was great his influence in the pulpit was even greater. He knew that his immense learning needed to be distilled in order to be dispensed to the less educated and intelligent of his hearers. There were ordinary people as well as university students in his congregation. These needed to be fed with solid and substantial food but in a form more easily digestible. Perkins had the ability to popularize theology by bringing it down to everyone's capacity. He was as H.C.Porter wrote, 'a theological artist in full control, and with the developed technique of the popularizer.'

If Perkins was adept as a scholar he was just as skilled as a preacher. Thomas Fuller, a seventeenth-century church historian, wrote:

> This may be said of Master Perkins that as a physician orders an infusion to be made by steeping ingredients in them and taking them out again, so that all the strength and virtue remain [in the liquid] yet none of the bulk or mass is visible therein, he [the preacher], in like manner [referring to Perkins] did distil and soak much deep scholarship into his preaching, yet so insensibly that nothing but familiar expressions did appear. In a word his church [in Cambridge] consisting of the University and town, the scholar could hear no learneder and the townsman no plainer sermons. ('Anglican and Puritan Thinking', Westminster Conference, 1977, Dr Martyn Lloyd-Jones, p.99)

One way in which he was able to capture the rustic mind was in the use of illustrations. He seemed to have a natural flair for encapsulating everything in a picture. For pungency and power they were very effective. The people could not miss his meaning as he elaborated on the mysteries of God's kingdom by the examples of nature. When he wanted to describe faith and its development he took an infolded bud which gradually opened to reveal the leaf and flower. This was a natural progression just as assurance is a natural progression from faith. Within faith there is assurance which first has to grow before it is revealed or unfolds itself.

His approach to preaching became the standard Puritan style. He was one of the first men to write anything on homiletics. He set out in detail what a sermon should be. It was a homiletical appraisal and many of the next generation of Puritans followed in his footsteps, though they had never actually heard him preach. They read his book,

The Art of Prophesying: or, a Treatise concerning the sacred and only true method of preaching, where they found the elements of a truly expository ministry defined and defended. Here in essence lay the Puritans' whole approach to preaching. They were always, first and foremost, preachers. What Perkins did in his *Art of Prophesying,* was to crystalize the Puritan ideal of preaching. All preaching had to originate out of a true exposition of God's Word. This is what gave it its power and pungency. For Perkins, like all Puritans, preaching was the gift 'par excellence'. It was used of God to spearhead his attack against the forces of evil and heresy. It is, he wrote, 'that Engine which, as it has shaken the foundation of ancient heresies, so it has in these few by-passed years cut asunder the sinews of that great Antichrist. Wherefore it be demanded which is the most excellent gift of all, doubtless the praise must be given to Prophesying [preaching].'

The stress of his preaching lay in its application or its 'use'. This became the hallmark of all Puritan preaching. What could legitimately be culled from the verse or verses and be applied to a person's everyday life was what mattered. A teacher may be able to express the essence of the text but the preacher needed to go further. He had to see its usefulness for daily living. It was the practical outworking of doctrine not just the doctrine alone that concerned him. Dr Lloyd-Jones defined Perkins' views under four main heads: (i) to read the text distinctly out of the canonical Scriptures. (ii) to give the sense and understanding of it, being read, by the Scripture itself. (In other words, your exposition must be scriptural. You must compare scripture with scripture.) (iii) to collect a few and profitable points out of the natural sense. (iv) to apply (if he have the gift) the doctrines, rightly collected, to the life and manners of men in a simple and plain speech.

Undoubtedly, Perkins was a preacher to the conscience. He attacked the mainspring of every man's life. He pointed out his faults and failings, the areas of deficiency and inadequacy. He wanted to impress upon his congregations the dread of rejecting Christ, that hell and damnation awaited all who refused him. For many this was too close to the bone to leave them comfortably listening to him. If they attended his services out of traditon or ritual they left them feeling disquieted. They would, for all the world, have been happy to be left alone and asleep, happy to listen to a drowsy, monotonous talk on morals, rather than listen to the arousing appeals of this preacher. John Cotton, who heard him preach towards the end of Perkins' life, resisted the inner stirrings it provoked . . . when the toll sounded in Cambridge announcing Perkins' death, he rejoiced that the man who had pained his conscience so much would no longer do so again. Cotton was later converted under Richard Sibbes' ministry and regretted not heeding those earlier feelings aroused in his ignorance.

Perkins did not restrict himself to preaching within a church. He had a vision for the masses, and an outdoor pulpit was erected at Stourbridge Fair where he felt there was an opportunity to reach many who never dared to enter church precincts. Clearly, he did not despise any means of doing good to souls. How many were savingly impressed at such times is unknown, but they could not avoid the earnestness with which the preacher explained the gospel. The vividness of eternal realities weighed so heavily upon him that he 'pronounced the word damn with such an emphasis as left a doleful Echo in his auditors' ears a good while after', wrote Thomas Fuller. There was no escaping the fact that this man was fully convinced of the awful consequences of 'neglecting so great salvation.'

Perkins' influence was not confined to ordinary people. Many ministers came seeking his help. They recognized in him one unusually endowed with gifts and graces to aid them along the way. Considering his premature death he must have made a strong impression on his peers regarding his spirituality.

Theologically, Perkins was a strict Calvinist. He saw man completely unable to do anything to save himself or remotely pleasing to God. The whole bent of his nature was away from God. It was only the elect who after being saved were able to offer something pleasing to God. By faith they rendered worship; by faith they offered service; by faith they lived and in faith they died. With poignancy and power he drove these lessons home to his hearers. With the stroke of an artist he described the children of God and the children of the devil in this world.

A master of music has his house furnished with musical instruments of all sorts; and he teaches his own scholars artificially to use them, both in right tuning of them, as also in playing on them: there comes in strangers, who admiring the said instruments, have leave given to them of the master to handle them as the scholars do: but when they come to practise, they neither tune them aright, neither are they able to strike one stroke as they ought, so as they may please the master and have his commendation. This world is a large and sumptuous palace, into which are received, not only the sons and daughters of God, but also the wicked and ungodly men: it is furnished with goodly creatures in use more excellent than all the musical instruments: the use of them is common to all: but the godly man taught by God's Spirit, and directed by faith, so uses them, as that the use thereof is acceptable to God. (H.C.Porter, *Puritanism in Tudor England,* p.268)

Perkins used every means available to instruct his congregation – charts, diagrams and visual aids. He also constructed a catechism. Many of the things he introduced became standard practice for subsequent Puritans. If they were not so enthusiastic about his visual aids they were keen to adopt his notion of a catechism. This dealt with main points of theology, the essentials of the faith. It was drawn up for adults and children alike and systematized their faith, all of which was backed with proof texts.

He also led the way for a casuistic style of preaching and pastoring. This dealt with 'cases' or problems of conscience. Those afflicted with a sensitive conscience on certain ethical issues were the main target of its emphasis. Its intention was to draw a line of demarcation between the godly and ungodly. By close examination in the light of Scripture people could read the signs of regeneration within themselves and know whether or not they were really God's people. It's approach was penetrating. Cases of conscience were of particular concern to Puritan pastors as they ministered to those lacking an assurance of salvation. These were encouraged to examine themselves to see if they were in the faith. This meant looking for the marks of life within and needed a keen spiritual discernment to see them. This casuistic approach was an attempt to distinguish between the righteous and unrighteous, the wheat and chaff, the sheep and goats, the living and the dead professor, those in the light and those still in darkness. It was born out of a pastoral concern for the true child of God and the belief that a person could not enjoy real peace until there was a measured sense of assurance.

To help God's children to discover their inheritance there was need for practical instruction. 'In God's Church,' he wrote, 'commonly they who are touched by the Spirit, and begin to come on in Religion, are much troubled with fear, that they are not God's children . . . and are not quiet until they find some resolution.' In 1602, his book *The Whole Treatise of Cases of Conscience* was published. It was a strange move, seeing that the Reformers had buried casuistry as a Roman Catholic device, but Perkins must have felt there was a real need for its resurrection for him to have broken with the Reformers' practice. Perhaps the changing scene called for a change of approach. Whatever the reason, it gained acceptance with the rising generation of Puritans.

Perkins died on the 22 October 1602, after several weeks of suffering. His immense loss was felt by all but none more than his friend Samuel Ward who wrote: 'God knows his death is likely to be an irrecoverable loss and a great judgment to the University, seeing there is none to supply his place.'

11
Richard Baxter
(1615-91)

Richard Baxter, wrote J.I.Packer, was 'the most outstanding pastor, evangelist and writer on practical and devotional themes that Puritanism produced.' He was one of the leaders of the Nonconformists after the restoration of Charles II to the English throne in 1660. He was a Puritan who, like all Puritans, wanted to see drastic changes in the Anglican Church. The need was felt for the Church of England to become totally Reformed and cast aside its old Romanist garb for that of Geneva. But his attempts to bring about these changes floundered on the rocks of an implacable church hierarchy. The bishops opposed any change of form or structure.

About the time of Baxter's birth, 12 November 1615, his father was converted. This was to have dramatic consequences on the family. Where, before, he would have met the other villagers for their weekly Sunday dance around the maypole, he now began spending his Sundays studying the Bible. This caused many of his neighbours to ridicule him as a hypocrite. Of course, unbelievers have no true concept of what is involved in conversion. To them the person has become religious and they do not understand the nature of the change which has taken place within. What they see is the effect and not the cause of that change. Unmoved by his neighbours' taunts Baxter's father continued to instruct his children in the ways of God. The consistency of his walk with God made a lasting impression on young Richard. Unfortunately, his tutors were not half as sincere or devout as his father. These curates were drunkards who shamed their profession and office by the way they lived.

When he was about fifteen years old Richard also was converted. He had experienced several religious impressions under his father's instruction but none were lasting. There was no real change in his life, no striving against sin or striving for holiness. These childhood impressions continued for a while before eventually evaporating.

What happened later was more lasting. His spiritual concern was induced by a long-drawn-out illness. For two whole years he had suffered from what looked like a consumptive complaint. One day he coughed so violently that it caused him to vomit blood. This began a whole train of illnesses which were to dog him throughout life. Startled by this on-going condition he began to seek God in earnest. His greatest fear was that he was not sincere enough or sensible enough of his real need. 'I was not then', he wrote, 'sensible of the incomparable excellence of holy love, and delight in God; nor much employed in thanksgiving and praise; but all my groans were for more contrition, and a broken heart; I prayed most for tears and tenderness.'

After his conversion theology became central to all his studies. Though he was never an expert linguist he was always an able student. He had the kind of mind that revelled in the niceties of theological distinctions. As a theologian he fell short of becoming a full-blooded Calvinist. He could never accept the idea of a sub-stitutionary atonement confined solely to God's elect. He saw it as more universal and dependent upon the faith of the recipient.

One problem which dogged him after his conversion was his inability to state a time or place when it happened. This perplexed him and made him become introspective and depressed. Later, the more experienced Baxter knew that the way to Christian joy is found not so much in looking within as in meditating on things above.

> I was once wont to meditate most on my own heart, and to dwell all at home. I was still poring over either my sins or wants, or examining my sincerity. But now, though I am greatly convinced of the need of heart-acquaintance and employment, I see more the need of higher work; and that I should look oftener on God, and Christ, and heaven, than upon my own heart. (William Orme, *The Life and Times of Richard Baxter*, p. 12)

As a young man he was dissuaded from entering the ministry and encouraged to leave his native Shropshire and seek a post in London. After a short time he saw through the shallowness of life there and decided to return home to look after his ill mother. After her death his desire to enter the ministry returned with renewed vigour.

Throughout this time Baxter remained a staunch conformist. He, perhaps, was prejudiced by the London preachers who often openly and publicly attacked Dissenters. He believed at the time that their

Richard Baxter

arguments in favour of remaining in the Church of England were
overwhelming and that no unprejudiced person could ever reasonably
oppose them. From this position he was eventually to become one of
the leaders of Nonconformity. After meeting such men as Joseph
Symond and Walter Cradock, he became convinced that if the bishops
persecuted such people they, the bishops, could not possibly be
followers of the loving Christ. Their godliness was so conspicuous
that it showed conclusively their spiritual condition. This change of
attitude was not simply a matter of meeting some strong personalities.
It came after examining all the evidence. This would finally sway him
and win him over to the Nonconformist view. But in the meantime his
aim was to purge the Church of every vestige of Rome, and that from
within.

It was not until he became a teacher in Dudley, Worcestershire,
that he began preaching. After teaching for a year he became the
assistant pastor in Bridgnorth, Shropshire. Though his labours were
blessed and souls were saved he was still dissatisfied with this meagre
harvest. His biographer says, 'that he was then in the fervour of his

110

affections, and never preached with more vehement desires for men's conversion; but the applause of the preacher, was the only success he met with from most of the people.' Sadly, they loved his eloquence but loathed his message.

From Bridgnorth, he went to Kidderminster, a name ever to be associated with Baxter. This invitation came in March 1640, when he was twenty-four. His ministry there was to extend over seventeen years. After two years he became a chaplain in Oliver Cromwell's army. Several years were to pass before he would return to Kidderminster to resume his ministry there. Baxter was no supporter of Cromwell or the Commonwealth regime of 1649 to 1660, but was a convinced Royalist. In this he never wavered even although he testified later that he had enjoyed more liberty under the Commonwealth than ever he knew under a restored monarchy.

It may seem strange then that a man of Baxter's persuasion should have enlisted as chaplain in Cromwell's army, but his main reason for joining was purely practical. He intended countering the multiplying of religious sects (Baptists and Independents included) within its ranks. This state of affairs horrified him. But it also concerned him to see so few of the clergy prepared to suffer the hardships of a military campaign in order to protect the purity of the gospel. He knew the only antidote for error was the truth. With this in mind he embarked on his own spiritual campaign.

When Baxter enlisted Cromwell gave him a very cool reception. This was due to his previous rejection of a proffered commission by Cromwell himself. The relationship between Cromwell and Baxter was always strained, with Cromwell having as little to do with Baxter as possible. Perhaps things might have improved had Baxter not been such a prickly character. He was a man born for contention, the exact opposite of a diplomat. In the army he often argued with some sectarians and republicans simply to hold them up to ridicule before the other soldiers. It is a sad fact that Baxter possessed little or no religious toleration at this time. Like all men he was a man of his time and had feet of clay.

Baxter remained in the army for two years before ill health forced him to resign. Before returning to Kidderminster he spent three months recuperating in Leicester. He began writing one of his best known works, *The Saints' Everlasting Rest,* at this time, and completed it within six months, although it was not published until 1649. He wrote as a man on the brink of eternity believing his time to depart had come. One of his most famous sayings was coined as a result of his constant brush with death, 'The preacher should preach as a dying man to dying men.'

The resumption of his ministry in Kidderminster in 1647 was as a lecturer and not as the holder of the living. This second episode was to produce dramatic results. Within the next thirteen years Kidderminster was changed beyond all recognition. The buildings and streets remained the same but the people were transformed. The spiritual and moral impact of his ministry was so universally effective that barely a home remained untouched. His description of these events was no exaggeration.

> Before I entered the ministry, God blessed my private conference to the conversion of some, who remain firm and eminent in holiness to this day: but then, and in the beginning of my ministry, I was wont to number them as jewels; but since then I could not keep any number of them. The congregation was usually full, so that we were fain to build five galleries after my coming hither; the church itself being very capacious, and the most commodious and convenient that ever I was in. Our private meetings, also, were full. On the Lord's days there was no disorder to be seen in the streets; but you might hear a hundred families singing psalms and repeating sermons as you passed through them. In a word, when I came thither first, there was about one family in a street that worshipped God and called on his name, and when I came away, there were some streets where there was not one poor family in the side that did not so; and that did not, by professing serious godliness, give us hopes of their sincerity. (Orme, *The Life and Times of Richard Baxter,* pp. 118-19)

Baxter attributed this remarkable change to several factors. At its heart was the public and private instruction of the people. In 1556 was published his great work, *The Reformed Pastor*, which indirectly shows the extreme thoroughness by which he himself pastored his people, by constant and unrelenting preaching, visitation and chatechizing. But that was not all. Christians were also living godly lives which quickly silenced their enemies. There was an apparent unity among believers which gave an attractive appearance to Christianity. He helped the poor, supported some through university

112

and gave away his books without charge. Previous ministers had not preached the gospel in its fulness or freeness; neither had they appealed to the people's consciences. This meant, in practical terms, that they were not gospel-hardened. He found a refreshing openness to his preaching which he had not known before. Each of these points helped contribute to promote the cause of Christ.

But Baxter had no foolproof methodology. He saw that ultimately the true cause of blessing was in God. Circumstances at Kidderminster may have contributed to the blessing, but did not create it. With gratitude, he wrote of God's sovereign dispensation in other places.

> God was pleased also to give me abundant encouragement in the lectures I preached about in other places; as at Worcester, Cleobury, &c., but especially at Dudley and Sheffnal. At the former of which, being the first place that ever I preached in, the poor nailers, and other labourers, would not only crowd the church as full as ever I saw in London, but also hang upon the windows and the leads without.

He goes on to say:

> I must here, then, to the praise of my dear Redeemer, set up this pillar of remembrance, even to his praise who hath employed me so many years in so comfortable a work, with such encouraging success. O what am I, a worthless worm, not only wanting academical honours, but much of that furniture which is needful to so high a work, that God should thus abundantly encourage me, when the reverend instructors of my youth did labour fifty years together in one place, and could scarcely say they had converted one or two in their parishes! And the greater was the mercy, because I was naturally of a discouraged spirit; so that if I had preached one year, and seen no fruits of it, I should hardly have forborne running away, like Jonah; but should have thought that God called me not to that place. (Orme, *Richard Baxter,* p. 120)

Another cause of his success in Kidderminster, which he does not mention, was his own intense evangelistic concern. He felt a pressing need for sinners to be converted. Not everyone living in Kidderminster attended the church, but as the local minister he had access to their homes. When he wrote his *Call to the Unconverted* in 1657, he gave a general introduction and a more specific one to the inhabitants of Kidderminster. His aim was essentially to confront them with the claims of the gospel and convince them of their need of salvation. The strains of his impassioned pleading stand out throughout the book. Even his introduction breathes the air of a plea to win them:

> Miserable souls . . . who has bewitched your minds into such madness, and your hearts into such deadness, that you should . . . go on so obstinately towards damnation, that neither the word of God nor the persuasions of men can change your minds, or hold your hands, or stop you, till you are past remedy! Well sinners, this life will not last always; this patience will not wait upon you still. Do not think that you shall abuse your Maker and Redeemer, and serve his enemies, and debase your souls, and trouble the world, and wrong the Church, and reproach the godly, and grieve your teachers, and hinder reformation, and all this upon free cost. You know not yet what this must cost you, but you must shortly know, when the righteous God shall take you in hand, who will handle you in another manner than the sharpest magistrates, or the plainest dealing pastors did, unless you prevent the everlasting torments by a sound conversion and a speedy obeying of the call of God. *(Call to the Unconverted,* p. 6)

If this sample of his writing breathes such pathos, what must his preaching have been like?

These memorable years of blessing in Kidderminster continued unabated throughout the whole Commonwealth period, and up to 1661. When the country reverted to a monarchy, events dramatically changed. Cromwell, the Protector, had died leaving his weak son Richard to succeed him. Unlike his father, Richard lacked the charisma and strength of character to hold together the varying factions within the realm. Eventually, he chose to stand down to allow the exiled son of Charles I to return and take control. The resumption of the monarchy effectively ended all the religious freedom and tolerance enjoyed under Cromwell's rule. For all his faults Cromwell possessed great virtues, none more, than his intense desire for religious liberty. In this, he was a man ahead of his time. Years were to pass before his contemporaries captured his vision.

To Baxter, Cromwell was nothing more than a usurper, and he told him so. His bias towards the monarchy and implacable prejudice against Cromwell always tended to slant his vision. Had he spoken half the things against Charles II that he did against Cromwell, Baxter would now be remembered more as a martyr than a preacher. They differed in so many ways that agreement between them was impossible. Their interpretations of God's providence regarding the monarchy were completely at variance. After preaching a highly provocative sermon before Cromwell and the Parliament, which Baxter himself says, 'they put up with', he was summoned before Cromwell a few days later. In the ensuing discussion the monarchy came under consideration. Cromwell maintained, that God had seen fit to change the government. Baxter retorted that it was the divine right of kings to rule, adding that he could not understand how the nation had 'forfeited that blessing.'

If history is to stand as judge and jury in the matter, its verdict would be that the Commonwealth period saw an unprecedented number of evangelical ministers. In August 1662, at the introduction of the Act of Uniformity, over 2000 of its best ministers were forced to leave the Church of England on grounds of conscience. It was the blackest hour of the Church. Suddenly, the replacement of immoral and ill-equipped ministers which had been taking place for years, for spiritual and godly preachers, was put into reverse. The Savoy Conference of 1661, where Baxter played a leading role, failed to secure a compromised solution to the divisions within the Anglican ranks. This meant that the Nonconformist secession was becoming almost inevitable.

Throughout this turbulent time Baxter continued a staunch monarchist. Clearly, his position was one of principle not policy. Soon after Charles II ascended the throne Baxter was made one of the King's chaplains. He was also offered a bishopric which he refused in order to stay at Kidderminster. To him there was nowhere on earth like Kidderminster. Over the years he had seen what few servants of God are ever privileged to see, a dramatic spiritual and moral change of a whole community.

St Bartholomew's Day in August 1662 was a sad day for Baxter when the 'Act of Uniformity' became law and the vast majority of evangelical minister, including Baxter, left the Established Church and lost their livings. But if August was blackened by this sad event, September was brightened by another more personal and providential event, his marriage. He was then forty-seven years of age and his bride, Margaret Charlton, was only twenty-two or twenty-three. The disparity in their ages caused quite a stir at the time. The report of his marriage, he says, 'rung about every where, partly as a wonder, and partly as a crime'. This was not only because of the difference in their ages, but also because of his previous disapproval of the marriage of ministers, which he maintained had 'no sort of necessity'. For all that, it was a happy union. His wife supported and encouraged him throughout his difficult years until her untimely death on 14 June 1681.

One of Baxter's quirks was to preach over the heads of his congregation once a year. For someone whose prime concern was to convey truth as simply as possible this practice needs explaining. It was no rash or impulsive move but quite the reverse. He deliberately intended the people not to understand everything he said.

> I did usually put in something in my sermon, which was above their own discovery, and which they had not known before; and this I did that they might be kept humble, and still perceive their ignorance, and be willing to keep in a learning state. For when preachers tell their people of no more than they know, and do not show that they excel them in knowledge, and scarcely overtop them in abilities, the people will be tempted to turn preachers themselves, and think that they have learned all that the ministers can teach them, and are as wise as they. They will be apt to contemn their teachers, and wrangle with all their doctrines . . . to their own undoing, and to the disturbance of the church; and thus they will easily draw disciples after them. (Orme, p .128)

Baxter, like so many others, could not conform to the demands of the Act of Uniformity, and in 1662 he had to leave his beloved Kidderminster. From then on he had no regular stated ministry but was forced to travel. He suffered the plight of all Nonconformists and was chased from pillar to post. The whole state polity was arrayed against them. They must either conform or be crushed. He underwent short spells in prison, in 1662 and then in 1685 and 1686, due to his preaching activity. Most of his time he lived privately in or near London and spent his time mostly in writing.

Sometimes there was a temporary reprieve from restriction to preach, either from state necessity or leniency. When the Great Plague struck London in 1665, the Conformist ministers fled for their lives leaving the Nonconformist ministers to care for the dying. In

1664 the Conventicle Act was passed, the act which declared illegal all meetings or 'conventicles' in private houses or elsewhere of more than five persons for worship other than that prescribed by the Book of Common Prayer. When this act was eventually repealed crowds again attended his preaching. His renown as a preacher meant he could always muster a large congregation wherever he went. Even in the countryside, if it was known beforehand that he was to preach, people struggled to hear him. 'Those heard, who had not come to church for seven years; and two or three thousand heard, where scarcely an hundred were wont to come, and with so much attention and willingness as gave me very great hopes that I never spake to them in vain.'

Before his death on 8 December, 1691, he was put in prison again. This was by order of the infamous Judge Jefferies, and was a complete travesty of justice. Some of the Conformist ministers themselves were moved to complain of his treatment. But these two years proved more relaxing for Baxter than his previous seasons of trial. After his release, he lived long enough to see the overthrow of the Stuart regime and the coming of William of Orange to the English throne. When the Act of Toleration was passed in 1689, granting once again freedom of worship to Nonconformists, it was too late for Baxter. He was now too old and crippled with various ailments to profit much from it. Towards the end of his life his ministry was restricted almost entirely to those who came to his home in Charter-house Square.

As he lay dying people continued to visit him. They wanted to see how the great man would die? Again he used the opportunity to preach to the people a practical lesson on death.

> You come hither to learn to die; I am not the only person that must go this way. I can assure you, that your whole life, be it ever so long, is little enough to prepare for death. Have a care of this vain, deceitful world, and the lusts of the flesh; be sure you choose God for your portion, heaven for your home, God's glory for your end, his word for your rule, and then you need never fear but we shall meet with comfort.

His friend Dr Calamy who visited him during the last year of his life said of him later, 'He talked in the pulpit with great freedom about another world, like one that had been there, and was come as a sort of express from thence, to make a report concerning it. He delivered himself in public as well as in private, with great vivacity and freedom, and his thoughts had a peculiar edge.' Baxter never returned to Kidderminster, but his work there remains immortalized in the annals of church history.

12
John Bunyan
(1628-88)

Bunyan's Dream
From the Fourth Edition 'Pilgrim's Progress' 1680

There can be few people who have not heard of John Bunyan's *Pilgrim's Progress*. It is hailed as an allegorical masterpiece. But allegories need interpreting, and the key to Bunyan's classic is his own spiritual experience. It is a testimony of his own spiritual life and walk. It was not written for amusement or literary reputation but as a spiritual aid to help others who, by faith, would walk the same spiritual path. Before this he had already written an autobiographical sketch of his conversion in his *Grace Abounding to the Chief of Sinners*. This was a simple, straightforward account of events leading up to and following his conversion. These two books are probably his best known works, although his literary output was enormous.

To most Bunyan is just a figure in history, remembered simply for his exceptional book. Little personal detail is known of him. Few realize how much he suffered and how long he was imprisoned for his faith. His cross has too often been hid behind the glory of *Pilgrim's Progress*.

He was born in November 1628 into a poor family in Elstow, near Bedford. His father was a poor brazier or tinker who tried to do his best for his son by sending him to school, but to what degree he was educated is not known. Whether or not he attended the local grammar school is uncertain. Looking back he was grateful that his parents had allowed him to acquire at least the rudiments of reading and writing. Though he confessed to being a 'bad boy', some have questioned it. They think that he was exaggerating and was never really as bad as he describes himself. But he states 'that from a child, I had few equals, especially considering my years, which were tender, for cursing, swearing, lying and blaspheming the holy name of God.'

After learning his father's trade, he was recruited by the Parliamentary army in 1644, and was stationed at Newport Pagnell. If he saw any military action he does not mention it. As a soldier he would have been issued with a Soldier's Pocket Bible which was published the year before. Whether he read it or not is not known, but one thing is sure – he could not have avoided the army's preachers who preached regularly to all the soldiers.

Upon leaving the army, he returned home to find a wife. Unlike himself, Mary Bunyan came from a godly background. She was brought up in an atmosphere of faith with Christian parents. Though Bunyan did not realize it at the time, it was a blessing for which he was to be thankful later. Mary was highly sensitive and very sympathetic towards him as he struggled under the conviction of sin. When he was all but crushed by his guilt she would encourage him.

When they were married they were extremely poor, but although they had nothing to call their own they loved each other. If Mary had come without a fine dowry, she brought with her a wonderful heritage – she knew the way to heaven. Through his wife, her father, and some good books, including *The Plain Man's Pathway to Heaven,* he was made to consider religion. He began to attend church, which made him feel good. But in reality he was nothing more than a hypocrite: in church he could sing as well as the next man but outside he lived as if there was no God. His faith did not affect his lifestyle, and there was no real spiritual or moral change.

Bunyan could have remained happy with this sham profession but for a sermon he heard on Sabbath-breaking. He went home feeling uncomfortable, but after a good meal the effect of the morning sermon began to wear off and he decided to go and play 'Cat' on the village green with the other men. 'Having struck it a blow from the hole, just as I was about to strike it the second time, a *voice* did suddenly dart from Heaven into my soul, which said, Wilt thou leave thy sins and go to Heaven, or have thy sins and go to Hell?' He was so startled at this that he stood motionless. He said nothing but felt his heart become heavy, and the burden intensified.

The following month he continued playing the hypocrite by going to church, but deep down he knew that all was not well with his soul. With his growing burden he left his outward sin and sought comfort in a life of moral rectitude, (that is, as he describes in *Pilgrim's Progress*, to ease his conscience he went to Mr Legality, the man who lived in the town of Morality). This may have suited his friends, who already considered him to be very religious. But he was still unhappy and unsaved and remained in this state for another year.

Because there was insufficient work in Elstow, he began travelling to Bedford in search of work. As he walked the streets crying out for articles to mend he met a group of women talking about spiritual matters. This proved a real eye-opener for him. He thought it would be easy to enter into their discussion seeing that he too was religious. Instead he had the poverty of his own religious experience exposed. In his book, *Grace Abounding*, he writes:

> I came where there were three or four poor women sitting at a door in the
> sun, and talking about the things of God . . . I drew near to hear what

they said, for I was now a brisk talker also myself in the matters of religion, but now I may say I heard, but understood not, for they were far above out of my reach. Their talk was about a *new birth*, the work of God in their hearts, as also how they were convinced of their miserable state by nature; they talked how God had visited their souls with his love in the Lord Jesus, and with what words and promises they had been refreshed, comforted, and supported against the temptations of the devil; moreover, they reasoned of the suggestions and temptations of Satan in particular, and told to each other by what means they had been afflicted, and how they were borne up under his assaults. They also discoursed of their . . . unbelief, and did contemn, slight and abhor their own righteousness as filthy and insufficient to do them any good. (*Grace Abounding*)

Such words struck fear into his heart. Their talk made plain to him his true spiritual plight. When he left them he was under no illusion. 'I was greatly affected with their words, both because I was convinced that I wanted the true tokens of a truly godly man, and also because by them I was convinced of the happy and blessed condition of him that was such a one.'

This conversation with these uneducated women put him on the right track as his search for spiritual reality intensified. The one thing he longed for was to know he belonged to God's elect. He wanted assurance and certainty and could not be happy with anything less. He became friendly with these godly people of Bedford and their minister John Gifford. They became inseparable. Eventually, after months of searching, he felt his burden roll away. He had come to Calvary, the fountain that has been opened for sin and uncleanness.

When he was twenty-six he became a member of the Bedford church. He still had his doubts but the fellowship there were in no doubt as to where he stood. For a considerable time his spiritual life was turbulent, an ongoing fluctuation of emotions. It was a desperate battle and one he could ill afford to lose. Relief came through reading Luther's *Commentary on Galatians,* a book, Bunyan said, 'that was fit for a wounded conscience.' But his fears were not wholly removed. He was tempted to think he had committed the unpardonable sin, only to find he had not. It was a continual struggle to retain his peace and joy in the gospel.

Convinced of the ordinance of baptism by immersion, Bunyan was baptized, but he could not be called a strict or strong Baptist. His criterion for membership in God's Church was not baptism but regeneration and faith. If he could discern these in a person, for him that was sufficient. Baptism was a recognition that these two things were already present, but it did not convey them. It was the sign and seal of grace, and not its dispenser.

> The saint is a saint before, and may walk with God, and be faithful with the saints, and to his own light also, although he never be baptized . . . I am for communion with saints because they are saints . . . Shew me the man that is a visible believer . . . and though he differ with me about baptism, the doors of the church stand open for him, and all our heaven-born privileges he shall be admitted to them. (Frank Mott Harrison, *John Bunyan*, p. 55)

Eventually, he moved from Elstow to Bedford with his wife and family. Not long after this transition he went through a trying time. His wife died; so too, John Gifford. Naturally, their deaths affected him deeply, and for a time he laboured under a cloud. His concern for his children, especially his blind daughter Mary, and the church in Bedford weighed heavily upon him. But he reminded himself of the dying words of his departed pastor to the church: 'Spend much time before the Lord before choosing a pastor.'

As the church sought the Lord's guidance concerning their future, Bunyan continued to grow spiritually. It became obvious to the church that he was no ordinary convert but that the hand of God was upon him. His grasp of the truth and his remarkable knowledge of the Bible made him above the ordinary. Unaware of it himself, he was encouraged to speak to the people. At first he refused. He was too bashful and embarrassed to stand before the church preaching God's Word. But their persistence finally won the day and he was persuaded to attempt it, even if he failed. Afterwards, he preached in and around Bedford with much acceptance. There had been within the heart of Bunyan an ever increasing bent towards preaching. He had begun reluctantly but now there was a yearning for it. At first he thought it was the devil trying to deceive him and lead him astray. Later, he came to see that it was the Lord and not the adversary who was promoting these good desires.

For the next two years Bunyan continued to preach. His past experience had made him so knowledgeable about the workings of his own heart that he was able to use it to good effect. His simple preaching soon struck a chord in the hearts of the people. He spoke from the heart to the heart with great effect. 'I preached,' he said, 'what I smartingly did feel.' As the people continued coming to hear him he thought there must be some reason other than his preaching which drew them. But he was mistaken. His preaching was highly appreciated. His congregation did not despise his low birth or poor condition but desired 'the sincere milk of the word' which he gave them.

Bunyan's ministry was not always readily accepted. Sometimes he met with opposition. Once, as he preached in a barn, a Cambridge professor took exception to his bluntness, especially when he said that he knew that his hearers were mostly unconverted people. The disgruntled doctor challenged him at the end of the service, as to how he could say such things of people who were baptized. Bunyan reminded him of the Lord's parable of the sower. The Cambridge man also criticized him for preaching at all, and asked how he could justify it in the light of Paul's words in Romans 10:15, 'How shall they preach unless they are sent?' Bunyan replied that he had been sent by the church in Bedford. 'That being a company of lay people,' said his opponent, 'they had no more right to send than a tinker had to preach.'

If this had been the only kind of opposition, Bunyan might have lived a tranquil life. But things were brewing politically, a state of affairs that would have serious implications for Nonconformists like himself. With the restoration of the monarchy in the person of Charles II in 1660, the believers in Bedford were forced to leave the parish church and find new premises. Coupled with this, John Burton, Gifford's successor, had also died, leaving the church without a leader. He highly regarded Bunyan as a Spirit-taught if not a college-taught man. It was a sad time for the church with all these upheavals.

With the Act of Uniformity on the horizon, Nonconformists were put under tremendous pressure. They were watched, even spied on, by their enemies. Bunyan himself was aware of this. Yet he persisted in his preaching. His main concern was not for himself but his children. Should he be imprisoned who would look after them? The answer, he felt, was to remarry. His second wife, Elizabeth, was a young but godly woman, and she was faithful in caring for his and their children.

On 12 November 1660, Bunyan was arrested for preaching at a farmhouse in the hamlet of Lower Samsell, about thirteen miles south of Bedford. It came as no surprise to him. His enemies had shadowed him, biding their time, picking their moment. As the warrant was put in his hand he turned to the congregation and said:

> Brethren and sisters, we are prevented of our opportunity to speak and hear the Word of God, and we are like to suffer for this attempt to do so, but I do desire that you shall not be discouraged. It is a mercy – it is a mercy, I say, to suffer upon so good account. For might we not have been apprehended as thieves and murderers, or for other wickedness? But, brethren and sisters, blessed be God, it is not so! We suffer as Christians for well-doing; and we had better be the persecuted than the persecutors. (Harrison, *John Bunyan*, p. 88)

Then he was taken and put in the County Prison in Bedford.

The following January Bunyan was made to defend himself before a court in Herne Chapel, in Bedford. Towards the end of the proceedings he was asked whether or not he confessed to the indictment. 'This I confess,' he replied, 'we have had many meetings together, for prayer and exhortation, and we have, too, the sweet comforting presence of the Lord among us for our encouragement – blessed be His name! I confess myself guilty in no other way.'

One of the things they disagreed upon was the use of the Prayer Book. It was inconceivable to these magistrates that prayers could be made with complete disregard for the nicety of words and neat phrases. They thought that prayers should be written well and read clearly. To Bunyan, this was to undermine the whole spirit of prayer. How could one write a prayer today for the problems of tomorrow? Prayer should be born out of living experiences. Formal prayers only succeed in binding the Spirit and Inspirer of prayer. Bunyan later explained his position on prayer in his treatise on 'Praying in the Spirit.' He took his cue from 1 Corinthians 14:15: 'I will pray with the spirit, and I will also pray with the understanding.' It begins like a reply to a question in the Westminster Shorter Catechism. 'Prayer is a sincere, sensible, affectionate pouring out of the heart or soul to God, through Christ, in the strength and assistance of the Holy Spirit, for such things as God has promised, or according to his Word, for the good of the church, with submission in faith to the will of God.' With such clearly held beliefs it is little wonder the magistrates could get nowhere with him. His belief in the presence of God in preaching and the power of prayer dominated his teaching. To submit was to deny what he knew to be true.

Twelve long years were spent in prison for conscience' sake. The first six had just begun. At first there was hope of an early release but this soon faded as his appeals were repeatedly ignored. Throughout this time he was kept busy writing. He also had a certain amount of freedom during his first six months custody. Then the authorities found out that he was preaching again and his jailor was severely reprimanded for allowing him out. Had he been prepared to relinquish preaching and return to his trade Bunyan could have been released. This was the choice set before him, but to stop preaching meant disobeying God, and Bunyan would not become a turncoat for the satisfaction of the magistrates. They thought that he was nothing more than an obstinate and intractable fellow. They had no sympathy for a man bound by conscience. Compromise would have been the easiest solution, but for him there was no giving way.

After six long and weary years Bunyan was set free. As he resumed his preaching activities the spies were again alerted. Within no time he was again caught preaching, arrested and put in prison for a further six years. These years were lean years. He felt the monotony of his custody and it was at this time that his blind daughter, Mary, died. Most of the time he had a dry pen and wrote nothing until his imprisonment was almost at an end. For all that, he did not lose heart. 'I have determined,' he said, 'the Almighty God being my help and shield, yet to suffer if frail life might continue so long, even till the moss shall grow upon mine eyebrows, rather than thus to violate my faith and principles.'

It was not until 1671 that religious freedom was granted to the Nonconformists. The King, Charles II, had signed the Declaration of Religious Indulgence in December 1671. Early 1672 saw the release of Bunyan as he came home to his family and to become the church's new pastor. The people had already met for prayer and conference to ascertain the mind of God concerning their situation. They were in no doubt as to their choice. On his return Bunyan was formally appointed to the position. In May 1672, he was given a preacher's licence. After securing a further twenty-five licences for other preachers he became known as 'Bishop Bunyan', much to the hilarity of his friends. How long this freedom would last, nobody knew. All he could do was to continue preaching the Word.

In 1675 the Declaration of Indulgence was repealed and all preaching licences were revoked. This meant Bunyan and his friends were again placed under renewed threat. It was inevitable that such a well-known figure as Bunyan would become the target of attack. As they opened the door to the heavy pounding of the constables, Bunyan was again parted from his family and carted off to prison. As he lay in prison that first night Bunyan dreamt of his whole life passing before him. The end result of this was his writing of *The Pilgrim's Progress*.

Through the unexpected intervention of the renowned John Owen his time in prison was comparatively short. The following summer he was released. Owen had a very high regard for Bunyan as a preacher and told Charles II that he would 'willingly exchange all his learning for the tinker's power of touching men's hearts.' Whenever Bunyan preached in London, John Owen always tried to hear him. When he consulted him on his new literary project, *Pilgrim's Progress*, he gave him his hearty approval and recommended him to his own publisher. This must have encouraged Bunyan tremendously, especially after hearing others describe it as a frivolous production. This bestseller gave Nathaniel Ponder the printer the nickname of 'Bunyan Ponder.'

In 1685 James II came to the throne and the passing of a renewed Indulgence Act meant that Bunyan was allowed to preach openly. His trips to London attracted much attention. His books, especially *The Pilgrim's Progress*, had made him famous. Huge congregations met to hear him. Charles Doe, a comb-maker, and later publisher of his posthumous works, described his popularity. 'If there were but one day's notice given, as many as twelve hundred persons would attend a morning lecture at the early hour of seven on a working day, in the dark winter time.' He also mentions that about three thousand who came 'one Lord's Day at London, at a town's-end meeting-house, so that half were fain to go back again for want of room, and then himself [Bunyan] was fain at a back-door to be pulled almost over people to get upstairs to his pulpit.'

Bunyan received many invitations to go to London, but he remained faithful to his little flock in Bedford. They were his prime concern and nothing could draw him away from them. Having added the second part to *The Pilgrim's Progress* his time was fast running out. Diligent in preaching and writing, he had another manuscript ready for publication, *The Acceptable Sacrifice*. As he prepared to take it himself to the publisher, his wife had a premonition that he would never return alive. Though she tried to dissuade him from going he comforted her and said:

> Be of good cheer, lassie-mine. The God of all comfort and peace be with thee and our children. Go to Elstow, wife, and place this rose . . . on the grave of our poor, dear, blind girl Mary! Blind, did I say? Why, her eyes are open now, as she sees the King and the glory of the Home Above. How we shall greet one another when we meet! (Harrison, *John Bunyan*, p.185)

And with these words he was away, riding into the distance as his wife retreated to cry over her departing husband.

Before he reached London the weather had broken and he found himself travelling through torrential rain, thunder and lightning. By the time he reached his destination he was soaked through, shivering and feeling the effect of his ride. This resulted in a fever, and though he was not fit to preach he kept his appointment. Afterwards he returned to his friend's home and to bed. For the next ten days the fever raged. After telling his friends that he 'desired nothing more than to be with Christ, which is far better,' he raised his hands to heaven and cried, 'Take me, for I come to Thee!' The next moment he was across the river heading towards the gates of the Celestial City.

13
Samuel Rutherford
(1600-61)

Samuel Rutherford lived at a time of tremendous political and religious upheaval in England and Scotland. He belonged to the Scottish Covenanters, Presbyterians hostile to an enforced rule by bishops. They were defenders of the crown rights of the Redeemer to rule over his Church, and they helped to change the political and religious history of a nation.

Rutherford was born in 1600 during the reigns of James VI of Scotland and Elizabeth I of England. His father was a farmer in Jedburgh, county Roxburgh, not far from the English border. He described the district as 'the place to which he owed his first breathing', and that 'his soul's desire was that it might blossom as a rose.' His education began in part of the old Jedburgh Abbey which was used as a school.

From Jedburgh he went on to study in the University of Edinburgh in 1617. His course lasted four years when he graduated as a Master of Arts. All lectures and discussions were conducted in Latin, which meant that every student had to be proficient in it in order to make progress. As a student Rutherford showed remarkable intellectual ability. Within two years of completing his course he was appointed Lecturer of Latin Language and Literature in the University. This was in spite of stiff opposition from two other nominees. However, this position lasted a very short period. When he was twenty-five, two years after his appointment, a dispute developed between himself and the University. This came after his marriage, which is thought to have been the cause of the disagreement. The rift deepened until he was finally forced to resign.

At the same time as this dispute was going on Rutherford was experiencing real concern for his soul. But the struggle was soon ended when he became a Christian. He often regretted that he had lived so long without Christ and that twenty-five years had passed without thought or desire for him. 'Like a fool as I was,' he wrote, 'I suffered my sun to be high in the heaven, and near afternoon, before ever I took the gate by the end.' Yet the ground that was lost was soon made up.

After his conversion he took a course in theology which was completed in 1627. Afterwards he presented himself for ordination. At the time it was not easy for evangelicals to enter the ministry. It meant submitting to ordination by bishops. Many who objected on grounds of conscience had no choice but to remain outside the ministry rather than subject themselves to this usurpation. They were Presbyterians and believed that ordination took place by the laying on of hands by presbyters or elders. On rare occasions the bishop could waive his right, which happened in Rutherford's case. Gordon of Kenmure, later Viscount Kenmure, a gracious man, was attracted to Rutherford. He admired his preaching and respected his godliness. After conferring with the parishioners of Anwoth he offered Rutherford the living. He applied to the Bishop to allow Rutherford to be ordained in the Presbyterian mode, which he did. Whether he consented to this willingly or not is not known. Perhaps the Bishop felt pressurized by Gordon's social and political influence.

Anwoth, in Galloway, was to become the name most closely associated with Rutherford, and for the next nine years he laboured there. Before his coming the people were starved of spiritual food. They had but one sermon every other week. Now, with their own minister, they were given more than adequate food. His biographer gives this description of a typical Sunday service.

> As one stands inside the ivy-clad ruin, it is not difficult even now to fill in the main features . . . the galleries at either extremity of the house, which were occupied by the titled families and principal proprietors of Anwoth, such as the Lennoxes of Cally, and the Gordons of Cardoness and Rusco; and lining every other part of the sacred edifice, the densely packed seats of the farmers and peasants, who sat listening for hours to Rutherford's melting eloquence, and were often raised above themselves by the almost seraphic strains of his adoration and prayer. (Andrew Thomson, *Samuel Rutherford*, pp. 20-21)

These times were precious to his people. There was nowhere they would prefer to be on a Sunday than in the sanctuary of God with

Rutherford preaching. His whole demeanour reflected his high office and holy calling. Sunday by Sunday they gleaned from his harvest. His congregation felt there was no place in Scotland or on earth so blessed as Anwoth! This was reinforced on communion Sundays when the whole parish came to hear him. The church was as a city set upon a hill where men and women congregated to feast themselves upon fat things. If his voice was a little shrill it did not detract from his message. His sermons, like his letters, had an inimitable style – oriental, luscious, rich, almost too extravagant in their expression. But they were a reflection of his heart, a heart consumed by love and passion for his Saviour. Thomson, his biographer, writes:

> His sermons were usually radiant with Christ, as incarnate, suffering, dying, risen, glorified and reigning, and in all his various saving relations to His people. It is a matter of tradition that much of his conversation glowed with this ever-welcome theme, that he sometimes fell asleep with the name of Jesus upon his lips, and that the subject often shed a heavenly light over his dreams. And when, in his pulpit, the unsearchable love of Christ in one of its many phases was the matter of his discourse, especially at the holy festival of a communion season, his animation not infrequently grew to rapture, and it seemed as if he might almost have said, 'Whether in the body, or out of the body I cannot tell.' (Andrew Thomson, *Samuel Rutherford*, p. 23)

If ever a man lived on the love of Christ it was Rutherford. It was a constant theme in his preaching, thoughts and letters. He could see nothing more lovely than the Man of Calvary. The sense of Christ loving him and giving himself for him filled his whole horizon. Such ardency of feeling could not be concealed, and where best to reveal it but from his pulpit in his preaching. When an English merchant visited Scotland he went to hear him preach and wrote, 'I came to Irvine, and heard a well-favoured, proper old man [David Dickson], with a long beard, and that man showed me all my heart. Then I went to St Andrews, where I heard a sweet, majestic-looking man [R. Blair], and he showed me the majesty of God. After him I heard a little fair man [Rutherford], and he showed me the loveliness of Christ.'

For all his intense feeling and thought on the love of Christ, Rutherford was an immensely practical man. He habitually rose at three o'clock for prayer, meditation and study. Between the manse and the church he had a favourite spot where he would ponder spiritual things. This became known as 'Rutherford's Walk'. 'There', he wrote, 'I wrestled with the angel and prevailed. Woods, trees, meadows and hills are my witnesses that I drew on a fair meeting betwixt Christ and Anwoth.'

However, things were not always easy for him at Anwoth. Though he was revered by his people he was not untouched by trials. He had personal and family problems to contend with. He suffered from a severe fever which laid him low for several months. His children all died young. His wife was soon to follow when she died in 1630 after a long illness which affected her both physically and mentally. When his aged mother moved to Anwoth to be near her son and to comfort him in his bereavement she rapidly deteriorated and became totally dependent upon him. These sad and painful experiences taught him to live closer and depend more on the strength of Immanuel.

After living in Anwoth for nine years he came under the scrutiny of the Church's leaders. This was precipitated by a treatise he had written against Arminians, who controlled most of the Church in Scotland. He was accused of nonconformity and summoned to appear before the Court of High Commission, who removed him from his ministerial office. Not content with this, his malicious enemies also accused him of treason. After a three-day trial, where his opponents failed to prove their case, the Bishop of Galloway swore that if they did not find Rutherford guilty he would put the case before the King. This threat swayed the judges sufficiently to condemn him on a majority vote.

In July 1636 Rutherford was debarred from preaching anywhere in Scotland and banished to Aberdeen to await the King's pleasure. The thought of not being able to preach dismayed him. But he rejoiced in the knowledge that he was suffering for Christ's sake. 'There is no quarrel', he said, 'more honest or honourable than to suffer for truth. That honour my kind Lord has now bestowed upon me, even to suffer for my royal and princely king, Jesus. I go to my king's palace at Aberdeen; tongue, pen, and wit cannot express my joy!'

Almost eighteen months were to pass before Rutherford would leave Aberdeen. When he did it was not at the 'king's pleasure' but in spite of it. While he was there he was often pointed out as 'the banished minister'. This episcopal stronghold had no love for the Lord's anointed. Deprived of liberty to preach he expressed his feelings in his letters. Of his three hundred and sixty-five recorded letters about two hundred and twenty were written from Aberdeen. This was the only way he could continue to minister to his flock in Anwoth. But the tide of change was coming. This forced separation of Rutherford and his people did not quench their mutual love. When his escort and delegation from Anwoth left him in Aberdeen to return home they wept bitterly. During this time he would say, 'I am for the present thinking the sparrows and swallows that build their nests in Anwoth blessed birds.' Anwoth always remained his first love.

At Aberdeen he was disturbed by the thought that he had in some way displeased his Lord and that his banishment and silence were a direct judgment from God. As he daily searched his heart he thought he saw the reason for God's judgment – a loss of fervour in his last two years in Anwoth. He confessed and prayed for God to forgive him. In the end he was left to wait God's time to reveal why he was sent there. Who knows, but that the reason for this situation was to give the Church at large those letters which have enshrined his name in the hearts of spiritual people everywhere. Spurgeon described Rutherford's *Letters* as, 'the nearest thing to inspiration which can be found in all the writings of mere men.'

In February 1638 Rutherford was able to return to Anwoth. Events had developed which were to have dramatic repercussions upon Scotland. King Charles I through William Laud, Archbishop of Canterbury, wanted to force a new liturgy on the Scottish Presbyterians. This intention was against the sound advice of those who knew better the Scots' intense feeling regarding their religion. This coercive measure was met with a hostile reception. When the new Prayer Book was used in St Giles' Church, Edinburgh, on 23 July 1637, a woman in the congregation, a Jenny Geddes, stood up and threw her stool at the Dean's head, narrowly missing him. This action prompted all those opposed to this royal intrusion to stand up and be counted. Soon the whole city was in uproar. The King, unprepared to stand down, accused those involved of rebellion against himself, a capital offence. Things got worse between the two parties until an irreparable rift developed.

On 28 February 1638, a National Covenant, drawn up by Alexander Henderson and Archibald Johnston, was presented to the people of Scotland for their adoption. Rutherford hastened to Greyfriars, Edinburgh to be there at its inauguration and to sign his name in support of the measures proposed, thus identifying himself with those who became known as the 'Covenanters'.

Charles I, unprepared to bow to their requests, played for time. He wrote to the Duke of Hamilton, his Commissioner in Scotland, encouraging him to use flattery to win them until such time as they would be suppressed. He had no intention of yielding to their demands.

These developments ended with the downfall of this inflexible King. That which began as a clash of religious rights ended in a clash of arms. Stuart absolutism was something the free-thinking Scots could not tolerate. When all peaceful means of settlement were exhausted, Charles led an army against the unyielding Scots. They, meanwhile, had mustered their own army and confronted the King at Newburn-on-the-Tyne. A battle took place on 28 August 1640 when the English army was severely defeated. For the time being the victorious Scots had humbled the haughty monarch.

While discussions were in progress between the King and Covenanters, before that eventful day in August, Rutherford had hoped to go back to his beloved Anwoth, but he was kept in Edinburgh to help promote the Covenanters' cause. He preached in Edinburgh and in Glasgow with exceptional blessing. A contemporary wrote that he was 'preaching to congregations exceeding great, among whom were many of the nobility.'

His usefulness as a preacher and gifts as a teacher were to draw him to the attention of the General Assembly. They were looking out for men of notable ability to take the vacant chairs in their universities. First Edinburgh, then St Andrews vied for his services. Eventually St Andrews won the day and Rutherford was instated as Professor of Divinity in October 1639. His departure from Anwoth was a sad event for pastor and people alike. 'Never,' he said, 'did I so much long for death. The Lord help and hold up sad clay.' It was not until the General Assembly had expressed its support of his nomination that he yielded to the request. Even then, he only agreed on condition that there would be no 'silent Sundays.' The thought of not being able to preach Christ crucified was more than he could bear.

Rutherford's coming to St Andrews was to reap great rewards. Within a few years the whole spiritual climate was changed. His lectures and preaching transformed the students' understanding and appreciation of the truth. One of his admiring students wrote: 'God did so singularly second his indefatigable pains, both in teaching and in preaching, that the University forthwith became a Lebanon, out of which were taken cedars for building the house of the Lord through the whole land.'

Within a short time of entering the University Rutherford remarried. He had been a widower for some ten years. His second wife was a very gracious and pious woman who cared and looked after him until his death.

In June 1643, 'the Long Parliament' as it was called, summoned an assembly of theologians to consider ways of reforming the Anglican Church and bringing it more into line with the Scottish and European churches. This event culminated in the 'Westminster Assembly of Divines.' Their brief was to discuss church government and its doctrine. The bulk of those who attended were Presbyterians at heart. They invited theologians from Europe and Scotland to witness the transactions and make limited suggestions. The Scottish contingent was made up of four of its best men, Rutherford along with Alexander Henderson, George Gillespie and Robert Baillie. Sessions of this Assembly sat for four and a half years, their work when they met going on for about nine hours daily from Monday to Friday, with preaching on Sundays. Throughout this time Rutherford only once returned home.

It was during his attendance at the Assembly that he wrote his famous work *Lex Rex*, Latin for 'The Law and the Prince'. Its subheading was *A Dispute for the Just Prerogative of King and People*. When it first appeared it caused an unprecedented stir among the educated. It contained a forthright denunciation of the King's absolute sovereignty.

Lex Rex is the plea of the Covenanters for the majesty of the people; for the truth that the law, and no autocrat on the throne, is king; for the creed that limitless sovereignty is the property of God alone. This was directed generally against Stuart absolutism, which held that by a 'free monarchy' is meant that of a king who is above the law and not bound by any bonds of

135

constitutional obligation. Such a king would be free to modify or overrule, to dispense with or set aside, the law. (J.D.Douglas, *Light in the North,* p.50)

Before Rutherford's death his *Lex Rex* was burnt by the public hangman for its treasonable teaching. But as was commonly agreed 'it was much easier to burn than it was to answer.' Charles II, another Stuart despot, positively hated it. Yet for all its claims it did not pose a real threat to monarchical rule; it only placed it in its proper context. Kings were just as much subject to the law as were peasants.

In fact, it was the Scots who offered Charles II the throne of Scotland. They had been outraged by the brutal execution of his father Charles I in 1649. Their revulsion was not just because of the King but because the English had gone back on a solemn promise that when the Scots handed over the King to them they would not execute him. The Scots had as early as 1643 entered into an agreement with Cromwell and Parliament to defend freedom and oppose Stuart tyranny. But with the final defeat of the Royalists it seemed unjustifiable to them to execute the King.

The contrast between Rutherford's *Letters* and *Lex Rex* could not have been greater. The one reveals his heart, the other his mind. He was a man who had heaven in his heart while his finger rested on the national pulse. When he returned to Scotland in 1647, it was with the plaudits of the Westminster divines. They had appreciated his many talents and contributions to their discussions.

His last years in St Andrews were quiet years. The previous turmoil had ended with religious toleration. Yet peace was not to reign long in Scotland. With the death of Cromwell and the abandoning of the Protectorate by his weak son Richard, Charles II came to the throne. In no time he revealed all the traits of a true Stuart. One of the first things he did on regaining the throne was to revoke all Acts of Parliament since 1638. He also violated his promises to the Scottish Church to protect it and its worship. As for Rutherford, he lost his position in St Andrews and was deprived of his pastoral charge. It seems he was picked out for persecution and accused of high treason on account of his *Lex Rex.* One of his closest friends testified at this time that the state of the Church 'lay so heavily on his heart as to sink him into his grave, as not able to outlive the departing of that glory which was already in a great measure departed.'

When the summons finally came for him to appear before the court, it was too late. Rutherford was dying. His response was characteristic of the man. 'Tell them', he said, 'that I have got a summons already from a superior judge and judicatory, and I behove to answer my first summons, and ere your day arrives, I will be where few kings and great folks come.' The day before he died, 29 March 1661, he told his attendants that he would be away before five o'clock the following morning, and thus it was. His last words were, 'Glory, glory dwelleth in Immanuel's land', words immortalized in Anne Ross Cousin's hymn. How well she enters, not only into his words but into the very spirit of Rutherford:

> The sands of time are sinking;
>> The dawn of heaven breaks;
> The summer morn I've sighed for,
>> The fair, sweet morn, awakes:
> Dark, dark hath been the midnight,
>> But day-spring is at hand,
> And glory, glory dwelleth
>> In Immanuel's land.

> I am my Beloved's
>> And my Beloved's mine;
> He brings a poor vile sinner
>> Into His house of wine.
> I stand upon His merit;
>> I know no other stand,
> Not e'en where glory dwelleth
>> In Immanuel's land.

> The King there, in His beauty,
>> Without a veil is seen;
> It were a well-spent journey,
>> Though seven deaths lay between;
> The Lamb with His fair army
>> Doth on Mount Zion stand,
> And glory, glory dwelleth
>> In Immanuel's land.

14
Jonathan Edwards
(1703-58)

Of all the glowing testimonies that have been written about Jonathan Edwards, the one by Dr Martyn Lloyd-Jones ranks as one of the best. He was an avid reader of Edwards and said of him:

> I have to put him ahead even of Daniel Rowland and George Whitefield. Indeed I am tempted, perhaps foolishly, to compare the Puritans to the Alps, Luther and Calvin to the Himalayas, and Jonathan Edwards to Mount Everest! He has always seemed to me to be the man most like the apostle Paul. Of course, Whitefield was a great and mighty preacher as was Daniel Rowlands; but so was Edwards. Neither of them had the grasp of theology that Edwards had; neither of them was the philosopher he was. (Westminster Conference Paper, 1976, p.108)

Edwards belonged to a preaching family. Just as kings have their natural successors he followed in the family tradition. But it was not simply a matter of tradition for him: he was called and equipped of God for the ministry. From a boy he showed signs of a remarkable intellect. He had an analytical mind which suited very intricate and closely reasoned arguments. Had he not been a Christian and theologian he may well have become America's greatest philosopher. However, his mind was taken up with other, greater and better things – the knowledge of God.

Born into a Christian home on 5 October 1703, at East Windsor, Connecticut, he remained unconverted until he was almost eighteen years of age. His conversion left an indelible impression on him and made him familiar with the inner workings of God's Spirit in the new birth. With his peculiar cast of mind he was able to discern every change of mood within himself and have an insight into the human heart rarely given to most men. But he was no inquisitive introvert, unhealthily preoccupied with his own feelings and emotions. His search was for a deeper, more profound realization of God.

Brought up to be religious, he made several attempts to live the life of a Christian devotee, but always failed miserably. His chief difficulty was in maintaining a devotional spirit which could effectively check sin's deadening influence. This he found impossible. No matter how hard he tried, his zeal for God proved fleeting. He knew that he needed more than religion if he was ever to be saved and live for God. He needed a complete change of heart, a new birth, a new life.

This change took place one day as he was reading his Bible. Suddenly he had an insight into the glory of God which he had never known before. This event kindled within him a new kind of relish for God. God's revelation of himself in the Bible now became the chief pursuit of Edwards' life. His whole inner frame was changed and charged with new aspirations for God. What once appeared almost meaningless took on a whole new dimension. He was now seeing with new eyes and the sight was glorious. His earliest memory of sheer delight in God, which he was often to experience later, sprang from reading the words in 1 Timothy 1:17:

'Now unto the King eternal, immortal, invisible, the only wise God, be honour and glory for ever and ever, Amen.' As I read the words, there came into my soul . . . a sense of the glory of the Divine Being; a new sense, quite different from anything I ever experienced before . . . I thought with myself, how excellent a Being that was, and how happy I should be, if I might enjoy that God, and be rapt up in him in heaven, and be as it were swallowed up in him for ever! I kept saying, and as it were singing over these words of scripture to myself . . . From about this time, I began to have a new kind of apprehensions and ideas of Christ, and the work of redemption, and the glorious way of salvation by him. An inward, sweet sense of these things, at times, came into my heart; and my soul was led away in pleasant views and contemplations of them. And my mind was greatly engaged to spend my time in reading and meditating on Christ, on the beauty and excellency of his person, and the lovely way of salvation by free grace in him. (Iain Murray, *Jonathan Edwards: A New Biography*, pp.35-36)

These words were written by a man who was at the time involved in scientific investigation. Science was his first love and held a peculiar magnetism for him. But from now on the experiential knowledge of God was to dominate his thoughts, his time, his energy. To him there was nothing quite like it; it was incomparable. It offered a subject of investigation which far surpassed anything and everything else. It was the study of God rather than his works, the Creator rather than his creation. The cosmos, at its very best, only reflects the glory of God even when it unfolds some of its deepest secrets. Theology, on the other hand, took him to the very heart of God, the Mastermind of the universe.

God, he learned, was not so transcendent as to exclude all self-communication. What is known of him is derived not by human investigation but by spiritual illumination. What he has chosen to reveal of himself can only be known by man in a renewed state. This renewal comes through the Holy Spirit, 'the eyes of your understanding being enlightened' (Ephesians 1:18), as Edwards' experience illustrates. There was nothing new in the words he read. The newness was in himself.

However it was only as he looked back that he realized how great the change had been. It needs to be remembered that this was no strange inner mystic light separate from all concrete reality. It came through God's written revelation, the Bible. Edwards believed that any true knowledge of God must come solely through this medium.

He wrote:

> I had then and at other times, the greatest delight in the holy Scriptures, of any book whatsoever. Oftentimes in reading it every word seemed to touch my heart. I felt a harmony between something in my heart, and those sweet and powerful words. I seemed often to see so much light exhibited by every sentence, and such a refreshing food communicated, that I could not get along in reading; often dwelling long on one sentence to see the wonders contained in it, and yet almost every sentence seemed to be full of wonders. (Iain Murray, *Jonathan Edwards*, p.41)

This vision of God prepared him to become one of the finest writers on experiential Christianity. His deep experience of God coupled with his writing skills laid the foundation for his treatises on the revival in Northampton and his *Religious Affections*.

Trained to write down everything of worth, he formed the habit almost to an obsession. He would sometimes get out of bed or off his horse in order to record something that struck him. At the beginning of his ministry his sermons were always written in full in tiny letters. Some have concluded that because of this they must have been read word for word. The largely mythical picture we have is of Edwards preaching his famous sermon, 'Sinners in the Hands of an Angry God', which portrays him as clutching a candle in one hand and his sermon in the other, totally abstracted from his congregation. He did read his sermons but they were written just as much for his own sake as for the congregation. Yet he was no slave to them. If a new thought came to him while he was preaching he would break from his script into an impromptu delivery.

After almost twenty years in the ministry he changed his method of preparation. Instead of writing his sermons in full he began writing notes. This developed out of a conviction that something was lost in their transmission if the preacher simply read his sermon. Samuel Hopkins, Edwards' first biographer, said of this transition that Edwards considered it, 'a defect and infirmity . . . he was inclined to think it had been better if he had never accustomed himself to use his notes at all'. It is worth noting that this change took place during a time of revival.

Edwards, it could be argued, was one of the founders of modern-day preaching. He was not afraid of change. Instead of following the

Puritan style he developed another far less involved, his new structure being far more adaptable to a rising generation. The Puritan method of divisions and sub-divisions may well have been acceptable a generation earlier, but it had now become too cumbersome. Behind Edwards' new approach lay a significant difference of opinion concerning the aim in preaching. The Puritans stressed its informative side. Adults and children alike were encouraged to memorize sermon headings. This approach did not find a friend in Edwards. He saw preaching as more than just imparting knowledge: it was to impress and change a person. How and when he came to this conviction is unknown.

In his *Thoughts concerning the Revival in New England*, Edwards draws a comparison between the old view of preaching and his own:

> The frequent preaching that has lately obtained, has in a particular man-ner been objected against as unprofitable and prejudicial. It is objected, that, when sermons are heard so very often, one sermon tends to thrust out another; so that persons lose the benefit of all. They say, two or three sermons in a week is as much as they can remember and digest – Such objections against frequent preaching, if they be not from an enmity against religion, are for want of duly considering the way that sermons usually profit an auditory. The main benefit obtained by preaching is by impression made upon the mind at the time, and not by an effect that arises afterwards by a remembrance of what was delivered. And though an after-remembrance of what is heard in a sermon is oftentimes very profitable; yet, for the most part, that remembrance is from an impression the words made on the heart at the time; and the memory profits, as it renews and increases that impression. (*The Works of Jonathan Edwards,* Vol.1, p. 394)

His conversion had taken place during his undergraduate days at Yale. After taking his Master's degree in 1722, a year earlier than was normal, he went as a supply preacher to a recently established church in New York. He began his ministry there in August 1722, but it was short-lived. By the following April he was on the move. This was not due to any friction between himself and the people. Rather his church had originated as a breakaway group from another nearby church, but after reconsidering the situation, some of his people began thinking they may have acted too hastily in separating and were considering returning. One major hindrance to this was his position within the church. They felt they could not just ask him to go. To help facilitate this reunion he resigned his pastorate, which effectively removed the one obstacle which stood in its way.

After leaving New York he came home to his father's manse in East Windsor. Before coming to Yale as a lecturer in 1724, he probably lived and studied at home. During this time he experienced an accelerated intellectual development. Again, his stay was short-lived. In 1726 he left Yale forever to come to Northampton, Massachussetts, the place which was to immortalize his name in church history.

Northampton was a fast developing town when Edwards lived there. He had come first as an assistant to his ageing grandfather, Solomon Stoddard, who pastored a large Congregational church, a church which had become too large for him to handle on his own. A previous attempt to secure a suitable assistant had ended in disaster. This made the congregation more wary of engaging anyone on a permanent basis. After a three-month trial period he was asked to stay. The people recognized in him one well able to step into the shoes of old Stoddard after his time.

Unlike his grandfather, Edwards was very reserved. If people wanted to see him they had to come to the manse. He used to spend thirteen hours a day in his study. Reading, prayer and sermon preparation were to him of the greatest importance, since preaching allowed him to deal with people collectively, rather than use up time in endless rounds of visitation. In this way many of their problems were resolved in one go. But his hours in the study were not all taken up with reading and preparation. New England manses were often used as centres for itinerant preachers and visitors were often lodged there. The church members would also make frequent visits there for his advice and help. Samuel Hopkins, one of his biographers, said that Edwards 'believed he could do more good conversing with persons under religious impressions in his study where they might be sure to be allowed easy access to him.'

When Stoddard died in February 1729, after a fifty-seven year ministry in Northampton, his grandson took up his mantle. Towards the end of 1734 revival broke out. This brought Edwards to the attention of both the English and Scottish church leaders. In his book, *A Faithful Narrative of the Surprising Work of God*, he tells how God had suddenly begun to stir the church, and of its sequel. One biographer wrote:

> The year 1735 opened on Northampton in a most auspicious manner. A deep and solemn interest in the great truths of religion, had become universal in all parts of the town, and among all classes of people . . . So extensive was the influence of the Spirit of God, that there was scarcely an individual in the town, either old or young, who was left unconcerned about the great things of the eternal world. This was true of the gayest, of the most licentious, and of the most hostile to religion. And in the midst of this universal attention, the work of conversion was carried on in the most astonishing manner. Every day witnessed its triumphs; and so great was the alteration in the appearance of the town, that in the spring and summer following, it appeared to be full of the presence of God. There was scarcely a house which did not furnish the tokens of his presence, and scarcely a family which did not present the trophies of his grace. (*Works,* Vol.1, p. xliii)

From 1739 to 1742 a far greater and more extensive revival took place, what has been called 'The Great Awakening'. Like all revivals this had its friends and foes alike. Some wrote attacking it, while others defended it. Edwards became its chief advocate. Whatever others thought or wrote he was convinced that what had happened was a real work of God. Unfortunately, its opponents steadily increased. Whereas they had begun attacking it under anonymity, later they came out of the shadows. Increasing support gave them added confidence and they became far more vocal. Their position was strengthened by the lack of restraint of some extremists. These were too extreme in their claims of the Spirit's impulses and revelation, and brought the whole work into disrepute.

The leader of this fanatical group was a preacher called James Davenport, a good but misguided man. He later repented and publicly denounced his former actions, but by then it was too late and the damage had been done. He stirred the people into a frenzy with his vitriolic attacks upon other ministers.

Edwards found himself at the centre of this controversy fighting on two fronts. On the one hand there were the formalists who wanted the Church to go back to sleep. They opposed any form of living Christianity. On the other hand, there were extremists like Davenport who refused to listen to reason. They had become so entrenched in their false notions that they were beyond recall. To Edwards, both positions were extremely wrong. He saw them as two strands of a single attack, behind which he saw the Devil, whose strategy was to keep them asleep and if he failed here then to push them into an unrestrained zeal. The pendulum swung from one extreme to the other. Edwards' position was clear, the revival was of God, even if there were deviations. He did not agree with those who were fanatical, but neither could he agree with the formalists who spoke ill of the revival altogether. He walked a middle road and presented a more balanced view.

The fruit of the revival in Northampton meant that most of the male population became attached to the church. At this time Edwards' position in the church was unassailable. The people loved and revered him, even though he was a little detached from them. He held New England's prize pulpit while others just looked on. He was the best-paid minister in New England. This was to present a major problem for him later in securing another pastorate when he was forced to leave the church. Other churches felt unable to offer him anything comparable to what he had been accustomed at Northampton.

However the tide of popularity quickly changed. His new position regarding who was eligible for partaking in the Lord's Supper created an immediate reaction among the people. His grandfather had opened the table to allow those with weak consciences, but lacking full assurance of salvation, to partake. Gradually this had deteriorated into a custom and tradition in the church. The original intention became so abused that it allowed people access to the Lord's table irrespective of the quality of their lives.

Stoddard also believed that an open table could aid a person in salvation, and that by coming they might believe and be saved. This position actually proved itself counter-productive. Instead of people being made aware of their lost condition and the substitutionary nature of Christ's death for sin, they became complacent. They began to think that partaking was the same as being saved. This situation gave them a false sense of security. It made them think that they were spiritually sound when they were actually lost. By closing the table,

145

Edwards believed he would confront some with their true condition, being religious but lacking reality. He did not expect or demand perfection or even full assurance. All he wanted was for partakers to have a credible profession borne out by their lives. When some of the people refused to change their lifestyle it provoked a crisis in the church.

Unfortunately, there was something more sinister about this situation than a theological difference. There was also an underlying current of discontent within the church. His opponents saw this as an ideal opportunity to oust Edwards. Due to their influence both in the church and town they were able to affect others. Edwards, wanting to clarify his position, offered to preach a series of sermons on the subject, but was refused. He also wrote a book explaining his views, though few read it. When the church came to decide on the matter a huge majority voted for Edwards' expulsion. In his farewell sermon there was no hint of any animosity. Behind this whole affair he saw the hand of a sovereign God thrusting him out. What grieved him most was the spiritual implications for the church. Contentions within a church never make for a happy church. Far from it. In fact, it positively hinders the Spirit's operation among a people. He told them:

> A contentious people will be a miserable people. The contentions which have been among you, since I first became your pastor, have been one of the greatest burdens I have laboured under in the course of my ministry – not only the contentions you have had with me, but those which you have had one with another, about your lands and other concerns – because I knew that contention, heat of spirit, evil speaking, and things of the like nature, were directly contrary to the spirit of Christianity and did, in a peculiar manner, tend to drive away God's Spirit from a people . . . Let the late contention about the terms of Christian communion, as it has been the greatest, be the last. I would, now I am preaching my farewell sermon, say to you, as the apostle to the Corinthians, 2 Cor.13.1: 'Finally, brethren, farewell. Be perfect, be of one mind, live in peace; and the God of love and peace shall be with you.' (*Works,* Vol 1, pp.ccvi-ccvii)

Due to this tragic event the Church at large became the beneficiary. Had Edwards remained in Northampton we may never have had his best theological works. His *Inquiry into the Freedom of the Will* and *The Great Christian Doctrine of Original Sin Defended,* were written in the seclusion of Stockbridge, the frontier town to which he went. The church there could not have been more different from that in Northampton. It consisted mainly of the native Indians who were the majority in the town with only about a dozen white people living there. Its isolation gave him far more time to devote to his studies and writing. There were fewer interruptions which allowed him more freedom to bring his long researches to a fitting conclusion.

His ministry in Stockbridge was brief compared with his twenty-three years at Northampton. It lasted from August 1751 until early 1758 when he became the new President of Princeton College, New Jersey. This offer came after the tragic death of his predecessor and son-in-law, Aaron Burr. His first sermon preached at Princeton was on Hebrews 13:8, 'Jesus Christ the same yesterday, today, and for ever'. Those who heard it were amazed to find that he had preached over two hours. The effect was tremendous!

Though Edwards was a profound scholar he never succumbed to the idea that truth was simply a matter for the mind. Its effect upon the heart was what most concerned him. And the truth did affect him. When George Whitefield preached in Northampton for the first time in 1740 the revival was at its height. Of that memorable occasion Whitefield wrote, 'Preached this morning, and good Mr Edwards wept during the whole time of exercise. The people were equally affected; and, in the afternoon, the power increased yet more.'

Edwards died on 22 March 1758, as the result of a smallpox vaccination. He allowed himself to be vaccinated because smallpox was so rampant around Princeton at the time of his coming. At first everything went well until he suddenly took a turn for the worse. As he lay dying his daughter Lucy continued to nurse him. After leaving messages for his wife and family he told her 'to seek for a Father who will never fail you'. Later he said, 'Now where is Jesus of Nazareth, my true and never-failing Friend?' He died soon after, to enter that glory which even his great mind found incomprehensible.

15

John Wesley

(1703-91)

John Wesley was the father of English Methodism. Both branches, the Wesleyan and Calvinistic, stemmed from a group of earnest 'Methodists', derisively called 'the Holy Club', which met in Oxford. The nickname 'Methodist' was derived from their rigid method of study and strictly regulated lives. Charles Wesley, John's brother, acknowledged that he had wasted his first year at college, then began a course of study for which he said, he received 'the harmless name of Methodist.'

Those associated with the Holy Club set out certain rules for systematic study to which they tenaciously adhered. They were a serious group of young men whose sole aim was to save themselves and the world. Though they were keen and zealous and thought they were Christians, their religion was not true Christianity. It was a mere shadow of what was to become the hallmark of their faith – assurance. George Whitefield wrote of them in his *Journal*:

> Never did persons, I believe, strive more earnestly to enter in at the strait gate. They kept their bodies under even to an extreme. They were dead to the world, and willing to be accounted as the dung and offscouring of all things, so that they might win Christ. Their hearts glowed with the love of God, and they never prospered so much in the inward man, as when they had all manner of evil spoken against them falsely without.

Of its two leading lights, one, Charles Wesley, was to become famous for his hymns, the other, John Wesley, for his organizational skills. John was a born leader, not the sort of man to take a back-seat in anything, especially when he could claim seniority. On his return to Oxford, after spending six months at home in Epworth, he immediately took charge of this little group of devotees. However it was Charles who had given it its original impetus. He had begun it the year before in the absence of his brother.

John Wesley

John was born on 17 June 1703, in Epworth, Lincolnshire. His father, Samuel Wesley, was the resident vicar. His mother, Susanna, a strict disciplinarian, took it upon herself to educate the children in their early years. She was particularly concerned with John's development because of a near disaster that had struck the family home. When he was only six years of age, the manse in Epworth was burned to the ground and John was remarkably saved. He was in an upper room and had to jump to safety as the bottom floor was engulfed in flames. A painting depicting this horrific event was given the motto, 'Is not this a brand plucked from the burning.' His mother felt that she had 'to be more particularly careful of the soul of a child whom God had so mercifully provided for.' Afterwards, John was taken to his father, who rejoiced that all his children had been spared.

'Come, neighbours,' he said, 'let us kneel down! Let us give thanks to God! He has given me all my eight children; let the house go, I am rich enough.'

If it was literally true that John was 'a brand plucked from the burning' it was almost another thirty years before it became true of him spiritually. The intervening years were to be years of searching. John was discontented with himself, his religion and his prospects. He laboured on earth to secure a place in heaven, but to no avail. No matter what he did he could find no rest for his soul. Within, there was agitation and perplexity. Even his earnest quest for holiness could not satisfy him.

After his education at home John went to Charterhouse, and on to Christchurch, Oxford. He was then seventeen years of age and possessed a remarkable reasoning faculty. His mind was always logical and systematic. Everything had its proper place, whether in his rooms or in his head. There was order and structure about everything he did.

Wesley graduated in 1724. On 19 September, the following year, he was ordained as a curate. Taking up the challenge of the ministry made him more thoughtful about practical holiness. He read several books upon it which profoundly affected him. Though his lifestyle was meticulous and he hated idleness, he still lacked inner peace. He did his best in the hope that God would choose the best for heaven. But his best, he later learnt, was never good enough.

Wesley's trouble stemmed from his constant fear of not knowing whether he was saved or not. There was a yearning in his heart for some certainty about his salvation, but it always seemed to evade him. For him, this element of uncertainty was disconcerting and meant a life of perpetual dread and remorse. Somewhere, somehow, there seemed to be a fundamental flaw in his faith. He wrote to his mother:

> If we can never have any certainty of our being in a state of salvation, good reason it is that every moment should be spent not in joy but in fear and trembling; and then undoubtedly in this life *we are* of all men most miserable! God deliver us from such a fearful expectation as this! (A. Skevington Wood, *The Burning Heart,* p.45)

When his father died in April 1735, John was expected to take his place in Epworth. He was now a Fellow of Lincoln College and as such financially independent. He was also lecturing to the under-graduates and felt that he was fulfilling an important role. Earlier, in December, he had already made known to the family that he could do more good in Oxford than in Epworth and was fully intent on staying there. As a result, the living passed from the Wesley family to another, much to the displeasure of his elder brother, Samuel.

Not long after, John received an invitation from the Society for the Propagation of the Gospel to go as a chaplain to Georgia, in America, to preach the gospel to the Indians and colonists there. This missionary call opened up a new opportunity to do his soul good. 'My chief motive,' he wrote, 'to which all the rest are subordinate is the hope of saving my own soul.' It did, ultimately, lead to this but in a way he could not have conceived beforehand. Up to this point Wesley never considered himself saved or fit to die. Even the Methodism of the Holy Club offered no real assurance of heaven. In fact, this whole system, although sincere and spiritually motivated, was nothing more than a human institution, built upon human ideas, and devoid of any real spiritual comfort. 'Their iron-clad regime,' wrote Arnold Dalli-more, 'was one of human effort, that provided no assurance and left the all-important salvation of the soul a distant uncertainty.'

Humanly speaking the Georgia experiment would be a complete disaster and would end with Wesley running away. Yet, for all that, it began a chain of events which ultimately led him to that much desired peace with God. On his outward journey, Wesley met a group of religious people called the Moravians. They were travelling from Germany to the New World. What struck him most about them was their obvious lack of fear in the midst of a terrible storm. As the waves beat against the ship, they remained calm. While he was filled with terror that any moment might be his last, they sang hymns; their serenity in the midst of imminent danger affected him deeply. These people had no fear of death. Little wonder that he was attracted to them.

When they eventually reached Georgia, Wesley was introduced to the Moravian leader in the colony, August Gottlieb Spangenberg. Wesley was immediately drawn to him and held him in high esteem. They discussed different aspects of religion. What surprised Wesley most was the directness of Spangenberg's question, especially, when he asked Wesley whether or not he was saved? This direct approach was something completely alien to him and embarrassed him.

When he finally returned to England in early 1838, Wesley was full of misgivings. He was confused as to what to do.

> I went to America to convert the Indians; but, oh, who shall convert me? Who, what is he that will deliver me from this evil heart of unbelief? I have a fair summer religion. I can talk well; nay, and believe myself, while no danger is near. But let death look me in the face, and my spirit is troubled. Nor can I say, 'To die is gain'! Oh, who will deliver me from this fear of death?

At home he met another Moravian, Peter Boehler, who became his spiritual adviser. When Wesley began to feel he should not preach because he was unconverted, Boehler encouraged him to continue. 'Preach faith till you feel it, and then, because you have it, you will preach it.'

However what affected him most was the way Boehler united faith and assurance, that a person should know he was saved the moment his sins were forgiven. Wesley argued with him over it, but to no avail. As Boehler pointed him to the Scriptures Wesley's whole life crumbled before him. He realized that he was full of self-trust and self-righteousness. Depressed by this he laboured on until that eventful day of 24 May 1738, when he wended his way to a meeting of a society in Aldersgate Street, in London. He felt encouraged that morning by reading in his Bible, 'Thou art not far from the kingdom of God,' but there was no lasting peace. That night, as he sat listening to someone reading from Luther's preface to Paul's Letter to the Romans, something wonderful happened.

> About a quarter before nine, while he was describing the change which God works in the heart through faith in Christ, I felt my heart strangely warmed. I felt I did trust in Christ, Christ alone, for salvation: and an assurance was given me, that he had taken away my sins, even mine, and saved me from the law of sin and death.

What had happened to him was everything he had been looking for. He had found the Saviour and in finding him he had found forgiveness of sin and peace with God. Boehler's words were no longer mere theories to him but a living reality. No amount of words or arguments could have convinced him of this wonderful experience. Now he had 'tasted that the Lord is gracious' all his misgivings were dispelled. This assurance revolutionized his life and became the future hallmark of Methodism.

Soon after he was on his way to the Moravian centre in Germany, where he met their leader, Count Zinzendorf. On his estates in Herrnhut, Saxony, a small colony of Moravians lived together. They were religious communists or communalists. Here Wesley found, 'living proofs of the power of faith: persons saved from inward as well as outward sin, by the love of God shed abroad in their heart.' Though he was attracted to the Moravians, and in a sense owed them his soul, he could never get along with their leader. Their first meeting was friendly and Wesley heard Zinzendorf preach. Later, a wedge was driven between them because of a dispute which had erupted in the Fetter Lane Society, London. Then again, when Wesley and Zinzendorf disagreed on many points of theology, the rift widened.

Wesley's future remained uncertain. It was almost a year before he began his outdoor preaching campaign. Prior to this he had confined himself to the churches. However, as time passed fewer churches were prepared to allow him to preach in them. Doors, which were once opened, were now firmly closed. Before very long a door was to open which would become the chief means of reaching the unchurched masses.

To the old bigoted cleric, outdoor preaching would have been sinful. Even the new Wesley was not fully convinced of its propriety. The remnants of a strict churchmanship still remained to trouble him when Whitefield first approached him to take charge of the thriving work in Kingswood, Bristol. His own words show the inner turmoil this new method of doing things created. 'I could scarce reconcile myself at first to this strange way of preaching in the fields . . . having been all my life (till very lately) so tenacious of every point relating to decency and order, that I should have thought the saving of souls almost sin, if it had not been done in church.' It was only after consulting his friends, who failed to agree, that a conclusion was finally reached. His decision was made not on the grounds of its orthodoxy, or that of reason, but by casting lots. Wesley asked God whether or not he should go? Had the reply been unfavourable Wesley might never have preached in the open air. However, as it happened, he was free to go forward.

153

It took a tremendous amount of courage for Wesley to preach outdoors; as already indicated there was something in his make-up which made it appear repugnant. Apart from his own initial prejudice there was also the thought of its irregularity, but after overcoming his scruples he launched out into what was to become his lifelong work as an evangelist. 'I submitted to be more vile,' he said, 'and proclaimed in the highways the glad tidings of salvation, speaking from a little eminence in a ground adjoining the city, to about three thousand people.'

Wesley's mission was not for his own benefit. From the human standpoint, it was demanding. He would be vilified from all directions, not least from within the Church. His natural inclination would have led him to maintain a rigorous respectability, but for the good of souls and the glory of God he embarked on his crusade. Seeing the effect his outdoor preaching produced he was forced to acknowledge that God was in it. If, after professing the true gospel, he had increasingly felt the alienation of his collegues, what would be their attitude to this unusual action? Even within his own family he met with hostility on this matter. His brother, Samuel, resented what he was doing. But once he had begun, there was no turning back. The evident success of his preaching was positive proof that God was with him.

For someone who had become a field preacher, not out of conviction but out of necessity, it proved revolutionary. The open air gave him a platform from which he could reach those who ordinarily never came into contact with the gospel. In any case, the kind of congregations he attracted were too large to be accommodated in traditional buildings. Thousands, even tens of thousands, attended these gatherings.

Having broken the mould of his churchmanship and broken with the Moravians, Wesley now came into his own. His role as a leader and his natural talent for organizing enabled him to introduce society meetings among the Methodists. These societies were close-knit groups watching over and caring for one another. They were to be disciplined in the faith, to support each other in crisis, and discipline each other in conduct. This was the formation of a church within a church. It was like a baby taking shape in its mother's womb before its inevitable separation. Wesley's conception of these meetings reached its maturity in 1743.

Such a society is no other than 'a company of men having the form and seeking the power of godliness, united in order to pray together, to receive the word of exhortation, and to watch over one another in love, that they may help each other to work out their own salvation.'

This attitude had practical implications for the whole body. There was toleration but not to the impenitent. They would sympathize with the weak but had no pleasure in the sinner. Falling, was one thing: deliberate sin, quite another. Those who fell were encouraged to repent and seek forgiveness. Throughout, their aim was to maintain the purity of the society and develop practical godliness.

These are the General Rules, all which we are taught of God to observe, even in his written word, the only rule, and the sufficient rule, both of our faith and practice. And all these, we know, His Spirit writes on every truly awakened heart. If there be any among us who observe them not, who habitually break any of them, let it be known unto them who watch over that soul as they that must give an account. We will admonish him of the error of his ways; we will bear with him for a season. But then if he repent not, he has no more place among us. We have delivered our own soul.

This was the kind of after-care these young converts received. They were not left to fend for themselves but encouraged by the group, whose purpose was to establish the novice in his Christian walk. Though this cellular form was partly borrowed from the Moravians, Wesley could not have realized the importance it would have within Methodism itself. This close shepherding kept a tight rein on the flock and stopped them from wandering. Many of its leaders were laymen who were expected to maintain a strict watch over their small flock.

If Wesley had parted company with the Moravians he was soon to part company with the Calvinists. These were highly supportive of Whitefield, who had led Wesley into field preaching and had entrusted him with the work while he returned to America. Early in 1739, Wesley published his sermon on 'Free Grace'. This was to create a rupture between the two groups who had up until then been happily living together. Though Whitefield tried to persuade him to restrain himself, Wesley carried on his attack against Predestination.

Methodism now became the mother of two. Instead of one body there were two factions, the Calvinists and the Arminians. Wesley gave his supporters their distinctive brand of theology. If he preached Free Will, he also advocated Perfectionism. Not that he ever claimed it for himself. This naturally disrupted the work for a while as the chasm widened. Instead of drawing together they drifted apart until the rift was too wide to bridge.

From here on Wesley went his own way. Though the Methodists remained under the wing of the Church of England, they were really a different people. It was like a living member in a dead body. Where there was putrefaction all around, with a few exceptions, there still remained these living cells, acting as salt to preserve the whole from decay.

What makes this development so strange is that Wesley did not realize what he had done. Whereas others could see it, he seemed to be oblivious to it. As the years passed and the work increased the young fledgling church should have flown from the nest, but Wesley remained a true churchman. If he was initially rejected by the Church, that was no reason for abandoning her altogether. He instructed his followers not to absent themselves from the established churches, and gave orders that the society meetings were not to be held at the same time as church services. Whenever possible, he himself, would attend these to receive the communion.

It was never Wesley's intention to withdraw from the Anglican Church to establish another. Yet, within the compass of Methodism there was a growing discontent towards the Church. Most of them were Methodists first and churchmen second. All they really wanted was for Methodism to flourish. Within the Church it was restricted. Some hoped that when Wesley died that Methodism would also die with him. However they did not understand the nature of Methodism: it was not of man, but of God. The vibrancy of the faith of Methodists was sustained by the inner assurance or witness of the Holy Spirit. He confirmed them in their faith, that whether in or out of the Church, Methodism would survive.

Before his death on 2 March 1791, Wesley had set the wheels in motion for a Methodist exodus from the Church of England. His concern for the barren fields of America prompted him to ordain elders and superintendents. The War of Independence had ended in 1784, with the expulsion of the Anglican clergy, who had supported England in her struggle. With the loss of its sovereign rights the Church had been greatly reduced in influence. The expulsion of the

Anglican clergy had left a gaping hole in the churches' life in the colonies.

As there was little hope of convincing the Bishop of London to ordain men for the newly-freed states of America, Wesley took the unprecedented step of ordaining them himself. Wesley wrote to the Methodists in America:

> Lord King's account of the primitive church convinced me many years ago, that bishops and presbyters are the same order, and consequently have the same right to ordain. For many years I have been importuned, from time to time, to exercise this right by ordaining part of our travelling preachers; but I have still refused, not only for peace' sake, but because I was determined as little as possible, to violate the established order of the national church to which I belonged.
>
> But the case is widely different between England and North America. Here there are bishops who have a legal jurisdiction. In America there are none, neither any parish ministers. So that, for some hundred miles together, there is none either to baptize, or to administer the Lord's Supper. Here, therefore, my scruples are at an end; and I conceived myself at full liberty, as I violate no order, and invade no man's right, by appointing and sending labourers into the harvest. (Richard Watson, *The Life of John Wesley,* p. 352)

This act of ordination hastened the eventual withdrawal of the Methodists both in America and England from the established Church. It was never Wesley's intention to withdraw from the Church which he considered 'the best-constituted national church in the world'. However, the writing was on the wall even if Wesley had not read it. The Church which was called by his name, was to stand as a lasting tribute to his preaching and governmental powers.

Wesley's ministry extended over sixty years. To quote J.C.Ryle:

> It would be useless to dwell on one year more than another. For fifty-three years – from 1738 to 1791 – he held on his course, always busy, and always busy about one thing – attacking sin and ignorance everywhere, preaching repentance toward God and faith toward our Lord Jesus Christ everywhere – awakening open sinners, leading on enquirers, building up saints – never wearied, never swerving from the path he had marked out, and never doubting of success. Those only who read the Journals he kept for fifty years can have any idea of the immense amount of work that he got through.

157

He journeyed up and down the land, London, Bristol and Newcastle-upon-Tyne representing the three points of a triangle within which he incessantly organized and preached. His journeys also included ministering in Scotland as well as preaching at various places in Wales on his way to Ireland, besides visiting Wales specifically over thirty times.

As a preacher he was not as overwhelmingly eloquent and powerful as Whitefield, but he possessed great clarity of expression, a simple and direct style, and perhaps excelled Whitefield in reasoning ability. Here is part of his concluding paragraph in a sermon on justification by faith, the text being Romans 4:5, 'But to him who justifies the ungodly . . .':

> Thou ungodly one who hearest or readest these words . . . I charge thee before God, the judge of all, go straight unto Jesus with all thy ungodliness. Take heed thou destroy not thine own soul by pleading thy righteousness more or less. Go as altogether ungodly, guilty, lost, destroyed, deserving and dropping into hell; and thus shalt thou find favour in his sight, and know that he justifieth the ungodly. As such thou shalt be brought unto the blood of sprinkling, as an undone, helpless, damned sinner. Thus look unto Jesus! There is the Lamb of God, who taketh away thy sins! Plead thou no works, no righteousness of thine own! no humility, contrition, sincerity. In no wise. That were, in very deed, to deny the Lord that bought thee. No! Plead thou singly the blood of the covenant, the ransom paid for thy proud, stubborn, sinful soul. (J.C.Ryle, *Christian Leaders of the Eighteenth Century,* p.93)

16
George Whitefield
(1714-70)

George Whitefield has had his place in evangelical history re-established in recent years. Because of the Wesley brothers, John and Charles, and the rise of Wesleyan Methodism in England, Whitefield has to a considerable extent been overlooked. He was converted some time before the Wesleys, and had already preached acceptably and powerfully in England and in the colonies of Georgia and New England before returning home to lead the evangelical upsurge within the Anglican Church. This work he later handed over to John Wesley to consolidate, while he returned to his travelling ministry in Britain and America.

Whitefield was born in Gloucester on 16 December 1714, the last of seven children. His parents were the owners of the Bell, the most prestigious inn in Gloucester. When he had just turned two his father, Thomas, died, leaving his mother to care for the inn and the children. His mother had great difficulty in delivering him and was laid aside for several months afterwards. She took this as a sign for good, and believed that she would derive more comfort from him than from any of her other children.

An inn, in such an immoral age, could not have been the best environment to bring up a young boy. He saw life in the raw. Even the better quality inns attracted the lower kind of person. There was no restriction on visitors and all sorts would have entered the premises. For sixteen years he lived there. In spite of all this, as a boy he used to think of preaching and often play-acted the part of a preacher. 'I was always fond of being a clergyman,' he wrote, 'and used frequently to imitate the ministers reading prayers.'

His mother had good intentions for her youngest son. He was educated at St Mary de Crypt, a grammar school in Gloucester. His remarkably retentive mind and elocution meant that he was often chosen to make the speech before the Corporation's annual visit.

Sometimes the pupils were expected to act out plays, an activity which he thoroughly enjoyed. Looking back, he remembered it with embarrassment because he sometimes had to dress up and play the part of women. 'The remembrance of this', he wrote, 'has often covered me with confusion of face, and I hope will do so, even to the end of my life.'

Due to some financial straits within the household, Whitefield was obliged to work in the Bell Inn for eighteen months, but deep within his heart there was a yearning for better things. His education also suffered a temporary setback, and when it was suggested that he go to Oxford to study with a friend, he was almost broken-hearted to be told he could not go.

During this time his elder brother had taken charge of the Bell. Unfortunately, George and his sister-in-law could never agree, and he was forced to leave. Later he realized that the hand of God was in it and wrote of his departure, 'little thinking that God by this means was forcing me out of the public business, and calling me from drawing wine for drunkards, to draw water out of the wells of salvation for the refreshment of His spiritual Israel.' For a short time he stayed with another brother in Bristol. Here he took on a religious aspect, only to find that when he returned home to his mother's house in Gloucester it quickly evaporated. Not knowing what his future held, and finding every opportunity of employment closed to him, he was left to himself. This made him think that God had something unusual in store, and that was made known through a friend who had just returned from studying in Pembroke College, Oxford. He happened to call on Whitefield's mother and mentioned how he had been able to pay his way through college as a servitor. This information caused Whitefield's mother to cry out, 'This will do for my son. Will you go to Oxford, George?' 'With all my heart,' he replied. Soon he was back at school preparing himself for Oxford.

Whitefield began his course in Oxford in November 1732. For the next three years he would live as a servitor, doing the menial tasks for those who had the means to live comfortably there. Servitors were considered the lowest of the students and were often made to feel it. They served others in order to have free tuition. His past experience in the Bell Inn stood him in good stead for these college chores. At Oxford, unlike many of the other students, he studied hard. He also sought to maintain his religious principles, which his brother told him would soon disappear once he reached Oxford. So diligent was he in performing them that his fellow students thought him an 'odd fellow'. They were so preoccupied with enjoying and indulging themselves that they thought it strange that he did not join them.

Instead, Whitefield's mind was on other things. Those who were stigmatized as 'Methodists', and generally ridiculed, he strenuously defended. Hidden deep within his heart there was a longing to know these despised religious zealots. Yet it was more than twelve months before this was to happen and that under the most tragic of circumstances. He had secretly sent a message to Charles Wesley informing him of a woman who had tried to commit suicide, requesting him to visit her. Charles soon found out who had sent him the message and invited him to breakfast. This was his first real contact with the Methodists, though he had often seen Charles about Oxford.

Unknown to Charles Wesley this meeting was to end in Whitefield's conversion. He loaned him several religious books, which he avidly read. Afterwards, he gave him Henry Scougal's, *Life of God in the Soul of Man*. This, for the first time, confronted Whitefield with experiential Christianity. He read there that true religion was not just a matter of going to church, hurting no-one, being constant in prayer and helping one's neighbour. 'True religion', he read, 'is union of the soul with God, and Christ formed within us.' Immediately, he realized that he had to become a new creature.

In his keenness to share this new-found revelation, he wrote to his family telling them of it. Instead of being overjoyed at the news, they simply ignored it. Worse, they thought him a little mad! In an attempt to enter God's kingdom by the 'strait gate' he made himself dangerously ill. He fasted to the point of starvation. Due to these extremes he finally succumbed and lay at death's door for seven weeks. Soon after his recovery he was converted and came into the clear light of the gospel. A new joy filled his heart which he had not known before. The weight of sin, which had so oppressed him, was now removed.

Soon after this, I found and felt in myself that I was delivered from the burden that had so heavily oppressed me. The spirit of mourning was taken from me, and I knew what it was truly to rejoice in God my Saviour; and, for some time, could not avoid singing psalms wherever I was; but my joy gradually became more settled, and, blessed be God, has abode and increased in my soul, saving a few casual intermissions, ever since. (*Journals*, p.58)

After experiencing this new-found joy, he was encouraged by his tutor and doctor to spend some time in the country recuperating. This was considered essential before resuming his studies. Whitefield, reluctantly, returned home to Gloucester rejoicing in his Saviour. Here he began to study his Bible on his knees, praying over every line and every word. Matthew Henry's *Commentary* also became his constant companion as he searched the Scriptures daily. If his soul was beginning to grow, so too was his usefulness. Though he was spiritually comparatively young, God made him instrumental in the conversion of several people in Gloucester.

Whitefield continued in Gloucester for the next nine months, during which time something remarkable happened. After about seven months he was unexpectedly summoned to an audience with the Bishop of Gloucester. Somewhat confused, he made his way to the Bishop's home. For some time he had been considering the possibility of entering the ministry but was fearful that he might have been running before being sent. He was conscious that a man needed to be called of God before taking up this office. To his great surprise the Bishop told him that ordinarily he never ordained anyone under twenty-three years of age but in Whitefield's case he would make an exception and ordain him whenever he wished. Whitefield returned home wondering what it all meant. His scruples, which had previously held him back, were now resolved as he looked forward to enter the ministry.

On 20 June 1736, Whitefield was ordained. The previous day he had spent preparing himself by prayer and fasting for this major event. The following week he preached his first sermon in the church of St Mary de Crypt. This met with exceptional results. A huge congregation had gathered, something which he attributed to curiosity. But if curiosity had drawn many of them they certainly went away convinced that the preacher believed everything he said. Those who knew him were struck by the change they found in him. It was a momentous occasion for Whitefield, who knew something of God's help in his delivery.

As I proceeded, I perceived the fire kindled, till at last, though so young and amidst a crowd of those who knew me in my infant childish days, I trust I was enabled to speak with some degree of Gospel authority. Some few mocked, but most for the present seemed struck, and I have since heard that a complaint has been made to the Bishop that I drove fifteen mad the first sermon. The worthy Prelate, as I am informed, wished that the madness might not be forgotten before the next Sunday. (Arnold Dallimore, *George Whitefield*, Vol.I, p.97)

After his ordination he returned to Oxford to finish his studies and receive his Bachelor's degree. He remained there to take charge of the Holy Club which he had joined after meeting Charles Wesley, and also to further his studies. He also preached in London for two months. Then, after returning to Oxford, he went to Dummer in Hampshire, where he decided to go as a missionary to Georgia, in America. It was a major decision on his part, as he had just received an invitation to a rich curacy in London. The contrast between these two places could not have been greater, yet the one held little attraction for him while the other challenged him to leave all for Christ. Developments in Oxford also meant he could leave that field of operation for the far more difficult one in Georgia. However, it was to be almost a year before he could set sail for that distant land.

The intervening time was to see his ministry expand. From being an unknown Oxford undergraduate he was quickly to rise to national fame through his preaching. When he returned to Gloucester to say goodbye to his mother and family he preached there on a few occasions, drawing large congregations and experiencing much of the blessing of God. He had reason to believe that a number were converted through hearing him. A few weeks later he was in Bristol. Again he met with the same response as he had in Gloucester. Soon, there were increasing numbers who crowded the churches in the hope of hearing him. Many had to go away disappointed because there was insufficient room to accommodate them. It is clear that this was no ordinary time. Something very unusual was stirring the masses. The Spirit of God was at work in him and in those who heard him. 'The arrows of conviction stuck fast,' he wrote, 'and my whole time, between one lecture and another, except what was spent in necessary refreshment, was wholly occupied in talking with people under religious concern.'

At times he speaks in his journal of his religious experience like a Christian mystic. The sense of the nearness of God was ever present with him. His soul seemed to be constantly absorbed with fresh visitations of God, and this was the real secret of his success.

> I found uncommon manifestations granted me from above. Early in the morning, at noonday, evening, and midnight, nay, all the day long, did the blessed Jesus visit and refresh my heart . . . Sometimes, as I was walking, my soul would make such sallies as though it would go out of the body. At other times, I would be so overpowered with a sense of God's Infinite Majesty, that I would be constrained to throw myself on the ground, and offer my soul as a blank in His hands, to write on it what He pleased. One night, was a time never to be forgotten. It happened to lighten exceedingly. I had been expounding to many people, and some being afraid to go home, I thought it my duty to accompany them, and improve the occasion, to stir them up to prepare for the coming of the Son of Man. In my return to the parsonage house, whilst others were rising from their beds, frightened almost to death, I and another, a poor, but pious countryman, were in the field, exulting in our God, and longing for that time, when Jesus should be revealed from heaven in a flame of fire! Oh that my soul may be in a like frame, when He shall actually come to call me! (*Journals,* pp.83-84)

Whitefield continued to preach regularly in Gloucester, Bath and Bristol. When he came to London he used to preach as much as nine times a week. The effect of his preaching was amazing. Nobody had ever seen anything on this scale before. His sermon on the new birth was published, causing a stir among the religious public, not least the Dissenters who thought it strange that an Anglican taught it. Though he was popular with the people, many of the clergy who had at first supported him withdrew from him.

In December 1737 Whitefield hoped to set sail for America. In fact, he had to wait until early 1738 before doing so. He had waited to travel out with General Oglethorpe, but when it became clear that he would not be going for some time, Whitefield decided to sail with some soldiers instead. Before leaving he had many invitations to stay. Doors opened in all directions as offers came for him to settle in England. But his mind was made up, and so he set sail for the unknown, confident that God had sent him. This was to be the first of

George Whitefield

thirteen transatlantic crossings he was to make during his lifetime.

As Whitefield set out for America, John Wesley was returning. What had been a disastrous adventure for Wesley became a glorious achievement for Whitefield. Where the one had failed the other was to succeed. Where Wesley was disliked, Whitefield was loved. Throughout his short stay an ever increasing number attended his services, and unlike Wesley, Whitefield was able to wind his way into the affections of these colonial settlers.

For all the excitement generated by his preaching Whitefield was not too distracted to consider others. When he arrived in New England he found there was a growing number of orphans in the colony. Agreement had already been reached, in principle, on the establishing of an orphanage, but the final arrangements had yet to be made. Whitefield took this project to heart and planned on bringing it to the attention of those in England. This orphan house, erected in Georgia, was to lay a heavy burden on Whitefield for the rest of his life as the constant need to raise funds became a matter of concern year after year.

When he returned to England, almost a year later, things had changed dramatically. Pulpits which had previously been open to him were now closed. The attitude of the clergy was generally hostile. They began looking at him with suspicion and branded him an enthusiast. This sudden change of climate resulted in him preaching outdoors. Had he been allowed to continue in the churches those great outdoor meetings which have been recorded for posterity might never have taken place. This turned out to be a blessing in disguise as there were no buildings big enough to house the huge congregations he attracted. A great work of God was under way which, sadly, few of the clergy were sufficiently alert to recognize. J.C.Ryle summed it up in these words, 'The plain truth is, that the Church of England of that day was not ready for a man like Whitefield. The Church was too much asleep to understand him, and was vexed at a man who would not keep still and let the devil alone.'

If his own Church rejected him the people received him gladly. His own account of these events shows an unusual degree of religious fervour. This was more than mere emotional excitement: revival had broken out. Wherever he preached there were conversions as hundreds, if not thousands, sought to speak to him. In characteristic fashion he wrote in his *Journals:*

> Expounded twice or thrice every night this week. The Holy Ghost so powerfully worked upon my hearers, pricking their hearts, and melting them into such floods of tears, that a spiritual man said, 'he never saw the like before.' God is with me of a truth. Adored be his unmerited goodness; I find His grace quickening me more and more every day. (*Journals*, p.197)

From his journal it is quite evident that he was kept very busy. Throughout this time he was conscious of God working within and upon him in a remarkable way. There was fresh light and life not only in the meetings but among the people. Tears were shed either because of a sense of sin or the forgiveness of it. There was so much to give thanks for that many a heart was broken in sheer delight at these wonderful events. Even areas which had seemed impregnable before were soon broken up. Where once sin reigned it was now being dethroned.

Whitefield described the effect of his preaching upon the ungodly colliers of Kingswood in Bristol.

> Having no righteousness of their own to renounce, they were glad to hear of a Jesus who was a friend of publicans, and came not to call the righteous, but sinners to repentance. The first discovery of their being affected was to see the white gutters made by their tears which plentifully fell down their black cheeks, as they came out of their coal pits. Hundreds and hundreds of them were soon brought under deep convictions, which, as the event proved, happily ended in a sound and thorough conversion. The change was visible to all, though numbers chose to impute it to anything, rather than the finger of God. (Arnold Dallimore, *George Whitfield,* Vol.1, pp.263-64)

Scenes like this were constantly repeated until he returned to America, leaving John Wesley in charge of the work at home. Before leaving for America he had come to Wales where he met Howell Harris, the evangelist. In America, the situation was almost identical to that in Britain. Revival was sweeping across the country. There was such an interest generated in his preaching that congregations could easily be gathered. Here he met Jonathan Edwards and the Tennents.

One impartial witness of his preaching in America was Benjamin Franklin, then living in Philadephia. He was a publisher and Quaker and had little real interest in Whitefield except as an orator. His message held no real attraction for Franklin, apart from its commercial value in print. He nevertheless gives a glowing report of the effectiveness of Whitefield's preaching and the change it made upon the populace.

> The multitudes of all sects and denominations that attended his sermons were enormous, and it was a matter of speculation with me, who was one of the number, to observe the extraordinary influence of his oratory on his hearers, and how much they admired and respected him, not-

withstanding his common abuse of them, by assuring them they were naturally *half beasts and half devils*. (Arnold Dallimore, *George Whitefield*, Vol.1, p.439)

Franklin was particularly impressed by the improvement in the habits and customs of the people, and by hearing psalms sung in every street.

When Whitefield returned to England in March 1741, it was a very different England from that which he had left behind. The general awakening which had taken place throughout the land had receded and disputes had arisen among the new converts. Two main theological camps were now discernible among the Methodists, the Calvinists and the Arminians. This division chiefly developed out of a difference of opinion on the doctrine of election. One side loved it, while the other despised it. This effectively split the Methodists into two irreconcilable parties. While John Wesley headed the Arminians, Whitefield refused to head the Calvinists. He sought to quell the dispute but to little avail. Between the growing rupture between himself and his old friend, the huge debt he was under because of the orphanage in Georgia, and the sudden boycott of his preaching by Wesley's supporters, Whitefield felt dejected. The only cheerful thing to happen was the response he had in his earlier preaching ground in Bristol. Here again, he felt something of God's blessing upon his labours.

Amidst all this disappointment he received an invitation from Ralph and Ebenezer Erskine to preach in Scotland. In August, he arrived in Edinburgh. Again he met with much wrangling, this time, among the Presbyterians led by the Erskines. They belonged to a group called the Associate Presbytery, which had been established after Ebenezer Erskine had been expelled by the liberal party of the Church of Scotland several years before. These wanted Whitefield to preach exclusively for them. However his sense of calling extended beyond all human boundaries and he would not restrict himself to any one group:

> I was asked to preach only for them until I had further light. I inquired why only for them. 'Because', said Ralph Erskine, 'they were the Lord's people.' I then asked were there no other Lord's people but themselves; and supposing all others were the devil's people, they certainly had more need to be preached to; and therefore I was more determined to go into

the highways and hedges, and that if the Pope himself would lend me his pulpit, I would gladly proclaim the righteousness of Christ therein. (J.R.Andrews, *Life of George Whitefield,* pp.132-33)

One memorable place Whitefield visited in Scotland was Cambuslang, where William McCulloch was the minister. Revival had already broken out among the people before he came. Whitefield found it easy to enter into the spirit of things. After preaching, McCulloch would sometimes have as many as fifty follow him home wishing to speak to him about their souls. Whitefield described the events that took place when he was among them:

Thousands and thousands have I seen, before it was possible to catch it by sympathy, melted down under the Word. Such a commotion, especially at eleven at night. For about an hour and a half there was such weeping, so many falling into deep distress; the people seem to be slain by scores. They were carried off, and came into the house like soldiers wounded in and carried off a field of battle. Their cries and agonies were exceedingly affecting. All night in the fields might be heard the voice of prayer and praise . . . My dear brother, God is still doing greater things for me than ever; the awakening here in Scotland is unspeakable. (J.R.Andrews, *Life of George Whitefield,* pp.163-64)

In many ways these early years were to characterize his whole life. His journeys took him time and again across the Atlantic. It is estimated that he preached some eighteen thousand sermons before he died. If ever a man burnt himself out in the service of his God, it was Whitefield. He was tireless and relentless in his efforts to win souls. Many other examples could be given to show the power of his preaching, the emotion it created and the number of souls that were saved, but it would only be a repetition of what has already been said. Throughout his life he enjoyed the presence of God in his preaching. Even on his last day in this world he preached, though he was very ill.

On 30 September 1770 Whitefield died of an asthmatic attack. He was greatly loved by the people and greatly admired for his oratory. He was a man whose sole desire was to preach Christ crucified.

17
Daniel Rowland
(1713-90)

Of all the great preachers of the eighteenth century, Daniel Rowland stands out as the most enigmatic. Born in 1713, about three miles from where he exercised his amazing ministry, he is like a man without a shadow because he had no contemporary biographer. It seems strange that such an omission should exist considering his dynamic and long ministry extending to his death in 1790. The task of writing a biography was left to a subsequent generation who had heard of his greatness but had never witnessed it. After his death some personal details of his life were gathered together by Selina, the Countess of Huntingdon with the intention of producing a biography, but these were irretrievably lost when she died.

Rowland's great stature as a preacher is by now generally recognised, but this was not always the case. For years he remained a spiritual giant solely in the minds of contemporaries and in the denominational and evangelical world of nineteenth century Wales (his reputation decreasing even in his own native land as evangelicalism lost its grip on the denominations in the twentieth century). Two main simple reasons account for this – geographic and linguistic. His ministry was almost entirely confined to Wales and conducted in the Welsh language. This meant that the English-speaking monoglot remained virtually ignorant of him. Historically, he stands out more like some huge mythical figure than a real person. The details surrounding his life are scanty. Yet his story bears repeating if only to remind us of what God can do, and to enlighten those who perhaps have not heard of his mighty exploits.

Rowland's life was anything but easy; it was often even humiliating. His brother John, whose spiritual condition remains uncertain, was, after their father's death, given his livings at Llangeitho and Nantcwnlle in Cardiganshire (part of the present Dyfed). Daniel became his curate and was paid a pittance of ten pounds a year to keep himself and his family. This harsh treatment was not the only insult he was forced to endure. When his brother was tragically drowned at Aberystwyth in 1760, everyone naturally assumed Daniel would succeed him. Much to their surprise, the Bishop of St David's refused to give him the livings. His reason was Rowland's preaching irregularities. His persistence in preaching outside his own parish was thought sufficient cause to withhold his right. The livings instead passed on to his son John, who was then only twenty-seven years old, while Daniel continued as his curate. It is ironic to see the son preferred before the father who was overwhelmingly the better preacher, with more experience and maturity. But intolerance of the Methodists (even of the Calvinistic kind) was not unknown among the bishops, who often hated anything like enthusiasm. Rowland was effectively reaping the reward of his own unrestrained zeal for Christ.

Rowland's spiritual pilgrimage had begun soon after his ordination in 1734. Until then he was one of those inadequate clerics who lack the most essential feature of a true servant of God – regeneration. No unregenerate man can be of any real service to God or his kingdom in this condition. Great gifts and abilities, or even personality, cannot compensate for its absence. Before his conversion Rowland was extremely wayward. As an Anglican curate he should have set the people an example of godly living. Instead, after leading them in their Sunday morning devotions he would then lead them in their sports. As a young man he was very energetic and a skilled sportsman. When he was about to be ordained in London on 10 March 1734, he walked to and from London, a feat rarely achieved by other ordinands!

Though he was strong physically he was also an astute scholar. He was no dim-witted curate but very bright and highly intelligent. He read Latin, Greek and Hebrew and endangered his health in his pursuit of knowledge. When he later reviewed his life he was grateful to God for his protective care. As a young boy he was almost killed when a huge stone landed where he had just been sitting. If it had struck him it would have meant certain death.

Rowland's conversion took place soon after his ordination and return to Llangeitho. He began to notice that many of his congregation were often absent from his Sunday services because they went to hear the local Dissenting minister, Philip Pugh, in Llwynpiod nearby. He was naturally curious to know what it was that attracted them. Eventually, he went to hear Pugh for himself. His motive was less than spiritual. He hoped to learn the secret of Pugh's success and copy it. Afterwards he concluded that it was because Pugh had 'thundered at the people'. He noticed that this kind of preaching had an unusual effect. It moved and stirred men in an amazing way. Taking his lead from Pugh he began preaching on some of the most alarming and terrifying verses in the Bible. He preached with such intensity that the people soon began to fill his church. Because of his violent attacks upon sin and the consequent doom of sinners he became known as, 'the angry clergyman'. Some thought he was actually mad and had taken leave of his senses. However, we should remember that though Rowland preached with such telling effect, he was still unconverted.

It was not until he heard Griffith Jones of Llanddowror that he felt any real concern for his soul. One day, as Griffith Jones was preaching, he happened to notice a very proud and arrogant looking young clergyman standing in his congregation. He was so moved by his attitude that he stopped preaching for a moment and prayed specifically for him. Rowland, along with the rest of the people, was staggered. But Jones' arrow was not shot in vain as Rowland felt it pierce his heart. It cut and cured him like a surgeon's knife. The old man died and a new was born within. God had suddenly taken hold of him to make him a channel of blessing to his native country of Wales.

For some time after his conversion his message remained the same. He preached on the wrath of God and eternal punishment but with little of the gospel's comfort. Eventually, Pugh pleaded with him to consider the people: 'Preach the gospel to the people, my dear sir. Apply the Balm of Gilead to their wounded spirits, and show their need of faith in a crucified Redeemer.' When Rowland confessed that he did not really possess that faith himself he was met with the reply, 'Preach it until you feel it. It will come without fail. If you go on preaching the law after this fashion you will kill half the population, for you thunder those awful curses in such a terrible manner that it is impossible for any man to stand before you.' Rowland heeded the advice, although Pugh was a Dissenter, and corrected this imbalance.

As soon as he did, many came to a saving knowledge of Jesus Christ. The law had made them ripe for the gospel picking.

Rowland's expanded ministry throughout South Wales began when a farmer's wife asked him to preach at Ystrad-ffin, near Llandovery. She was visiting her sister who lived near Llangeitho, and had heard of a strange preacher who lived there. Curiosity led her to go and hear him. Much to her sister's surprise she returned the following week to hear him again. Her visits became more frequent as Rowland's preaching affected her. Eventually, she persuaded him to preach in her home village where thirty people were said to have been converted under his preaching.

In 1763 the Bishop of St David's, not content to leave him alone, finally expelled Rowland from his curacy. His expulsion was not for any immorality or heresy, which would have been understandable. It was for a purely ecclesiastical reason – he did not toe the Church's party line. One Sunday morning as Rowland was about to preach he was handed an ultimatum: he must either stop preaching irregularly or suffer the consequences. After reading it aloud to his congregation he said, 'We must obey the higher powers. Let me beg you will go out quietly, and then we shall conclude the service of the morning by the church gate.' As the people followed him out of the church many were emotionally distraught while some gave way to unrestrained and audible crying. They felt that a great injustice had been done to this man of God because of his love for Christ.

This blatant act, intended to curtail his growing influence, only succeeded in promoting it. In fact, it proved far more detrimental to the Church of England, which Rowland loved dearly and served for over thirty years, than it did to himself. The people in support of him left the church *en masse* and built him a new commodious chapel in Llangeitho, not far from the church. This chapel still stands as a monument to his faithfulness to God.

His only crime had been a desire to relieve the spiritual needs of the surrounding people. How could he restrict his ministry to Llangeitho when there were so many other neighbouring areas crying out for the gospel? He felt compelled to extend his activities out of sheer necessity. Gospel preachers were still scarce and the people were in desperate need. The reason for this mass exodus from the parish church was not simply to show their solidarity with him and

Statue of Daniel Rowland in Llangeitho

disgust at this unfair treatment. The people knew that what lay at the heart of the matter was the gospel itself. Their action revealed their belief that the message was far more important than the organization. If the Anglican Church, whose first function it is to proclaim the gospel, begins to set obstacles and barriers in the way, then it has deviated from its divine intention and effectively ceases to be a Church. Instead of being a servant it has become the master.

After his conversion Rowland soon became one of the most

influential preachers in Wales, indeed a prince among preachers. His influence can be seen by the opinions of his contemporaries. When the ranks of the Welsh Calvinistic Methodists were severely split in 1751 over Howell Harris' Patripassianism, the teaching that God the Father suffered on the cross, the resulting parties became known as either Harris' people or Rowland's people, depending on whom they supported. Harris was in error in attributing the atoning death of the Son to the Father. This meant, in theological parlance, a confusion of the personal and individual identities of Father and Son within the Godhead. Rowland, who was by far the superior theologian, was appointed to confront Harris on the matter. Harris simply refused to listen. Instead, he dug in his heels and a rupture became inevitable. Fortunately, it was not permanent and the two groups were realigned later.

As a preacher Rowland was second to none. Many considered him, if not superior to George Whitefield, at least his equal. It seems strange that such a small country of minor political significance should raise up one of the greatest preachers ever known. Rowland was in the vanguard of a succession of outstanding Welsh preachers. One biographer wrote:

> A friend once asked an old gentleman of considerable intelligence, now dead, who had often heard both Whitefield and Rowland, respecting their comparative merits as preachers. He decidedly gave the preference on the whole to the latter. Whitefield, he said, was greater perhaps in the power of alarming the unconcerned. But Rowland excelled in building up, strengthening, and comforting the Christian. His sermons were more methodical, and contained more matter and more point. Whitefield's sermons would be soon forgotten; but those of Rowland would be remembered and retained through life . . . There is another point in which the superiority, according to this old gentleman's opinion, belonged to Mr Rowland. Whitefield, at times, when much animated, lost his matter, his feelings impeding the operations of his mind. But this was never the case with Rowland; the more animated he was, the greater was his matter, the more weighty was what he said; which is the summit of all excellence in an orator. (Edward Morgan, *Brief Memoir of T.Charles*)

Their difference can be explained also by the diversity of their ministries. Rowland was a resident pastor confined to one general locality. His sermons were preached almost entirely to the same congregation. They were studied and prepared specifically to edify and build up the people spiritually. Whitefield was essentially an evangelist. His primary aim was conversion, not consolidation. He was frequently on the move and unable to prepare new material and often preached the same sermon in different places.

Rowland attracted people from all over Wales – and did so for over half a century. This was especially so at the monthly communion services where thousands flocked to the small village of Llangeitho to hear him. Many walked for days just to attend these memorable gatherings, often having to run the gauntlet of harrassment from the populace on their journeys. To those who came Llangeitho was like the spiritual capital of Wales, as Jerusalem was of Israel.

Rowland's pulpit manner was exceptional. As the time of the service approached he would suddenly appear in the pulpit through a back door. He would announce a psalm to be sung, usually just one verse, which was sung in typical Welsh fashion with tremendous gusto. He then read a portion of the Bible from which he intended to preach while the people listened with bated breath. As he began to preach there would be a growing anticipation that something extraordinary was about to happen. His sermon was never a steady incline but full of undulations and modulations. There was no gradual ascent to an applicatory climax. Sometimes he would calmly relate relevant background material then raise the pitch time and again by his application. The tempo of his sermons was controlled primarily by their content.

Christmas Evans, another great Welsh preacher, used the blacksmith's shop to illustrate Rowland's preaching. He would place the iron in the fire until it became red-hot and pliable enough to work. Then he took it and hammered it on the anvil with sparks flying everywhere. This was the kind of ministry Rowland exerted. It was always heated by argument and hammered with passion. The congregation was moved, some to tears, others to rejoicing. There was often a mixture of emotions depending on the spiritual condition of his audience.

Rowland used notes but was never bound by them. He would glance at them from time to time and then resume eyeing the people. He applied his message not just at the end; there was application throughout. Emotionally, he rose and fell as the truth affected him. There was never anything of affectation. As the truth moved him he found no problem in moving others. He was never monotonous. His voice, emotions and body, seemed to be synchronized. Like some young sapling swayed by the wind he was moved by God's Spirit. The power and presence of God were the chief characteristics of his meetings. During these times God would become very real to the people. If anything of heaven could be known on earth, it was there, under the preaching of this great man.

During his ministry at Llangeitho Rowland witnessed several remarkable revivals. One of these began while he was reading the Anglican Litany. When he came to the words, 'By thine agony and bloody sweat, good Lord, deliver us,' of a sudden he was intensely gripped. As he repeated the words the congregation began to break down. Some cried out, others crouched on the floor in an agony of soul. This was not due to any extraordinary or vehement preaching; it was the mere reading of a service. Something, or better Someone, unseen drove these words home with irresistible force.

On another occasion time seemed to stand still in the little village of Llangeitho.

> The pathos and remarkable unction of Daniel Rowland's preaching would, at times, so absorb his hearers, that they would forget themselves and everything around them. It is said that he preached, on one occasion, for six or seven hours without a pause; and that neither himself nor the people perceived that the service was longer than usual (Thomas Rees, *History of Protestant Nonconformity in Wales,* p.392)

Yet Rowland was not without his faults. He was meticulous in his preparation but was prone to fainting fits if he felt inadequately prepared! When this happened it was virtually impossible to get him into the pulpit. He usually rose early, especially on Sundays when he avoided all human contact, to concentrate on his message. However, if he felt unprepared his bed became his retreat. He would feign being ill or say he could not possibly preach because he had no message from God. When he would be eventually persuaded to come to the church it was under duress from his servant. Often these times proved to be his best times. Rarely did he fail to rise to the people's expectations.

Critics often arise from many quarters, and Rowland had his

critics. One condescending, little known, Nonconformist preacher who heard Rowland preach wrote:

> Feb. 23, 1744. Went this afternoon to Clungwyn (near Carmarthen), to hear Mr D.Rowland. Ben.Thomas prayed before him; then he preached from Hosea ii.14. He did not much confine himself to the text, but was very earnest, endeavouring to win the affections. I think I found some efficacy attending his work, though he had some very weak expressions. May 24, 1744. Went to Caerphilly, where I met many of my old acquaintances. In my way home I heard Mr Rowland at Penygroeswen, from Judges v.23. His sermon was practical, but not critical; for he said several things which I think he would not have said, had he well considered the matter beforehand. (Thomas Rees, *History of Protestant Nonconformity in Wales,* pp.368-69)

These criticisms which came from within the ministerial frat-ernity were far removed from the general opinion of ordinary people. They were enthralled by his preaching. To them, there was only one Daniel Rowland. Only a dozen or so of his sermons remain in print today to give some vague impression of his preaching. His sermon material was always good, but what gripped the people most was the way in which it was delivered. There was not only light but heat, and plenty of it. It was impassioned preaching at its best.

Howell Harris, a contemporary of Rowland and friend of George Whitefield and the Wesleys, had ample opportunity of hearing him. Early on he gave this valued assessment:

> Though I have now been favoured with hearing and reading the works of many of God's ministers, I do not know, so far as I am capable of judging, that I have known any so favoured with gifts and powers; such a penetrating light to the spirit of the Scriptures, to set forth the mystery of godliness and the glory of Christ . . . Many counties partake of this blessing, he being indefatigable in going about, and I believe seldom, if ever, opens his mouth without a great blessing attending; this is not for a while, but has continued, to my knowledge, for nearly seven years . . . The visible effects on the people under the word and after, as well as the lives and conversations of them that are wrought upon, prove to such as have spiritual eyes, and do not shut them against conviction, that God is there in an uncommon manner. (Thomas Rees, pp.351-52)

In spite of their quarrel, Harris held him in very high esteem. In a letter to Whitefield, he gave this eyewitness account of his preaching and its visible effects on the congregation:

I was last Sunday at the Ordinance with brother Rowland where I saw, felt and heard such things as I can't send on paper any idea of. The power that continues with him is uncommon. Such crying out and heart breaking groans, silent weeping and holy joy, and shouts of rejoicing I never saw . . . Tis very common for scores to fall down by the power of the word, pierced and wounded or overcome by the love of God and sights of the beauty and excellency of Jesus, and lie on the ground . . . Some praising and admiring Jesus, free grace, distinguishing grace, others wanting words to utter . . . others falling down one after another for a long time together, praying and interceding, and you see and feel it is the Prayer of Faith, and that they are worshipping a God that they know, and love and delight in, and that now no veil is between. Others lie wounded under a sense of their piercing Jesus, so that they can hardly bear it. Others in triumph over all the enemies. Others mourning and wailing for the Comforter, and such love and simplicity that the spiritual eye must see and acknowledge that God is there. (*Selected Trevecka Letter*s, ed. Gomer M. Roberts)

This account should be put in context. Revival was in progress. The secret of his tremendous influence was not in himself but God. There was such a sense of God's all-pervading presence. Rowland himself wrote, 'I must tell you though I am in a great hurry; we enjoy the presence of God almost every Sunday! Oh! help us to praise him, he is altogether lovely. Blessed be his holy name, says your poor unworthy brother.'

Rowland died on 16 October 1790. His daughter gave this descriptive and fitting epitaph of him. 'My father was short, and of an iron constitution. He never spared himself. He was very swift of foot. He was very passionate. His heat was intense at times. In that intense heat he was awful. He was very great in prayer. It was impossible to get him out of his study.' This was how this great man lived and died to the glory of God.

18
Charles Simeon
(1759-1836)

When the veteran preacher of Huddersfield, Henry Venn, then living in Yelling near Cambridge, met the novice Simeon, he told him, 'Thou art called to be a man of war from thy youth.' This was particularly true of Simeon's early ministry in Cambridge. To the ordinary Anglican he was an odd rarity. He was zealous, enthusiastic, and full of substance, unlike the dozy, comfortable and naturally aloof vicars of his day.

What made him so different from the standard cleric was the message that gripped his heart. He was following in the footsteps of evangelical Anglican 'Methodists' like Whitefield, Wesley and Venn. They had a compulsion from within to preach a gospel which was alien to the vast majority of Anglicans. Yet in spite of this, there was no one more devoted to the Church of England than Simeon. He was a thoroughgoing Anglican who loved the Prayer Book.

Simeon presents us with a very colourful personality. He was slightly eccentric in many ways, exceptionally fastidious when it came to clothes and highly meticulous in everything he did. He was easily recognized in Cambridge by a huge umbrella he used to carry about. When this new invention was imported from France he was thrilled with it and was one of the first to possess one. Yet for all his peculiarities, he had the extension of God's kingdom at heart.

From the time of his birth on 24 September 1759, in Reading, Simeon lived a privileged life. He had wealthy parents who could lavish things upon him. Perhaps this accounts for his extravagant dress throughout life, clothes which made others think of him as something of a dandy. As a youth he was obsessed with horses, and loved riding even in his old age. But a shadow hung over his childhood – the death of his mother. She died while he was still a child, an event which left a profound mark upon him.

Belonging to the upper class he was sent to Eton, which he hated.

Looking back, he could find nothing good to say about it. Everything about it echoed of immorality and viciousness. It was both spiritually and morally a dreadful place. He said:

> It is often with me a matter of regret that the atmosphere of Eton is so unfortunate for health of the soul; and that amidst all the attention that is paid to the poets and philosophers of Greece and Rome, scarcely ever by any chance is the name of our blessed Saviour heard. (Hugh Evan Hopkins, *Charles Simeon of Cambridge*, p.14)

When he left Eton for Cambridge, he was glad to be away. On 29 January 1779, he enrolled in King's College. This was to change the whole direction of his life. Soon after his arrival he was informed that he had to partake in a communion service in three weeks. He was surprised and shocked to think that he must participate in his present condition. This became a turning point in his life. He began to prepare himself by reading Richard Allestree's *The Whole Duty of Man*. He was so impressed by it that he made himself ill by fasting, reading and prayers.

After this initial ordeal he knew that he had to partake again at Easter. With a renewed vigour he set about preparing himself. So keenly did he feel the weight of his sins that he envied dogs their mortality and wished he could have exchanged it for his own immortality. For some time he continued to grope in darkness, but without peace. However, as he read Bishop Wilson on the Lord's Supper he came across an expression which struck him, 'that the Jews knew what they did, when they transferred their sin to the head of their offering.' He later wrote:

> The thought came into my mind, What, may I transfer all my guilt to another? Has God provided an Offering for me, that I may lay my sins on His head? Then, God willing, I will not bear them on my own soul one moment longer. Accordingly I sought to lay my sins upon the sacred head of Jesus; and on the Wednesday began to have a hope of mercy; on the Thursday that hope increased; on the Friday and Saturday it became more strong; and on the Sunday morning, Easter-day, April 4, I awoke early with those words upon my heart and lips, 'Jesus Christ is risen to-day! Hallelujah! Hallelujah!' From that hour peace flowed in rich abundance into my soul; and at the Lord's Table in our Chapel I had the

sweetest access to God through my blessed Saviour. (Handley C.G. Moule, *Charles Simeon*, pp.25-26)

The next three years were lonely years. Due to his Methodism he became increasingly isolated. Cambridge was a traditional stronghold of formal Anglicanism. Even within his own family this new breed of religion was met with a cool reception. Only his sick elder brother, Richard, supported him. At Cambridge he had no spiritual confidant but God. There was nobody else he knew who stood where he stood regarding the gospel. Yet though the majority of Simeon's family were unaffected by his testimony they still retained an affection for Charles. He was loved in spite of his 'enthusiasm', which they hoped would diminish in time.

After finishing his course at King's, he was ordained a deacon at Ely Cathedral on 26 May 1782. This brought its own problems. His ambition was to enter the ministry but he did not know anyone who would be interested in having a 'Methodist' as a curate. He became so despondent that he almost offered himself gratis to anyone who would employ him. Fortunately, this expedient became unnecessary.

For a while he had attended St Edward's Church in Cambridge, where the minister, Christopher Atkinson, had mistaken him for a formal hypocrite. This misunderstanding was only corrected when he heard Simeon speak of himself as 'a poor, guilty, helpless sinner'. Soon afterwards Simeon was taken on as an honorary curate. When Atkinson was forced to be away for a long time, Simeon was left in complete charge of the church. This gave him an opportunity to exert himself freely. For seventeen weeks he preached and visited the people. They were struck by his sincerity and concern for them. As the weeks passed the numbers increased, filling the church, something unknown for over a century. His preaching was striking and impressive. When the vicar finally returned the church's clerk was so overjoyed to see him that he said, 'Oh, Sir, I am so glad you are come; now we shall have some room.' If his response lacked tact, it does reveal something of the humility and humour of the minister, who probably related the story.

During Simeon's curacy at St Edward's, Atkinson introduced him to the few existing evangelicals in and around Cambridge. He met John Venn, and later his ailing father, Henry Venn. This gracious old

Charles Simeon preaching in a barn

man overlooked Simeon's peculiarities and saw him grow and mature spiritually. After riding over to Yelling, about twelve miles west of Cambridge, to visit Venn, Simeon became the subject of criticism by one of his daughters. But the wily old man took them into the garden and asked them to pick one of the peaches which were not ripe at the time. They thought he was joking. 'Well, my dears,' he said, 'it is green now, and we must wait; but a little more sun, and a few more showers, and the peach will be ripe and sweet. So it is with Mr. Simeon.' Venn was not mistaken, and later commented on Simeon's growth in grace. His humility and affection endeared him to the older man, who valued his company greatly.

As he was waiting to know his next move Simeon heard of his brother Richard's death. Under a sense of bereavement he offered to go back home and take his place in the family. Yet no sooner had he suggested this than the incumbent of Holy Trinity, Cambridge, suddenly died. This new development evoked an impassioned plea to his father to use his influence with his friend the Bishop, to secure him the position. The probability of his preferment was very slight seeing Holy Trinity already had a curate whom the parishioners wanted to appoint. However, against the tide of public opinion, the Bishop gave his assent to his father's request and nominated Simeon. When he heard, nobody was more surprised than Simeon. He wrote:

> I had often when passing Trinity Church . . . said within myself, 'How should I rejoice if God were to give me that church, that I might preach the Gospel there and be a herald for Him in the University.' But as to the actual possession of it, I had no more prospect of attaining it than of being exalted to the see of Canterbury. (Handley Moule, *Charles Simeon*, p.37)

This unusual appointment provoked a crisis. A group of parishioners began to lobby the Bishop on behalf of their curate. But the unrepentant Bishop refused to listen to them. As a result the Bishop wrote to Simeon telling him that even if he were to refuse the offer he would never install the present curate. As for the parishioners, they were so incensed that they boycotted Simeon's services, locked the church pews and elected the curate as their lecturer. If they could not have their way regarding a minister, they would maintain their right to appoint a lecturer. It was twelve years before these two roles were combined, four years after Hammond, the curate, had left the church. Even when Simeon pleaded that he was a man of peace and had come to them in peace, it did nothing to quell their resentment of him.

His first sermon in Holy Trinity was preached on 10 November 1782, but it changed nothing. The growing anti-Simeon feeling continued unabated. For all this, the church continued to grow. He received letters of encouragement and advice from leading evangelicals such as John Newton, John Thornton and his new friend, Henry Venn. For Simeon, preaching once every Sunday was not enough. When he began a Sunday evening lecture at six o'clock, together with his morning service, the church officials were in uproar. They resisted him as much as they could, even to the point of locking the church doors. But this was not going to stop the impetuous preacher. He had a blacksmith come and open the doors. Afterwards he thought it better to stop these meetings for a while until these strong feelings had subsided.

Apart from this innovation, Simeon also began a mid-week meeting. This was held not in the church but in a room which he hired for the purpose. Again he saw the numbers increase until the room became too small and congested. This meant that another more spacious building had to be found. The reason behind this unusual action was his fear of losing his congregation to the Dissenters. His hearers had a hunger for the truth which could not be satisfied by one sermon on a Sunday morning. He felt that if he did nothing to meet their need then the situation could escalate into a minor crisis. As nowhere adequate was available in Cambridge they were forced to go outside the parish. This unorthodox approach was taken in the hope that the minister of that parish would not complain to the Bishop. If so, Simeon, a keen Episcopalian, would have submitted to the censure and left the place. Fortunately, this was overlooked and the meeting continued to flourish.

His influence in Cambridge steadily grew. If the people of Cambridge had turned their backs upon him he attracted a congregation from further afield. These came from the countryside every Sunday to hear him. There was also a large following among the undergraduates. He had an appeal for them seldom witnessed among other Anglicans. These became known as 'Sims,' a title of ridicule among the other students. For these faithful it was not the service or the sacrament that was the attraction but the sermon. Many of these themselves went into the ministry or out onto the mission field. The most famous was Henry Martyn, who went to India and then on to Persia where he died at the age of thirty-one. He had been Simeon's beloved curate at Cambridge for nearly two years. After hearing of his death he could not bear to look at a portrait he had of Martyn without breaking down in tears.

India had a particular attraction for Simeon. He often spoke of it as his 'diocese' or 'province.' Due to his connections in the East India Trading Company, he was able to recommend candidates to them to go as Anglican chaplains. Rarely did he send out missionaries in the strict sense of the word. This was because chaplains had certain rights where missionaries had none. As a result they had more protection to do their work as evangelists.

Due to his growing involvement with ministerial students, Simeon became aware of the need for their special training. Until then their education had been general. In the early years of his own ministry he remembered the struggle he had had with sermon preparation, not knowing where to begin or end. He devised a plan whereby he could instruct them on a fortnightly basis. They were invited to his rooms in the college for tea, cakes and discussion. Topics were presented in an informal way and then followed by debate. These meetings were presided over by Simeon himself who directed everything. They proved invaluable to many as he explained the aim and intention of a sermon and how best to prepare it.

One major boost he received to this enterprise came through a book written by the French Huguenot, Jean Claude, *An Essay on the Composition of Sermons*. Most of what he advanced Simeon had already adopted. What it did do, was to help him crystallize his own thoughts as they took shape in his mind. How he wished he had had something similar when he had begun his ministry. He knew that the faults of the fathers could be corrected by the children and that ministerial training was not sacrosanct. There is no definitive method whereby there is never a need for modification or alteration. After reading Claude's essay he decided to use it as his textbook. He wrote:

> From seeing my own views thus reduced to system, I was led to adopt the resolution of endeavouring to impart to others the little knowledge I possessed in that species of composition; and to adopt Claude as the ground-work of my private lectures; correcting what I thought wrong in him, and supplying what I thought deficient . . . For the space of about twenty years I have persevered in having a few young men to assist in thus preparing for that which is generally esteemed so difficult – the writing of their sermons; and from the many acknowledgements which have been made by ministers from time to time, I have reason to hope that my labours have not been in vain in the Lord. *(Great Anglicans, a* Composium)

The advice he gave to this up-and-coming generation of preachers he exemplified in himself. He was the living embodiment of everything he taught. Every time he preached they saw what he had been advocating. Simeon's whole approach to preaching can be summarized in three short maxims. 'Does it ,' he said, 'uniformly tend to humble the sinner, to exalt the Saviour, to promote holiness?' He also stressed the importance of avoiding an affected manner, unnatural intonations and an artificial professionalism, so common among the Anglican clergy. There was never anything artificial about him. Most of those who attended these meetings appreciated these practical lessons. For some his advice became the rule and practice of their ministries.

This concern for young preachers convinced him of the need for special aids and helps in the preparation of sermons. For several years he worked on what was to become his chief work, his *Horae Homileticae*. This was comprised of numerous sermons and sermon outlines on particular texts from every book of the Bible. The text, he maintained, should be allowed to speak for itself. This principle he aimed to apply throughout. The work consisted of twenty-one volumes, an immense undertaking. He said that 'if the readers will peruse one discourse every day of his life, the whole will occupy him exactly seven years.'

Simeon was much in demand as a preacher. He made several tours of Scotland, preaching among Anglicans and Presbyterians alike. Though the moderate party of the Church of Scotland was cool towards him, as they were to all true gospel preachers, the evangelical party clamoured to hear him. During his first visit in 1796, he became instrumental in the salvation of an unconverted minister, Alexander Stewart of Moulin. His sister, concerned about his spiritual condition, asked if Simeon and Robert Haldane, his travelling companion, could call and see him. How thankful Stewart was afterwards. He wrote to Simeon:

> Ever since the few happy hours in which I was blessed with your company, I have daily thought, with pleasure and gratitude, of the Lord's loving-kindness to me, in sending two of his chosen servants, so unexpectedly and so seasonably, to speak to me the words of life. (Alexander Halden, *The Lives of Robert & James Haldane,* p.140)

After his conversion a revival took place in and around Moulin. He again visited Scotland in 1798, 1815 and 1819.

By 1807 Simeon's health had began to break down. Worn out by ceaseless labour his voice became so weak that he could only preach with difficulty. After each service he found himself 'more like one dead than alive'. This weakness continued for thirteen years before he was fully restored. His renewal was sudden, almost miraculous, though he considered it providential. As he crossed the border from England into Scotland on his last visit in 1819 his strength suddenly returned. He was then sixty years of age. His own view as to what had happened was that he had been under God's chastening. He had always entertained the idea of strenuously labouring in his Master's vineyard until he was sixty and then easing up afterwards. However, when he had thought of retiring gradually from the field the Lord revived him, not only adding to, but multiplying his strength. He was enabled to continue as he had started for another sixteen years.

Simeon was very conscious of inner communion with God. This was the power which lay behind his ministry. He had a favourite walk on his rooftop where he would retreat to be alone with God. There, under the canopy of heaven and with complete privacy, he was undisturbed. He was alone and yet not alone, for God was with him. It was as if he had entered the chamber of God, to have an audience with the King of Glory. He often said that his favourite place was 'in the valley of humiliation.' There he knew what it was 'to walk humbly with his God.' Any unnecessary intrusion upon this sense of the nearness of God was resented. After he had preached in a church in Scotland where God had been unusually present, the resident minister began to ask him about his travels. Simeon's response was, 'Speak to me of heaven, Sir, and I can talk with you, but do not speak to me about earth at this moment, for I cannot talk about it.'

No doubt times like this prepared the ageing soldier for his final reward. These glimpses of glory acted as appetizers. The man who had been shunned by all at the beginning of his Cambridge ministry was hailed by all at his end. His last sermon preached in Holy Trinity was on 18 September 1836. After a few days he decided to visit the new Bishop of Ely but refused to wear his coat because of the mild climate. Later he became ill and died on Sunday, 12 November 1836. Before he died, writes his friend and biographer, William Carus, he was asked what he was thinking at that moment. He said, 'I don't think now; I am enjoying.' 'I am in a dear Father's hand,' he said later, 'all is secure. When I look to *him* I see nothing but faithfulness – and immutability – and truth; and I have the sweetest peace.' The joy and peace he experienced in life was also experienced in death. 'Yea, though I walk through the valley of the shadow of death, I will fear no evil; for you are with me; your rod and your staff, they comfort me.'

19
Robert Hall
(1764-1831)

When a vicar was once reproved for going to hear Robert Hall, he said, 'When God goes out of his way to make a great man, I'll go out of my way to hear him.' Robert Hall was a brilliant preacher, brilliant in his diction, brilliant in his eloquence. Though he preached extempore and later wrote his sermons out from memory, he had such a wonderful flow of language that it seemed to those who heard him, that even if he had written them out beforehand he could not have chosen better words to clothe his thoughts. They were always so appropriate and precise.

He was, above all others in his day, admired for his eloquence. To those most familiar with him he was incomparably the best. His preaching was like a meandering river, always moving forward at a steady pace, graceful, peaceful, unlike some preachers whose influence and power lay in their forcefulness. These appear more like Niagara Falls, loud and awe-inspiring, than a quiet river. To those who loved good English, it was a treat to listen to Hall.

Motion and movement were his strong points and that not in a physical or demonstrative way but in his vehicle of expression. He always seemed to have a superabundance of words. At times during his preaching he seemed unable to keep pace with his thoughts. Due to his opulent mind his sermons always appeared like a well-garnished meal, full of well-digested material.

When he preached it was common for preachers from all denominations to go and hear him. His flights of eloquence astounded them. Even his illustrations were exceptional, never distracting but always illuminating his themes. He seemed to grasp his subject so thoroughly and found illustrations so applicable, that they seemed almost inspired. Undoubtedly, Hall was a master of lucidity. In his sermon, 'On The Duty, Happiness, and Honour, of Maintaining the Course Prescribed to us by Providence,' on Acts 13:25 – 'As John fulfilled his course' – he begins with an illustration of life in general and gently drifts into eternity. Everything adds and expands our vision of life until there is nothing left to be said.

> The life of every individual may be compared to a river – rising in obscurity, increasing by the accession of tributary streams, and, after flowing through a longer or shorter distance, losing itself in some common receptacle. The lives of individuals also, like the course of rivers, may be more or less extensive, but will all vanish and disappear in the gulf of eternity. Whilst a stream is confined within its banks, it fertilizes, enriches, and improves the country through which it passes; but if it deserts its channel, it becomes injurious and destructive, a sort of public nuisance, and, by stagnating in lakes and marshes, its exhalations diffuse pestilence and disease all around. Some glide away in obscurity and insignificance; whilst others become celebrated, traverse continents, give names to countries, and assign the boundaries of empires. Some are tranquil and gentle in their course; whilst others, rushing in torrents, dashing over precipices, and tumbling in waterfalls, become objects of terror and dismay. But, however diversified their character, or their direction, all agree in having their course short, limited, and determined: soon they fall into one capacious receptacle; their waters eventually mix in the waters of the ocean. Thus human characters, however various, have one common destiny; their course of action may be greatly diversified, but they all lose themselves in the ocean of eternity. (*The Works of Robert Hall,* Vol. 6)

The effect of his preaching was dynamic. Congregations were known to rise unconsciously under it. They would not just sit on the edge of their seats but stood, leant forward, poised as if they were afraid of missing something. It began with a few and spread until the whole congregation was standing, completely entranced by his words.

He had read so widely that there was little he could not discuss thoroughly. His reading habits were excessive, at times from five in the morning until eight in the evening. Yet he enjoyed company, and often went on trips into the country with his friends who loved nothing more than to hear him hold forth on an endless variety of subjects. They were always fascinated by his stories and breadth of knowledge. It seemed as if there was nothing with which he was not familiar, from mathematics to politics.

This diversity of interest often brought him into conflict. He was sometimes attacked for writing on politics, especially when he wrote supporting those who had volunteered to fight against Napoleon. Many felt that he had exceeded the bounds of his calling and that he should confine himself to the spiritual domain and not to political or military concerns. However, he saw himself just as much a British citizen as a Baptist minister and used his citizen's rights to support his country. He believed Britain was the last great bastion left in Europe against the French despot.

For all his brilliance, Hall had his thorn in the flesh. He endured extreme physical suffering throughout life. From the age of seven he could not remember a day without pain. It was his constant companion. At night he almost invariably awoke, lay on the floor, smoked his pipe and read. This posture eased his pain, smoking helped him to relax, and reading took his mind off it.

Hall was born on 2 May 1764 in the little village of Arnesby, about eight miles from Leicester, and was the fourteenth child. His father was the minister of a small Baptist church there for nearly forty years, and was the author of the popular *Help to Zion's Travellers.* At birth it appeared Robert would not live. After seeing him his mother thought him already dead but he survived to become the ornament of her life. His intellectual acuteness began to emerge at a very early age. As a boy he would sneak off to the graveyard with his books and return home at dusk only under duress from his nurse. By the age of nine he had read Jonathan Edwards' treatise *On the Freedom of the Will* and his *Religious Affection*s. He also read Butler's *Analogy of Religion.* Though he was so young he was able to grasp the sense of their arguments.

He was naturally inquisitive and forever asking questions. After his first four years at Wigston school, four miles from Arnesby, his teacher asked his father to send him to another school. This was not because of any misdemeanour but because he was so demanding in his studies. To keep abreast of his best student his teacher often had to stay up all night just to prepare lessons for him. Eventually, he felt this could not continue, otherwise he would be completely worn out. At his second school, the famed Nonconformist academy of the Rev. John Ryland in Northampton, Hall was expected to write essays. These were so good that several of them were published, even before his twelfth birthday. Soon after he was forced to return home because of his increasing infirmity.

For all his intellectual ability he still kept his native boyish instinct. He enjoyed sport and a good prank. Once, his father was sent a young pig as a present from a farmer. The farmer's servant who had brought it happened to put it down for a moment. Immediately, Robert saw his chance, seized the bag and exchanged the pig for a dog. When his father opened the bag the servant was totally mystified. Though Hall was generally serious, he did have his humorous side.

Robert Hall

It seems he was converted quite young. His nurse used to say, 'I will answer for it that my dear Bobby knew the Lord before he was seven years of age.' When he was only fourteen, after giving an account of his spiritual condition, he became a member in his father's church.

After a few short years at home he entered the Bristol Baptist Academy, which was under the supervision of the Rev. Hugh Evans and later his son, Dr Caleb Evans, both Welshmen. At the time he was just fifteen years of age. Here, Hall had his first experience of preaching, which was disastrous. It was arranged for him to preach at Broadmead Meeting-house, Bristol. His text was, 'For this end we both labour and suffer reproach, because we trust in the living God, who is the Saviour of all men, especially of those who believe' (1 Tim. 4:10). He began well with the people very attentive. Suddenly he stopped, put his face in his hands and said to a startled congregation, 'Oh, I have lost all my ideas!' When he sat down he was still clasping his face. The following week he was again sent to preach in the same place and on the same subject. It was almost a repeat performance of the previous week. Afterwards, he rushed into the vestry saying, 'If this does not humble me, the devil must have me!'

It would seem that not every great preacher starts off in a whirlwind. The cultivation of any gift is as delicate an operation as the cultivation of a plant. Though he was a tremendous scholar, he was still very immature. Because of this the occasion got the better of him and he floundered. However, this first setback was only a minor delay and not a denial of his great gifts.

In 1781 he went to study in Aberdeen University. Here he met his lifelong friend Sir James Mackintosh, another brilliant scholar. These stimulated each other's literary enthusiasm. They read together and to each other. They also began a literary club which was euphemistically called, 'The Hall and Mackintosh Club'. Due to Hall's reticence Mackintosh often had to resort to a mild provocation to draw him into the debate. Once he was stirred to defend a moral principle he would become extremely eloquent. When their friends saw them walking together they joked, 'There go Plato and Herodotus'.

At the end of his course in Aberdeen he returned to Bristol to become co-pastor of the Baptist church in Broadmeads and to lecture in the Baptist Academy. It was a rather sad time for him, characterized by tensions between himself and his colleague and senior, Dr Caleb Evans, based chiefly on theological differences. Before his return a strict Calvinism, bordering on Hyper-Calvinism, had been taught in the church and Academy. He adopted a more Arminian stance. For this reason differing factions arose and after five years he felt constrained to leave.

Hall's theological alliance was often considered suspect, prompting Dr John Ryland who admired his preaching to say, 'O that God may keep that young man in the way of truth and holiness!' This suspicion was due to two main reasons. He did not always use orthodox expressions while preaching, and he had an appreciation for the writings of some unorthodox theologians. These were taken as sure signs of his own unorthodoxy. In fact he tended more towards the emphasis of Richard Baxter than to anything else and once told a friend, 'My father, sir, was very doctrinal in his preaching, and more attached to Calvinism than I am. If there are any sentiments to which I could subscribe, they are Baxter's.' It was this seeming unorthodoxy which helped promote his move to Cambridge in 1791, where he lived for fifteen years.

These years at Cambridge were years of great preaching, when his sermons both in the town and neighbouring villages, and in other parts of the country completely captured the attention of his hearers. Olinthus Gregory, one of his biographers, in looking back on the ministry of this 'extraordinary preacher' writes of these sermons:

> . . . these sublime exertions were made for the promotion of man's best interests – to warn the impenitent – to show to the sinner the fatal error of his way – to invite the self-condemned to the only, the all-effectual remedy – to console and encourage the faithful – to distribute the bread of life among those who must otherwise perish . . . when it is known also, that while men of taste and intellect were both gratified and instructed, the uncultivated rustic heard, and understood, and 'received the Word of Life', and went on his way rejoicing. (*The Works of Robert Hall,* Vol. 1, 'Memoir of his Life')

His preaching provoked widespread alarm within the hierarchy of the Church of England. They were concerned that many of their students were abandoning the Church to populate his chapel. They wanted to curb his influence in order to keep them within the establishment. It was so disconcerting for them to see so many being affected by this Dissenting minister.

For those who heard him for the first time his pulpit stance was quite distracting. Due to the perpetual pain in his back he stood with his chest resting against the pulpit cushion. At the same time he leant on his left arm and raised his right hand slightly towards the congregation. He became so engrossed in his message that even his pain could not distract him. When it was suggested that he publish his sermons he was surprised. He had never thought of himself or his sermons as anything other than ordinary. In reality, they were extraordinary. The first edition was soon sold and another edition quickly followed. He was amazed. He thought that they would have gone through one edition and then sunk into oblivion.

But the picture is one of tragedy as well as triumph. Sometimes his pulpit was occupied by less than orthodox preachers, a state of affairs which he never opposed. His mistake was in being far too liberal-minded theologically. As a young man he had imbibed liberal political principles, and these tended to bias and cloud his theological judgment. Sadly, he also experienced two bouts of insanity while at Cambridge. The first attack took place in 1804 and lasted about six weeks when he was taken to an asylum in Leicester to recuperate. Afterwards, he recalled his experience with horror. In the asylum he was abused and mistreated by the warders. One actually tied him hand and foot to the bedposts so as not to be disturbed through the night. After his recovery he returned to Cambridge.

His second attack came during the following year. One sacramental Sunday morning, in November, he was expected to preach but had failed to turn up. In the afternoon service he came to the church with a wild look in his eyes. When he entered the pulpit he gave out a hymn, read and prayed. Then he announced his text. The moment he began to preach it became clear that something was seriously wrong. His thoughts, normally so lucid and coherent, were completely muddled. Nobody could understand anything he was trying to say. Suddenly he realised that something was wrong, and putting his hand to his head said, 'My friends – I beg your pardon, my head is very bad this afternoon.' It was a pathetic scene.

By the time he came to conduct the communion service, all was lost. As he closed the service and the people began leaving the church he started to shout, 'Stop! I have something very important to say to you. I have to inform you that the millennium has come, the period which we have been hoping for, waiting for, and praying for so long; it has at length come! Let us all kneel down and bless God that we have lived to see this day.' The following day he was taken to Fishponds, near Bristol, where he again spent some time recuperating.

Towards the end of his stay a man who happened to call at the asylum recognised him. He was surprised to see him there and said, 'What! *you* here, Mr. Hall, *you* here! Whatever brought you here, Mr. Hall?' Hall replied, 'What will never bring you here, sir. *Too much up here, sir,'* tapping his head; *'Too much here.'*

Hall's general state of health always remained precarious. After leaving Fishponds he was given three instructions to follow if he wanted to retain his sanity and avoid a relapse: leave Cambridge because it affected his health, smoke to compose his mind, and get married to relieve his solitude. The first two were comparatively easy but not so the third. He had previously fallen in love in Bristol but it had come to nothing. For a long time afterwards he remained a wounded man. It soon became known that he was seriously seeking a wife. Because of his renown everyone assumed that he would marry someone of wealth, but he was never affected by money. When somebody told him that he had heard Hall was to marry a certain high-ranking lady, he indignantly replied, 'Marry Miss—, sir! marry Miss—, sir! I should as soon think of marrying the devil's daughter, and going home and living with the old folks!' When Hall did marry it was for love, not money.

In 1807 he moved to Leicester to become minister of Harvey Lane Baptist Church, and it was in Leicester that he found himself a wife. Though he could be abrasive, he was really a very gentle man. When he went to propose to his future wife it was in a true spirit of humility. There were many women who would have queued up to marry him but he was sensitive to a woman's feelings. He chose the maid of one of his best friends. When he visited this friend and divulged his intention, she suggested sending her maid into the living room so that he could speak to her in private. But he refused. He still believed in seeking the bride's hand and not having it sent to him. He went into the kitchen and asked her whether she loved Jesus, and could she love him also? Needless to say, she could. His time in Leicester was the happiest of his life. He was happily married though still suffering pain in his back. The pain was so persistent that he never knew an hour free from it, and to relieve this he frequently used laudanum, an opium-based medicine.

Like many intelligent men he could not suffer fools gladly. He had very little patience with 'clever men'. Once, as he described the powerful preaching and appearance of Christmas Evans, a Welsh Baptist minister interrupted him, 'But Mr. Hall, you remember that he had but one eye.' Hall's sarcastic retort was, *'One* eye! Why, sir, if I had a thousand eyes such as yours, I'd give them all for that one!' It was things like this that irritated him and brought the worst out in him. The tongue that was silver-lined was also razor sharp.

He also possessed a very dry wit. He was seriously humorous. When Christmas Evans was telling him how serviceable and descriptive the Welsh language was, and how he had wished John Gill's works had been published in Welsh, Hall remarked, 'I wish they had, sir; I wish they had, with all my heart, sir, for then I should never have read them. They are a continent of mud, sir!'

Hall returned to Bristol in April 1826. He was then sixty-two years of age and his life was fast coming to a close. His ministry there in the Broadmead Baptist Church was brief but bright. He ended where he had begun and had travelled in a complete circle. Yet it was a far different Hall who returned to Bristol. Where he had once failed he now triumphed. The novice had become the veteran and the church relished the thought of his return.

His death, like so much of his life, was martyr-like. Throughout his life he had sought never to grumble or complain of his lot. His affliction, he believed, was a sanctifying instrument of God. Towards the end of his life his suffering became more intense. But he was determined not to complain. Even when things became extreme and he was dying he could say, 'I have not complained, have I, sir? and I won't complain.'

As he lay dying his wife inquired as to his condition. He replied that he was comfortable, 'very comfortable! – only come, Lord Jesus, come!' He was then asked if he was suffering much. 'Dreadfully!' he replied. By now death had taken on an air of relief rather than fear. He knew it was the final escape from all his pain, and it was to be with Jesus.

In a conversation he had had with William Wilberforce a few years before, he had asked him, 'What is your idea of heaven, sir?' Wilberforce replied, 'Love, Mr Hall, *love!* What is yours, sir?' 'My idea of heaven, sir,' he said, 'my idea of heaven is rest, sir, *rest!'*

On 21 February 1831 Hall entered into 'that rest which remains for the people of God'. When a post-mortem was performed, they found that he had a twisted vertebra and a huge sharp stone in his right kidney. The doctor who carried out the post-mortem wrote in his report, 'Probably no man ever went through more physical suffering than Mr Hall.'

20
William Jay
(1769-1853)

When C.H.Spurgeon sat down to write a review of William Jay's works, he wrote, 'O for more Jays! We would give some two or three dozen of the general run of doctors of divinity for one such a Master in Israel as William Jay of Bath.' William was born in 1769. His father was a quarryman and stonemason. Due to their poverty he had very little formal education and, like many, he began work as a boy apprentice to his father. During this time he became interested in Christianity and was converted. Afterwards the other masons took great delight in ribbing him about his new faith. Usually this was nothing more than harmless fun. There was nothing malicious or spiteful in it. They were too attached to the lad to be hurtful.

At work William was often confronted with foul language. He found it hard to keep silent, and often condemned it. If he heard others cursing or swearing, he would challenge them; but his action was more than just a negative response to sin. He was equally pointed in explaining the gospel to them: how Jesus had died for sinners at Calvary.

His bias towards preaching soon became obvious, even to his ungodly workmates. They noticed his preoccupation with his religion and joked about it. Once, when William was slow in bringing up some mortar one of the masons joked, 'Hollo, Will! what's thee doing so long there? be'st thee making us another sarment? Let's have mortar now, and sarments when all's done!'

When Jay began work it was difficult for a person to rise above his station in life. Sons usually followed their father's livelihood in an almost endless procession. William soon showed signs of being something more than a stonemason. He possessed a meditative mind and enjoyed nothing better than a walk in the country where he could be absorbed in his thoughts. In later life he saw how providence's kind hand had lifted him out of obscurity to become a household name throughout the land. In a letter to his children he referred to this remarkable rise to fame: 'What probability was there that such a change as I have experienced would ever take place? No effort, no purpose of my own, or of my relatives, had the least concern in it. It resulted purely and entirely from the providence of God.'

God's normal way of working is through second causes – the human factor. In fact, he rarely ever violates this principle. In William's case Cornelius Winter was the human factor. He was a godly man who ran an academy for aspiring preachers at his home at Marlborough. While preaching at William's church one day he was struck by a young man listening very intently. When he returned the following year the same thing happened. Afterwards Winter made a point of speaking to him and suggested that, if his parents were willing, he could come and study at his academy. After receiving his parents' consent he moved to Marlborough to live with Winter, who was to become the greatest moulding influence in young William's spiritual life.

William became Winter's favourite pupil and Winter had a peculiar attachment to him. He treated him more like a son than a student. When he went for a walk or on some longer excursion William often accompanied him. These jaunts allowed them time to discuss the Scriptures and aspects of preaching. Jay always felt indebted to Winter for the interest he had shown in him, and it was at Marlborough that he first began to preach.

Today relatively few have heard of him though he was considered a prince of preachers in his day. What makes him so remarkable is the great length of his ministry, a ministry which lasted over sixty years. He began preaching at the age of sixteen and continued until his death in his eighty-fifth year. Of all the many privileges he knew, Jay prized his acquaintance with some of the early Methodist preachers above all. Many of his early associates had been converted under the ministries of men like the Wesley brothers and George Whitefield. Their depth of spirituality and godliness made an indelible impression upon him. Like many young converts, he was immensely influenced by the spirituality of the Christians he first met and Jay's life became almost a reflection of theirs. Jay was also on intimate terms with all the great preachers of his day. Because of this he was often asked to preach at their funerals, including those of the celebrated Robert Hall and Rowland Hill.

He had just reached sixteen when he preached his first sermon, and by his twenty-first birthday he had preached over a thousand. Students at the academy were expected to preach during the week as well as on Sundays. They were encouraged to use every opportunity to preach the gospel. It did not matter where they preached – a village green, a barn or a cottage – as long as they preached. They preached anywhere they could get an audience. Sometimes their preaching was disrupted by unruly locals, but more often than not they were left unmolested.

William soon became known as the 'Boy Preacher'. Most of those who went to hear him went because of his evident sincerity and simplicity. However, there were some who used his youthfulness as an opportunity to taunt him. Once, when he was to preach at Melksham, he stayed with an elderly man from London.

> I called upon him on the Monday morning. He received me rather uncourteously. He did not, indeed, censure my preaching, but rudely said, he had no notion of *beardless* boys being employed as preachers. 'Pray, sir,' said I, 'does not Paul say to Timothy, "Let no man despise thy youth?".
> And, sir, you remind me of what I have read of a French monarch, who had received a young ambassador, and, complaining, said, "Your master should not have sent me a beardless stripling." "Sir," said the youthful ambassador, "had my master supposed you wanted a beard, he would have sent you a goat."' (*The Autobiography of William Jay,* p. 44)

This reply illustrates one of Jay's chief characteristics: his sense of humour. He was very quick-witted and saw the ridiculous in almost everything. Unfortunately he sometimes over-used humour in his preaching. He never planned to be funny but because he preached from memory he sometimes allowed his guard to drop and let things slip. Fortunately for him, he had the ability to get away with it. If other preachers had tried to use some of his illustrations they would have been bombarded with apples. For example, when he wanted to make the point that, 'evil communications corrupt good manners,' he said:

> Two friendly neighbours bought each a favourite parrot. That of Mrs A. was a bird of grave deportment, and had been taught to speak a good many godly words; but Mrs B's. was an impious fellow, for his language

abounded in bad words. Now Mrs B. felt quite shocked at the irreverent talk of the parrot, and prevailed on her friend to allow the godly parrot to pay a visit to the swearer, in the hope of reclaiming the rogue by good example. Well; the two birds stayed together for about a month, and a great reformation was expected in the swearing parrot, from listening to his more decent neighbour; but imagine the consternation of Mrs A., on the return of her grave and decorous bird, to hear him swearing like a trooper! The fact is, that instead of teaching, he had been learning; and, from that sad day, his language was as bad as his scapegrace associate. (*Memoir*, p.82)

However it would be wrong to conclude that Jay's popularity was due primarily to his pulpit quaintness. This was the exception rather than the rule. Generally, he was far more guarded and reserved. Nobody could sustain such an influential ministry in one church on mere frivolous drivel, and Jay knew it. When his sermons appeared in print he had cut out all questionable humour.

Despite his ministry being unusually long, it was virtually confined to one particular church, Argyle Chapel in Bath. His ministry there lasted over sixty years to the year 1853, and though he received many offers to leave Argyle Chapel, he refused them all. He was never more at home than he was in Bath.

Jay's name has often been closely linked to another chapel, Surrey Chapel, London, a place which was made famous by the influential ministry of Rowland Hill and which became like a second home to Jay. His association with Surrey Chapel lasted throughout his life, diminishing slightly after Hill's death. Until then he felt bound to preach there during his summer vacations because of a promise he had made to Hill. His connection with Surrey Chapel began early in his ministry. As a young man he was invited to preach there and from the moment he arrived his preaching was an immediate success. This metropolitan congregation was immediately drawn to the country boy. Accustomed, as they were, to listening to the somewhat eccentric Rowland Hill, they soon warmed to Jay's youthful zeal.

Preaching there in 1851, after well over half a century of service, Jay reminded them of his longstanding connection with the Chapel and the effect of his first preaching. 'Six days ago', he said, 'I entered on my eighty-third year. When I first ascended these steps, with

William Jay

trembling knees, I was not nineteen. Many years have passed since then; many changes I have seen; yet have been upheld till now; who could hold me up but Thou!'

> Perhaps there are few if any persons here this morning, who heard my first address then, from the words of the apostle, 'God forbid that I should glory, save in the cross of our Lord Jesus Christ'. I was then young and tender. The work was great, and the Lord was pleased to afford assistance, and give me very considerable acceptance; so that I remember, when I had been taking my leave of the congregation here in my farewell sermon, still the crowd remained in the chapel-yard, and refused to disperse, till I opened the parlour window and addressed them again. From that time, for half a century, I annually served this chapel eight sabbaths for many years, and then for six, and then for four.' (*Memoir of W.Jay*, pp.10-11)

In an age of short ministries, his mammoth sixty years in one church seems incredible; yet he saw successive generations come and go. What is perhaps even more amazing is that his popularity as a preacher never waned. Argyle Chapel continued to flourish from first to last. His preaching was as lively and fresh at the end as it was at the start. Time had not eroded his powers or enfeebled him. During his ministry the chapel was rebuilt three times to accommodate the ever-growing congregation.

Jay's call to Argyle Street in 1790 came at the recommendation of their dying pastor, Thomas Tuppen. After preaching in Surrey Chapel, London (for the first time in July 1788) he had received several invitations to remain in London, but had refused them all. This was due to a sense of his own inadequacy. He felt the need of further preparation and wider experience. Instead, he accepted a call in the autumn of 1788 to a small village church in Christian Malford, near Chippenham.

With his fine gifts he could not long be kept concealed in such a small and obscure place as Christian Malford. As he travelled around preaching, the people flocked to hear him and, because of his growing popularity, the attention of Argyle Street Chapel was drawn to him. As Thomas Tuppen lay dying he was asked who should succeed him. His immediate response was, 'William Jay!' Jay was not only Tuppen's first choice, but also that of the church, who had merely asked Tuppen out of courtesy. When he received the invitation Jay quickly accepted it. He intuitively felt that this was the place of God's appointing. Until then he had never felt at home anywhere.

The chapel itself had recently been constructed and was a new building. Jay had preached at the inaugural services due to Tuppen's ill health. Out of respect for him the church delayed its opening in the hope of his recovery but, sadly, Tuppen never recovered sufficiently to preach there and died soon after it was opened. Apart from his short ministry of a little over two years at Christian Malford, Argyle Street was to be Jay's only church.

Theologically, Jay was a Calvinist, though this was more implied than stated, for his sermons were always textual. After choosing his text he would draw out all its relevant points and develop them by natural progression. Each point evolved from the verse and was never forced. The text always set the parameters to all his thoughts.

His method of preaching was determined early on. After his first visit to London he knew the kind of preacher he wanted to be. On his way to London he was looking forward to hearing some of the great metropolitan preachers. After mentioning it to a friend he was surprised to be told that if he wished to hear a good doctrinal sermon he must hear Mr – ; if an experimental he must hear Mr – ; if a practical, he must hear Mr – . And he well remembers simply asking, 'But is there no minister here who preaches all these? I should rather hear him.' To Jay, preaching was more than one thing. A well-balanced sermon must be as wholesome as a well-balanced diet. It must appeal to every part of the Christian – his mind, his heart, his life. Otherwise, he could easily become deficient in some area.

Jay always knew beforehand how his preaching would turn out. Experience had taught him that good preaching was dependent upon the preacher's own state of heart and mind. If he was distracted or had little time to prepare himself beforehand, he knew that preaching would be difficult. He needed time to reflect and make his sermon a part of him. For example, after visiting Scotland in the early part of the nineteenth century Jay returned home extremely disappointed with his preaching. On reflection, he pin-pointed the cause of his weakness as a lack of seclusion before the service.

> Here also I scarcely preached to advantage, and must have fallen short in some degree of the fame that had preceded me, and which was aided by the report of many who had, in a course of years, visited Bath and had heard me in my own pulpit. I was hurried and perplexed, and wanted that freedom from bustle, and that retirement, without which I never could feel or produce much impression. *(Autobiography,* p.136)

How well he understood the Psalmist's words, 'Be still and know that I am God.'

It was not until the latter part of his life that he resorted to sermon notes. At times, on special occasions, he even read his sermons, but he later regretted it. He felt that his memory had been such a good and faithful friend to him and now he had let it down. His increasing dependence upon his notes caused him to become less and less dependent upon his memory. Consequently, his mental recall was not as sharp or spontaneous as it used to be.

It is little wonder that he had had such implicit confidence in his memory. His knowledge of the Bible was encyclopaedic. His aptitude in selecting appropriate texts for almost any situation was proverbial.

The Bible had become an integral part of his make-up. His confidence in his memory is demonstrated in his use of biblical quotation. He could, at a moment's notice, summon passages of Scripture from almost anywhere in the Bible.

An eyewitness of his uniqueness as a preacher gave this description of him:

> The style of Mr Jay is one exclusively his own. He imitates no one; and no preacher whom I have ever heard resembles him. Usually, he commences his sermon with some abrupt, terse observation, which would seem to have little to do with his subject . . . He is not rapid in his delivery, but rather the reverse; his sentences are delivered with great emphasis. His discourses may almost be called conversational . . . Occasionally he produces a prodigious effect by a solemn strain of eloquence, immediately following some remarks which had, in spite of the sanctity of the place, provoked a smile; for . . . he has a flow of wit which cannot always be restrained. (*Memoir,* p.100)

Of all his many virtues as a preacher one stood out above the rest. Like his master before him he was genuinely sympathetic towards those who heard him. This was conveyed both in and out of the pulpit. As he preached, his heart was opened for all to see. Good preaching can often mean the preacher opening his heart to the people in order to explain the Scriptures. It was difficult, almost impossible, for him to hide his true self in the pulpit. One biographer said of him, 'As regards his voice: its tones can many of them never be forgotten. They were capable of stirring the deepest founts of feeling, and of exciting the finest sympathies of our nature. The expression of tenderness was, perhaps, the preacher's forte.'

Jay died on 27 December 1853, at the age of eighty-five. His joy throughout his long life had been to see successive generations grow up and flourish under his ministry. Not that he considered himself of any real significance. Like all preachers worth their salt, he knew that his sufficiency was of God. Even at his Jubilee service, after fifty years in the ministry, he could say, 'I feel the want of assistance rather than an assistant.' How well did his ministerial friend, T. Grinfield, capture him in a poem he composed for his Jubilee celebrations:

'Dear, venerable Pastor! whose career
Of labouring zeal hath loosed its fiftieth year,

Within those favoured walls, where once thy youth,
Where still thine age, hath taught celestial truth;
Well did thy flock, with grateful love, agree
To celebrate thy pastoral Jubilee;
Honouring their friend, their father, honouring Heaven,
Who such a father-friend so long had given.
Oh, in this changeful world, how few like thee
Have trained one church through half a century,
With undeclining constancy like thine;
Alone, unaided – save by strength Divine!
How well, in thee, was piety combined
With kindly converse and a master mind!
How well thy natural eloquence impressed
Wisdom, devotion, on the listening breast!
A spreading throng caught manna from thy lips;
Thy popularity knew no eclipse.
The wise, the good, still hailed thy faithful course;
And, with thy foremost friends, the sweet-souled *Wilberforce*.
Happy, like him, in enviable age,
With Canaan opening on thy pilgrimage!
Oh, golden sunset of a beauteous day!
Soon, in the clime of glory, thou, too, Jay,
Midst the bright host shall shine, a star of loveliest ray!'

(Memoir, pp.147-48)

But before he was to enter that celestial reward there remained still more than a decade of active service, and God kept and blessed his ministry to the very end.

21
Archibald Alexander

(1772-1851)

Archibald Alexander was a child of the second Great Evangelical Awakening in America. He was converted at its beginning and saw its growth and development throughout its entire forty-year history. Though he is best known as Princeton Theological Seminary's first professor, he was also an excellent preacher.

What makes his life so fascinating is his rise from an obscure little place in Virginia to the foremost seat in the Presbyterian Church of America. This was achieved without any extraordinary academic background. In fact, his education was very basic. After leaving school he never attended a college or university. Yet by the time he was twenty-four years of age he had been appointed joint-president of Hampden Sidney College, a position he held for over a decade.

His selection to this post came as a direct result of his rising fame as a preacher and self-taught theologian. His friends observed his exceptional intellectual potential and development. He had an insatiable thirst for knowledge. Due to the scarcity of books he came to appreciate and prize them. Everything he could lay his hands on, he devoured. Sometimes he read and re-read books simply because there were no others available. By the time the Presbyterian Church came to establish their first theological seminary to train ministerial students in Princeton, New Jersey, Alexander was renowned. His academic achievements had come through his own labour. He had no sabbatical rest or prolonged respite to build up his vast stores of knowledge. Instead, he had relentlessly pursued it.

When, in 1811, the General Assembly nominated him as the Seminary's first Professor of Theology nobody was more surprised than he, yet no one deserved it more. He had neither sought nor coveted it, neither had he any influential or wealthy friends who could lobby the General Assembly for him. But by its general consent he was elected. This call, he believed, was the hand of a sovereign God leading him into his life's work which was to last almost forty years.

Alexander was born near Lexington, in the colony of Virginia, on 17 April 1772, three years before the outbreak of the American War of Independence. His parents were farmers as were his grandparents before them. His ancestors were staunch Presbyterians who had moved to Northern Ireland at a difficult time in Scotland's turbulent history. Some of these emigrated to the New World in the hope of better prospects. When they came to America they brought their Presbyterianism across the Atlantic with them.

Like all Presbyterian children, Alexander was reared on the Westminster Confession of Faith, but it had very little real impact upon him. He was as ignorant of God as the worldlings among whom he lived. When he was converted he realized he was not the only one in that condition: many professing Christians were not so in reality. They had a name that they lived but were dead (Rev. 3:1).

After his seventeenth birthday his father arranged for him to become tutor to General John Posey's children in Wilderness, Virginia. Owing to its seclusion and the General's small library he was able to read to his heart's content. He enjoyed reading the history of the Roman Empire and of England, and he taught the Greek classics to his pupils. However it was not the intellectual advantages of Wilderness that figured most in his life but the spiritual advantage he obtained there. It was here he first met anyone maintaining the necessity of a new birth for salvation.

A Mrs Tyler who lived with the Poseys began speaking to him about spiritual things. Though he had read of regeneration, of being born again, in the Westminster Confession, it did not seem to have any clear relevance for him. He believed that anyone who was moral or religious was a Christian. Experiential Christianity was then almost a forgotten feature of Presbyterianism. It had retained a form of godliness but without its power. When revival came in 1790 this situation was quickly changed. Men and women were again made to feel the power of the gospel. There was a restoration of the true knowledge and sense of God. They came to realize that the essense of a living faith was through this new birth. Without it, man is 'dead in trespasses and sins' (Ephes. 2:1-3).

Mrs Tyler was an Anglican by birth but a Baptist by conviction. She often confronted Archibald with his spiritual condition and told him of her own conversion. He was impressed by her obvious sincerity and was convinced there was something more to regeneration than he had first realized. Encouraged by her, he began to attend Baptist meetings. However before he would come to any settled assurance of salvation a major struggle had to be fought within.

This godly woman used every possible means to bring him into contact with the truth. Due to her failing eyesight she asked him to read to her her favourite Puritan author, John Flavel. At first Alexander was reluctant and only agreed out of courtesy. But when he learnt that Flavel was a Presbyterian like himself he became more interested and read Flavel's treatise on *Justification by Faith and Regeneration* until he understood their significance. Eventually, his spiritual condition reached a climax and he entered into the clear light of the gospel. He saw that God could save sinners through the death of his Son on Calvary, that God could be 'just and the justifier of the one who has faith in Jesus' (Rom. 3:26). Until then the importance of the cross remained a mystery to him, but now everything was different because he was different. Life had taken on a new dimension with God at its centre.

After his conversion in 1789 Alexander had tremendous difficulties. He experienced profound emotional changes. Sometimes he would ascend above the clouds of doubt into the ethereal light of heaven where there was nothing between himself and the Sun of righteousness. But when he descended below them he found himself shrouded in darkness, perplexity and despair. His problem was one of maintaining his spiritual equilibrium. He was too often controlled by his emotions and not enough by the truth. If at any time he felt low he lost all sense of his assurance. When he learnt the practical value of the doctrine of justification by faith he never again entered the cloud. There were times when his salvation was not as clear as he would have liked, but these became rare exceptions.

Soon after his conversion he returned home and found a revival in progress. Special meetings had become common and were being held everywhere. He visited several revival scenes and was struck by what he saw. God was so evident among the people that they were full of joy and rejoicing. Hymn and psalm singing became the natural expression of God's praise. What one Psalmist had written was being fulfilled before Alexander's very eyes. 'When the Lord brought back the captivity of Zion, we were like those who dream. Then our mouth was filled with laughter, and our tongue with singing. Then they said among the nations, "The Lord has done great things for them." The Lord has done great things for us, whereof we are glad' (Psalm 126:1-3).

His first sermons were preached in this revival atmosphere. After being accepted by his presbytery as a candidate for the ministry he was immediately sent, with a friend, on a preaching excursion. Before embarking on his mission Alexander preached at home, an experience which he found particularly trying. Since he appeared weak and frail and did not look his age some began to call him, 'The Boy Preacher'. Fifty years later he gave this judgement of his early attempts at preaching:

My delivery in those days was fluent and rapid. I never appeared to hesitate or be at a loss for words; my thoughts flowed too fast for me. I laboured under two great faults as a public speaker; the first was extreme rapidity of utterance, not so much from indistinct articulation as neglect of pauses. I ran on until I was perfectly out of breath . . . the other fault was looking steadily down upon the floor. This arose from a fear of losing the train of my thought; for my sermons were closely studied, though not written. My voice, though not sonorous, was uncommonly distinct and clear, so that without painful exertion I could be heard in the largest churches, or by a great assembly out of doors. I preached but one other Sabbath in my native county . . . I had very little estimation in which my preaching was held, and was always surprised to hear of a favourable opinion expressed by anyone; for I was so conscious of my own defects, that often after preaching I was ashamed to come down from the pulpit, and wondered that any could speak kindly to me. (J.W.Alexander, *Life of Archibald Alexander*, pp.123-24)

This assessment of his preaching and its defects was written by the veteran preacher who had heard and trained many of the finest preachers of his day. Afterwards, as he developed, these flaws were corrected and his preaching vastly improved. It seems that God had concealed from him any sense of greatness. Instead, he was made to feel his weakness. God's order is always first to humble, then to exalt.

During these early years Alexander developed his gift of extemporary preaching. This began almost accidentally. As he was preaching one day a sudden gust of wind blew his notes off the lectern. Too embarrassed to descend from the pulpit to pick them up he carried on regardless. Afterwards, he was determined never again to take a paper sermon into the pulpit with him.

This extemporaneous ability was the fruit of prolonged concentration on his themes. As he rode from place to place, especially during his time as travelling missionary for the Synod of Virginia, he found himself constructing sermons. When a text gripped him he would churn it over in his mind until he understood the writer's drift. He then extracted its main points and formed them into a plan. He became so effective at this that he preached many of his early sermons throughout his life. Their substance and structure had become embedded in his mind.

Though he became a theological professor, Alexander never preached as one. His personality made it impossible for him to be staid or rigid when he preached. He was never heavy or dull. Neither was he too encumbered with theological niceties, so as to mar his simplicity. His particular style of preaching was learnt during his itinerant days. After seeing how ignorant the people were he realised he could not take too much for granted as to his congregation's knowledge.

One of his great attributes as a preacher was his ability to speak to children. He was always able to come down to their level and had such a simple style that he could hold them entranced. His manner, tone and words gripped them so intensely that they became like clay in his hands. He was a very good story-teller and children loved to listen to him.

In 1794, at the age of 22, he was ordained to the pastoral charge of a number of congregations in Virginia, and in 1796 he became President of Hampden-Sidney College, while continuing to act as pastor and preacher. Then in 1807 he became minister of Pine Street Church, Philadelphia, one of the largest congregations in the country.

During this time his preaching never changed. Even after coming to Princeton Seminary in New Jersey, in 1812, he kept his natural simplicity. Though he possessed a profound theological under-standing he never allowed it to intrude into his sermons. He left the intricacies of theological debate in the classroom. Not that he all theology from his sermons: theology was their bedrock and frame-work. To throw it out altogether would be like taking the skeleton out of a body. Instead, his preaching was permeated with theology, but it was taught in such a way that even the simplest of minds could understand it.

> Formal and elaborate argumentation on doctrinal points was not common in his sermons. It is true, he expounded and defended the great doctrines of the faith, but it was in a method which was homiletical and popular, rather than scholastically didactic . . . Even when his object was to establish doctrine, he preferred the textual method. His division and treatment of the subject were generally governed by the text. Any figure which it contained was apt to colour the whole discourse. (J.W.Alexander, *Life of Archibald Alexander*, pp.683-84)

Those whose chief interest in sermons was more in their structure than their content often found his preaching unimpressive. Because of their preoccupation with diction and style they disliked his common-place speech. They were neither spiritually alert nor theologically aware, but enjoyed preaching simply for its entertainment value. What they failed to realize was that true eloquence must flow from the truth. It is the truth which fires the passions and creates the heat to melt the heart.

In October 1816 the Synod of Virginia met in Fredericksburg. Alexander was there along with many of his friends. Preaching services were conducted both morning and evening. It also happened that the Superior Court was in session there during that week. Many of its most distinguished lawyers and judges were in attendance. They were proud of their profession and considered themselves the intelligentsia of the day. When they heard that Alexander was to preach, there was general excitement. They all wanted to hear the best preacher of the time, but their attitude was more curious than spiritual. It was his gift not his gospel they wanted to assess. Many of them were disappointed with him – one lawyer even left the building while he was preaching. But for those best qualified to judge, he was excellent. His friend Dr Samuel B. Wilson, Professor of Theology in Union Theological Seminary, comments on his graphic style:

> As he passed from the description of the Jewish passover, to the sacrifice of Christ, he said, bending forward and looking intently òn the communion table spread before him, where the bread and wine lay covered, 'But where is our Lamb?' At these words, so impressively uttered, and accompanied by a gesture so significant, an old French dancing master, who scarcely ever entered a church, rose from his seat near the pulpit, and gazed intently, to see if there was not something on the communion table, which he had not yet seen. An intelligent little girl, too, who sat before him, after she returned home, said: 'Aunt H. did you hear such a man? When he said, "Where is our Lamb," he seemed as if he was looking for a lamb on the communion table.' (*Life of Archibald Alexander*, pp. 409-11)

To Alexander preaching was more than a matter of mere words or oratory. He had seen and experienced the Spirit's operation. His knowledge of revival had taught him to look beyond the man in preaching. He was but a channel through whom God could work, the messenger not the conveyor of life. This was the Spirit's sovereign domain. He imparts life where there is death, light where there is darkness, and cleansing where there is sin.

> Far more than is common, and beyond what he ever explicitly declared, he seems to have believed in special aids, elevations and illuminations, conferred on the preacher during his delivery of the message; such

afflatus from the Spirit he was accustomed to distinguish from the personal graces of the preacher . . . Hardly anything could be augured from his beginning. He allowed himself to rise and glow in a manner almost imperceptible. As might be expected, he did not always soar; but when he did, it was without effort and without abruptness. As he kindled, his language became more vivid, ornate, and powerful; it even acquired an elegant fitness and accuracy, which is not found in his writings. Towards the close of his greatest sermons, the audience was usually in a state of rapt attention; nothing was more common than for people to say that they would gladly have listened to him all day. (*Life of Archibald Alexander*, pp.689-90)

Alexander always preached with a sense of expectation that God was about to do something wonderful. This attitude was a direct result of his revival experiences where preachers were given unusual liberty to preach. Not that God confined the Holy Spirit's operations to revivals, for God has his ordinary as well as extraordinary ways of working. Preachers can just as well know something of his power outside as well as inside revival.

Throughout his life revival was a subject of prime interest to him. He read, experienced, visited and wrote on it. His book, *The Log College*, deals with revival incidents in the first Great Awakening in America. If Jonathan Edwards is recognized as the eighteenth century's theologian of revival, Alexander should be recognized as that of the nineteenth. The spiritual life of the Church is always enhanced by such events, and she should always be looking and praying for such times.

When Charles G. Finney, the famous nineteenth-century evangelist, began to introduce new methods of evangelism, Alexander was opposed to them. Finney, like Alexander, had experienced revival but these new ways were considered highly dangerous. Finney's extreme emphasis on man's will, which almost meant the exclusion of regeneration, disturbed Alexander. To Finney, man's will was the bastion to conquer. He believed that salvation came more through natural persuasion than by supernatural regeneration. The whole process was seen entirely from a human and not a divine perspective. It increasingly became man-orientated instead of God-orientated as divine spiritual renewal became almost a thing of the past.

In another of his books, *Thoughts on Religious Experience,* Alexander attacks the psychology of this new evangelism. He shows how easy it is to manipulate people, given certain circumstances.

However it would be unfair simply to think of him as just another critic of these new ideas. He was just as critical of the old Presbyterian guard who were guilty of quenching the Spirit's operation among them. He sought to hold a balance between a cold, calculated, academic approach to salvation and a too simplistic, easy believism. What he wanted was for those who had come to faith to be sure they had undergone regeneration. He knew that those who made professions and later turned away were far harder to win back afterwards. They also supplied the enemies of the gospel with ammunition for criticism. These became extremely vociferous in their condemnation of preachers and the gospel.

When he died in Princeton, on 22 October 1851, he was still in harness at the Seminary. From his first year there in 1812 until the time of his death, 1,837 young men had been in his classes, one of the most famous being Charles Hodge. His career had been long and eventful. God had honoured and blessed his ministries as a preacher, pastor and professor. His work had grown and expanded alongside his spiritual and intellectual growth, and his life was never static but increasingly active as God opened up new avenues of service.

22
Adolphe Monod
(1802-56)

People tell me that I speak well: what matters it to me? Tomorrow I shall be laid in the tomb. What will it profit me then to have spoken well? Happy will it be if they can say of me: 'He served his Master; he died in harness; putting himself out of sight and glorifying God.' Speak no more to me of praise. Do not speak of it between yourselves; think only of what I tell you: and look to your soul's salvation. Already as I approach my half-century, I feel my voice failing and my imagination growing torpid; but it is more than ever on my heart to do the work of God, during the little time, and with the little strength, which remain to me.

Almost on his deathbed, this is what the most famous preacher in France at the time could write of his ministry. Not himself but God was to be glorified.

His full name was Adolphe Louis Frederic Theodore Monod. He was born in Copenhagen, Denmark, on 21 January 1802, the sixth of thirteen children. His father, who was Swiss, pastored a Reformed church there before moving to Paris, where he had received a call from the National Reformed Church. This move took place in 1808.

As a boy Monod was noted for his ready wit and clear speech. He was bright, intelligent and possessed all the qualities of a good speaker. After his first sermon his father remarked that he would become a preacher of distinction. He probably never dreamt that Monod would become one of France's most celebrated preachers. He also possessed a natural poetic talent. For his fifteenth birthday he composed a poem which was almost prophetic of his future career, even though he was not yet converted.

> No, not for thee, O world, I mean to live,
> Nor shall my heart to thy false joys aspire;
> Riches, vainglory, honours, from my sight
> Begone! too well I know your deadly charms.

God shall preserve me from your treacherous snares;
He, He alone, shall henceforth be my Guide.
Devoted to the obedience of His laws,
I'll teach my fellow-men to love Him too;
And, walking in my tender parents' steps,
I'll live, I'll toil, my brethren's souls to save.

Monod was educated under his father's supervision and with the help of some close family friends. After this initial preparation he studied at the College Bourbon and then at the College de France in Sorbonne. When he was eighteen he went to Geneva to study theology. Not long before his coming, Geneva had been a centre of Unitarianism which all its professors taught. However after the Scottish Baptist preacher, Robert Haldane, came there in 1816, there was a dramatic change in its spiritual climate. As he lectured to the students on the Epistle to the Romans, in his own apartments, there was a powerful movement of God's Spirit. Many of the students were converted, including Adolphe's elder brother Frederic who always considered Haldane as his 'spiritual father'. This led to a full scale revival. Calvin's city, the heart of Reformation teaching in Europe in the sixteenth century, was almost restored to its former glory.

Had Monod come to Geneva, even a short time earlier, he would have met with a far different theological environment. Many of his friends there were the fruit of the revival. For this reason his own faith, such as it was, was challenged. These people knew and loved their Bibles and believed in its inspiration. This shook him. His faith was more rational than spiritual. A conflict erupted not only with the supporters of the revival but deep within himself. This condition caused him many months, even years, of internal perplexity and pain. He was troubled by his sensitive conscience and his natural tendency to depression. Even at his ordination in July 1824, his dilemma had not been fully resolved. Three years were to pass before he enjoyed a clear assurance of the gospel.

It was not until the spring of 1826 that he was established as a full-time pastor. His first church was in Naples, which he had visited for a few months towards the end of the previous year. At the time he had acted as a pastor to a group of French-speaking Protestants living there. These were like sheep without a shepherd. His ministry in Naples lasted a mere eighteen months and were distressing days for him. He became depressed and disheartened by his spiritual condition and did not know what to do. Isolated from his family and unsure of what to preach, a deep melancholy set in. In this desperate state he was driven on solely by his conscience to perform his pastoral duties, but without a real faith to share and offer he began to despair. This arid spiritual state made him aware of his own emptiness. He was weary and heavy-laden but could find no relief. He did not know the One who had said, 'Come to me, all you who labour and are heavy laden, and I will give you rest' (Matt. 11:28).

To overcome his gloomy thoughts he threw himself into his work and began studying his Bible more enthusiastically. For all this, peace still eluded him. He began to long for his time in Naples to end, his presence there beginning to feel like a prison sentence. Yet his incarceration was not in Naples but in the barreness of his own deficient faith. He was sincere and conscientious but spiritually dead.

For all its gloom Naples became the birthplace of his new life. Here he came to trust in Jesus Christ as his Saviour and experienced God's love for him. This removed in a measure the bleakness of his mind. In a letter to his sister on 14 August 1827, he said:

> Renouncing all merit, all strength, all resources of my own, and confessing that I had no claim to His mercy but that of my own misery, I asked of Him His Spirit, to change my spirit. Since that day, which is now more than three weeks ago, I have had no return of melancholy. The reason is, that I was before without God, and depended for happiness on myself, now I have a God who undertakes to make me happy. This is enough for me. I am not yet very happy, nor constantly happy, because the sense which I have of the presence and the love of my God is not continual, nor lively.

His entrance into God's kingdom had not been easy. There was no simple solution to his problem. He was at the end of his tether and did not know what to do. All he could do was throw himself wholly upon God. Afterwards he used to remind himself of something he had read about God's preparations for usefulness and its obvious implication to himself at this time. 'When God sets apart one of His servants for a great undertaking, He begins by breaking his arms and his legs.' This he knew was a metaphorical way of stating it but it was true – God in breaking him was also preparing him.

In October, not long after his conversion, he left Naples and returned to Paris. While staying at his parents' home he was invited to preach in the vacant Reformed church in Lyons. The Consistory, who had the right to employ ministers, were delighted with his preaching and offered him the position. His ministry there began in December 1827.

At first his preaching was greeted with much applause from the Consistory. However they soon rued the day when they had called him. People were converted and he began attracting other evangelicals from outside the National Church to his church. These put aside their ecclesiastic differences in order to hear him. But it was his sermons on 'Man's Misery' and 'God's Mercy' which provoked the most hostile response. They were preached in February 1828. Before this he was just feeling his way along theologically, studying the Scriptures and praying for further light. After preaching these two sermons the Consistory's attitude towards him decidedly changed. They suddenly realised he was not the man they had hoped for, and even his great pulpit talents were not enough to compensate for his unpalatable message. From then on they tried to squeeze him out of the church.

This state of things lingered on for the next four years with the Consistory relentlessly opposing him. The only thing which helped to relieve his situation was his marriage to Hannah Honyman from Scotland. This took place on 2 September 1829, almost two years after his arrival in Lyons. She comforted and consoled him throughout all his difficulties. In fact, she became the mainstay of his remaining ministry there. His offence was the offence of the cross. It was this that had provoked the Consistory's discontent. The more clearly it was preached, the greater became their hostility. Writing to a friend in 1829, he said:

> The 19 of April (Easter-day) I preached a sermon, in which I showed that no one can die in peace, until he believes in free pardon through the blood of Jesus Christ. This sermon gave great offence, especially to the Consistory . . . On the 17 of May I preached on Romans 6 v.1, and showed that, far from good works being hindered by faith, not a single good work is possible with a soul which has not believed in free salvation by Jesus Christ. This sermon gave even more offence than the other.

It was this forthright presentation of the gospel which the

Consistory found intolerable. In March 1832 the conflict finally came to a head and he was forced to leave the church. Though he was expelled from his living he was not expelled from Lyons. His popularity as a preacher had grown and attracted much attention from those outside the Reformed Church. They rallied around him and pleaded with him not to leave the city but stay and form an independent evangelical church, and this he did. This expulsion meant losing his stipend and being thrown on the goodness of God's people. However the Lord undertook to supply his needs, even from distant places.

As he pastored these warm-hearted people he saw a steady increase in their numbers. Yet his concern for growth did not mean that he watered down his message. He was as much concerned for the quality of Christian profession as he was for the quantity of professions. There were many Roman Catholics who wanted to become Protestants and join the church, but they had little interest in the gospel. He advised them 'not to change their name but their hearts.'

Throughout his time in Lyons he always felt an inclination to the professorial role. While he was in the National Church it was suggested to him to apply for the vacant Chair of Moral Theology and Sacred Oratory in the Theological College at Montauban. This caused such a stir that the position was left empty for another four years. Those who opposed him did so on the grounds of what had happened in Lyons. The opposition he had provoked from the Consistory appeared more than adequate to debar him from this post.

As minister of the independent evangelical church in Lyons he received several invitations from the Evangelical Society in Geneva to become one of its Professors in their School of Theology. But these were always rejected. He felt the more pressing need of the newly formed church of gaining a measure of stability before he could leave it. It seemed certain that one day he would have his wish fulfilled. In August 1836 he was appointed Lecturer of Moral Theology and Sacred Rhetoric in the Protestant University at Montauban. This was a heart-rending experience for the church. They had waited so long in the shadows for him to leave the National Church and establish a new Church and now he was leaving them. His only reason for going was his belief that by then they were strong enough to survive without him. Someone else could just as easily be found to carry on the work, now that the foundation had been laid. The church finally submitted to the inevitable as his assistant, Georges Fisch, wrote, 'All exclaimed that this call came from God, and that he must go. It was a touching and solemn scene. Their hearts were broken, but they said: 'The will of the Lord be done.'

In Montauban his attitude towards his students was more than cordial. At the time it was unheard-of for professors to entertain students in their own homes. Monod broke with tradition as students came and went as they pleased. Many of these were impressed not only by the Professor but also by his wife. She attracted the admiration of the young collegiates, and together they won the students' hearts. Their aim throughout was to show the fruit of their faith in a very practical way.

One of the many benefits Monod derived from his new position was his long vacations. These allowed him to go on extended preaching tours. He preached in many parts of France and Europe. He also attended the inaugural meeting of the Evangelical Alliance in England, during August 1846, before going on to preach in Scotland. He loved visiting Protestant countries where the gospel had been faithfully preached for many years. He found something refreshing about it, a freedom unknown to many European countries where the gospel had been suppressed for centuries.

On one of his tours he arrived late in the evening at the home of a pastor friend with whom he was to stay the night. His friend, who was expecting him to preach said, 'At what o'clock would you like to preach tomorrow?' 'I can't preach here: I must start early, as I am expected elsewhere in the course of the day.'–'Well! you can hold a meeting this evening, can't you?'–'But all your folks must be gone to bed by this time.'–'Oh! that makes no difference. We'll ring the bell: you will have them all.' Within no time the church was full and the service began.

Though he enjoyed his lifestyle at Montauban Monod could not resist a call from the Reformed church in Paris in 1847. This was a golden opportunity to preach at the heart of the nation. One of its prize preachers was unable to continue his ministry due to age and fatigue. He proposed that Monod should come as his assistant and share the preaching. When the other ministers and elders of the city met to discuss the situation and vote on the matter, it was virtually unanimous with only one variant vote. He was now entering the last stages of his life and his end was in view.

In 1849, not long after his arrival in Paris, a secession took place in the National Reformed Church and was led by his brother Frederic. Though there was a severance in their church connections there was never a severance in their hearts. They remained as firmly attached to each other as ever. The point at issue was not great, but large enough to cause some to secede. The dispute revolved around the Church's Confession of Faith. Some wanted a new Confession of Faith to be immediately drawn up. Others, like Adolphe, agreed there was a need either for a new Confession altogether, or a revised version, but that the time was not ripe to raise the question. These voted to keep the *status quo*. When the split finally came Adolphe found himself on one side of the divide with Frederic on the other.

In many ways Monod could have used this opportunity to pay back the National Church for its harsh treatment of him by the Consistory at Lyons. It would have been easy to align himself with Frederic and his supporters but he chose to remain in the National Church. It was issues not personalities which he supported. As he saw it there was insufficient grounds to leave the Church. The reason why Frederic and Adolphe never fell out over the issue was their mutual respect for each other's spiritual integrity.

One strange thing to develop out of this affair was Adolphe's appointment to his brother's vacant pulpit.

'How comes it,' he said, 'that I am today taking the place of my elder brother, that faithful disciple of Christ, that pastor respected by all in his retirement, and honoured by all in the sacrifice which he made? It is vain for me to say to myself that my occupation of the post which he so long filled is another pledge of that fraternal affection which unites us as tenderly as ever. My heart breaks at the very thought of even an apparent separation. But after all . . . can we do otherwise than follow, each one, the path which we believe to have been traced for us by God?'

The omens for a prolonged ministry in Paris were not good. A few years after his arrival his health began to deteriorate. There were times of forced relaxation, which he hated, times when he had to take extended vacations in an attempt to regain his strength. He had a growing awareness of the brevity of life as he saw himself hastening towards eternity. By the middle of 1855 his health had completely broken down. He had preached what was to be his last sermon in May on Whit Sunday. By September he was confined to bed. His public ministry was at an end. His illness was a lingering death with no hope of recovery. The only thing left was to wait patiently for the end. For the next seven months someone attended him at his bedside day and night. Several medical students also took turns in sitting with him through his nightly vigils. These all loved him.

This last illness lasted until 6 April the following year, when he died. Though it was severe it was not his greatest trial. Throughout his life he had struggled with a melancholic temperament and was naturally prone to depression. It was only the light of the gospel that kept the spectre of despair at bay. From his sick bed he wrote to someone with a similar temperament:

> One day, July, 1827, [his conversion] as I was walking in the streets of Naples, oppressed as usual by inconsolable melancholy, the thought suddenly occurred to me: 'Others have been melancholy before you; they found peace in the Gospel; why should you not find it there also?' Urged by this thought, I returned home, cast myself on my knees, and prayed as I had never before prayed in my life . . . Hope had found an entrance to my heart, and when I once had struck into this path, the God of Jesus Christ, to whom I had learnt to commit myself, did for me the rest little by little. Under the cross of Christ, there remained for me only a general shade of sadness, which the pains that I now endure, and the prospect of death, have entirely dissipated . . . feeling from the bottom of my heart that I was miserable and helpless, I cast myself, without reasoning and without reserve, into the arms of a God of love, revealed to me by the Gospel . . . Who was it that then gave a new power of persuasion to a thought which had occurred to me a hundred times before? It was God, the good God; it was His Spirit, speaking to my heart on the day that He had fixed, after allowing me to remain in distress long enough to appreciate His deliverance.

His last remaining months saw a group of friends gather around him for what was to be his final ministry. They listened Sunday by Sunday as he struggled to speak. His messages were taken down and sent to his beloved church in Lyons. Several of these were headed 'A

Dying Man's Regrets'. The fact that he was on the brink of death added weight to his words. He also had time to reflect on his past life which to him upon review almost seemed fruitless. He was a preacher and pastor to the very end and these addresses show it. They were to become his last written work and were published just as they were spoken, unedited. As long as Christian, evangelical literature is read, *Adolphe Monod's Farewell* to his friends and to his church will be remembered as the most lasting monument he left to the glory of God.

23
Thomas Chalmers
(1780-1847)

Thomas Chalmers was unquestionably the foremost Scottish leader of the early nineteenth century. He commanded the respect of men of state as well as men in the Church. His intellect and eloquence made him stand out among his peers and attract the attention of the masses. He combined the mind of a Paul with the impetuosity of a Peter. Everything he did was done with all his might. His spirit was so highly pitched that he was ready to attack the most formidable strongholds of darkness with an enthusiasm bordering on fanaticism. There was no challenge too difficult and no obstacle too great for him to attempt. He invariably brought the best out of others and his command of people made him a natural leader.

Chalmers was born for publicity as some men are born for obscurity. From his earliest days he began to reveal his fiery temperament. He managed to do things which others could never have done because of his tremendous influence both in and out of the Church. From Chalmers sprung a whole new generation of Scottish Evangelicals.

His conversion introduced a new spiritual ethos into the Church. Men of renown emanated from his ministry. He was also one of the founders of the Free Church of Scotland. Yet for all his qualities as a leader and abilities as an administrator it was as a preacher that he excelled. Though science had been his first love he preached with all the passion of a poet. He was no cool, calculating mathematician but a man whose Celtic blood boiled to make the Saviour known to lost sinners.

Chalmers was born into a godly family in Anstruther, Fifeshire on 17 March 1780. His father was a shipowner, a general merchant and an elder in the Church of Scotland. At school Chalmers was remembered as, 'one of the idlest, strongest, merriest and most generous-hearted boys in Anstruther school.' Even when he went to St Andrews, near his home, at the age of eleven, to undertake an university course he was completely unprepared for it. One contemporary wrote that he was, 'volatile and boyish and idle in his habits, ill-prepared by previous education . . . for reaping the full benefit of a college course.' Yet from these small beginnings was to grow a strong, towering oak.

St Andrews, at the time of Chalmers' attendance, was the domain of the Moderates, the name given to those divines in the Church who tolerated patronage by the laity and who were critical of man-made creeds and confessions. They preached morality, with almost nothing of the supernaturalism of true Christianity. Chalmers himself defected from his father's strong Calvinism to a more philosophical approach to the Bible. It was rare to find any who still held to the old faith. William Hamilton Burns, father of William Chalmers Burns, a contemporary, was an exception. He held firm to his Calvinism and the Westminster Confession of Faith. 'We inhaled,' wrote Chalmers, 'not a distaste only, but a positive contempt for all that is properly and peculiarly gospel, insomuch that our confidence was nearly as entire in the sufficiency of natural theology as in the sufficiency of natural science.'

St Andrews was to open the vistas of his mind to an increasing interest in academic studies. His 1793-94 session was, as his son-in-law and biographer William Hanna wrote, 'Chalmer's intellectual birth-time.' Mathematics became his constant companion and was to him all-absorbing. When he should have been listening to a theological lecture he was so abstracted by his mathematical thoughts that he heard nothing of it. Theology held little attraction for him even though he was technically a theological student.

As a ministerial candidate he was expected to present written prayers for the morning and evening devotions. These were so good that many of the people of St Andrews would gather to hear them. He was still only sixteen when this took place. Yet in his broad Scottish accent they were memorable events. One of his auditors, W.H.Burns, after a lapse of fifty-two years could still remember the impression they made upon his audience.

> The wonderful flow of eloquence, vivid, ardent description of the attributes and works of God, and still more perhaps the astonishing harrowing delineation of the miseries, the horrid cruelties, immoralities, and abominations inseparable from war, which always came in more or less in connexion with the bloody warfare in which we were engaged with France, called forth the wonderment of the hearers. (Mrs Oliphant, *Thomas Chalmers*, p.8)

These prayers, needless to say, were more like sermons for men than addresses to God. Their aim was to give practical experience to the ministerial students. But instead of forming a true spirit of prayer they only succeeded in creating a professional clericism.

When Chalmers left university at the age of eighteen he began his career as a private tutor, but this was to end in wrangling. His hot-headedness and impetuosity forced him to resign. Soon after he was ordained into the ministry. His early entrance, at the age of nineteen, indicates his extraordinary abilities. If his theology was suspect his attitude toward the ministry was even more so. He saw it as a stop-gap before a Professorship, his chief ambition. To this young aspiring genius human accolades meant everything. When he was appointed to his first pastorate at Kilmany in 1802, after an assistant ministry in Cavers, Teviotdale, his thoughts were still on the Professorial role. As things happened he was also invited to assist Dr. Playfair in the Mathematics chair at St Andrews. This seemed a natural stepping-stone to the fulfilment of his dearest ambition. He accepted both positions, a pluralist indeed.

What a change of events can be caused by conversion. Here was Chalmers, destined to become the chief antagonist of pluralism, taking up both occupations. This was due to his low opinion of the ministry. He believed that a minister had five days in the week in which to pursue whatever studies he wished and that Saturday evening was more than ample to prepare his sermons for Sunday. His conversion was to drastically change his whole approach to ministerial work.

Much later in 1825 when the Plurality debate was at its height, one of its supporters quoted from a 'so-called' anonymous article. This was only a ploy to see how Chalmers would react to his own words written in defence of a previously held position. His reply ended in a public act of repentance. His opponent quoting him said, 'After the satisfactory discharge of his parish duties, a minister may enjoy five days in the week of uninterrupted leisure for the prosecution of any science in which his taste may dispose him to engage.' Chalmers replied:

> Sir, that pamphlet I now declare to have been a production of my own, published twenty years ago . . . Verily I believed that my unfortunate pamphlet had long ere now descended into the tomb of merited oblivion .
> . . But since that gentleman has brought it forward in the face of this House, I can assure him that I feel grateful to him from the bottom of my heart, for the opportunity he has afforded me of making a public recantation of the sentiments it contains . . . At the time when I wrote it, I did not conceive that my pamphlet would do much evil . . . I now confess myself to have been guilty of a heinous crime, and I now stand a repentant culprit before the bar of this venerable Assembly.

After rehearsing the background to what prompted him to write it in the first place Chalmers went on to say:

> Alas! Sir, so I thought in my ignorance and pride. I have now no reserve in saying that the sentiment was wrong, and that, in the utterance of it, I penned what was most outrageously wrong. Strangely blinded that I was! What, Sir, is the object of mathematical science? Magnitude and the proportions of magnitude. But then, Sir, I had forgotten two magnitudes – I thought not of the littleness of time – I recklessly thought not of the greatness of eternity. (William Hanna, *Memoirs of the Life and Writings of Thomas Chalmers,* Vol.3. pp.77-78)

This pamphlet had been written in defence of a minister's right to

229

academic pursuits other than those directly connected with his ministry. The attack had come from Dr Playfair, his old senior professor in Mathematics. It is little wonder that these two men never got on together. Things grew worse as the old doctor time and again insulted him. Eventually Chalmers, whose fiery temperament was always simmering, could stand it no more. When the classes were sitting their examinations he stood up and gave an unprecedented invective against his colleague, much to the chagrin of the other professors, who looked on in amazement. It is not surprising to find that he was dismissed from his post.

This dismissal did not bring an end to the conflict. 'Inefficiency as a teacher,' says Hanna, 'had been alleged as the ground of his dismissal; and if that allegation was received, his prospects of academic distinction would be blasted.' This so incensed the aspiring academic that he determined to go back to St Andrews as an independent lecturer in Mathematics and Chemistry, his eloquence and influence soon attracting a host of students around him. This action both irritated and annoyed the University faculty. Eventually, after proving himself to the faculty and students, he finally surrendered his crusade and settled down to a pastoral life in Kilmany.

Several years were to pass before Chalmers would experience salvation. After a year of searching and several months of ill health he read William Wilberforce's book, *Practical View*. This finally brought him to realise his own inadequacy and to acknowledge the sufficiency of the Saviour alone to save him. Where morality had failed the Mediator had succeeded. His conversion took place in 1811. It was at this time that he wrote in his journal: 'O God, make me feel the firmness of the ground I tread upon, and enable me to give all my mind to Thy Word . . . my sentiment was a total, an unreserved, and a secure dependence on Christ the Saviour.'

The following year he married, and at the comparatively young age of thirty-four he received a call from Tron Church, one of the most influential churches in Glasgow. Several of its members had attended a funeral service conducted by Chalmers where some unusual circumstances surrounded the death of the deceased. Because of this a huge congregation had gathered. He preached with such intensity that many of those present admitted, they had never heard anything like it. After the funeral the wheels of change began to turn.

A report was submitted to the Tron Church and Chalmers was put at the head of their list of candidates.

His new church gave him national fame while his preaching was unparalleled. Tron Church suddenly became the heart of the city. Even his midweek meeting, held during the day, filled the church to capacity. Merchants, students and the ordinary man of the street squeezed together to hear him give his 'Astronomical Sermons' based on Psalm 8:4, 'What is man, that you are mindful of him, and the son of man that you visit him?' At times even the church doors were forced open with the crush of people wishing to enter. For someone who always read his sermons his preaching was riveting. Only during his gatherings in the poor areas of Glasgow did he resort to impromptu speech, when a hundred to a hundred and twenty people were present. In his pulpit it was not unknown for him to stamp his foot in the excitement of his delivery. One highly acclaimed critic who was accused of 'slaying poets right and left' was totally bemused by him. 'I know not what it is,' he wrote, 'but there is something altogether remarkable about this man. It reminds me more of what one reads of as the effect of the eloquence of Demosthenes than anything I ever heard.'

On one occasion when he was expected to address the Church's General Assembly the building was surrounded hours before the meeting. Even the officials found it hard to gain access. The following year 1817, when he visited London to preach on behalf of the Missionary Society, the public's desire to hear him was overwhelming. Surrey Chapel was full four hours before the commencement of the meeting. For an hour and a half the congregation sat enraptured by him. Afterwards, all London was full of his praise. Even William Wilberforce noted that, 'All the world wild about Dr. Chalmers,' and 'The tartan beats us all.'

For all the attention he aroused and the clammering crowds he attracted, it was for those who never heard him that he was most concerned. Those teeming tenements in Saltmarket, Glasgow, where the poor lived, worried him. These never darkened the doors of a church from one year to the next. Though Tron Church was on their doorstep it was populated by the invading middle and upper classes from the suburbs. It was the ungodly people of the Saltmarket he set about to save. He organized his church members into groups of two to visit homes and speak with children and parents on spiritual things. He often spent four or five hours a day visiting the hovels of these destitute people. It is said that he had visited 11,000 homes in one year during this time.

In 1823 Chalmers left Glasgow and moved to St Andrews to become Professor of Moral Philosophy. Many thought it was a bad move to leave such an influential position for the dusty cloisters of the University. However Chalmers himself had already made it quite clear that the only thing that could draw him away from Glasgow was a Professorship. This hint was quickly taken up by St Andrews. To him the preparation of a few ministerial students was of greater importance than preaching to a multitude in Glasgow. It was one of his convictions that a changed ministry was the chief need if there was to be a general renewal in the Church. In this way a nation not just a city could be touched. It may have been easier for people to have understood if he had been offered the Theology Chair. They failed to see his reasoning in accepting Moral Philosophy. But he made his position quite clear: 'Moral philosophy', he said, 'is with me the philosophy of morals – the philosophy of duty!'

For someone as energetic as Chalmers, life in St Andrews must have appeared slow. Compared with his previous public ministry his new situation was one of partial obscurity. Even he had doubts at times as to whether or not he had made the right decision. But his light could not be hid for long. Neither could St Andrews keep such an illustrious figure. In 1828, after five years at St Andrews, Edinburgh University offered him its Divinity Professorship. This was a far more influential position than that of St Andrews, and Chalmers accepted it.

Through his lectures Chalmers affected a whole new generation of men who were to become influential in the Scottish Church. Preachers like Robert Murray McCheyne and missionaries like Alexander Duff were captivated by him. Andrew Bonar could write of him: 'New fields of thought were daily opened up.' His example remained before them even when they had left his care.

In 1834 developments in the Scottish Church took a new turn. For the first time the ascending Evangelical party gained a majority in the General Assembly and the supremacy of the Moderates came to an end. This change of fortunes allowed them to pass new Acts regarding church expansion. Chalmers was instated as the Convener of the Church Extension Committee. He was quick to devise a plan to promote the churches' influence. This consisted of seeking financial aid from the people to build new churches and acquiring a grant from the Government to pay for new incumbents. The Government, after hearing a Commission set up to investigate the plan, turned down their proposal. Chalmers' response was to go to the people alone for help. He travelled extensively throughout Scotland seeking funds to accomplish the programme. Between 1834 and 1841 two hundred and twenty-two churches were built.

During this time Chalmers accepted an invitation to speak in London on the 'Establishment.' As he entered the auditorium to address a very auspicious gathering he was greeted with rapturous applause. Over the next few days his series of lectures gave his hearers an increasing appreciation of his gifts. By the last day one of them wrote:

> The tide that had been rising and swelling each succeeding day now burst all bounds. Carried away by the impassioned utterances of the speaker long ere the close of his finest passages were reached, the voice of the lecturer was drowned in applause, the audience rising from their seats, waving their hats above their heads, and breaking out into tumultuous approbation. (Mrs Oliphant, *Thomas Chalmers,* p.193)

Another major development to come out of the 1834 General Assembly, was the introduction of the right of veto for heads of families on ministerial nominees. This new law was considered an infringement on the rights of patrons. Within no time two parties sprung up within the Church. Those who supported the veto were called the 'Non-Intrusionists,' while those who did not the 'Intrusionists.' This latter group maintained the absolute right of patrons to give livings to whomsoever they wished. This difference of opinion escalated into a full scale quarrel and was to end almost ten years later, in 1843, in what is termed the Disruption.

The main point at issue was the old vexed question regarding the crown rights of Jesus to rule in his Church. State interference was viewed as an usurpation of his authority. This recurring debate in Scotland has often proved one of its most sensitive and provocative. Yet the divide within the Church was not simply a matter of party loyalties between the Evangelicals and Moderates. Many of the Moderates also were in complete sympathy with the Non-Intrusionist position. After several test cases in the Courts, all met with the same result – the law was on the side of the patrons. Even the House of Lords favoured the Intrusionists. When the Moderates finally capitulated wholesale to the Intrusionists in 1841, a parting of the ways became inevitable.

Throughout this long and drawn-out battle Chalmers had remained at the head of the Non-Intrusionist party. Though he was an ardent supporter of the principle of a National Church he could not submit to the State's supposed supremacy in matters of church affairs. On 18 May 1843 he headed a group of nearly five hundred ministers and elders out of St Andrews Church, Edinburgh to establish 'The Free Church of Scotland', an event that became known as the 'Disruption'. Little did the opposition think that so many would have seceded. It was a triumph both for Chalmers and for freedom of conscience. Many of these men who came out left everything behind, church buildings, manses, stipend and security.

However, there were greater issues at stake than these, a conscience void of offence. The first thing Chalmers did was to organise a Sustentation Fund to support those ministers who had come out. Though he never agreed with 'Voluntaryism' (that is, that the support of the Church was the sole responsibility of its members apart from state aid), he saw no other way for the emerging Church to remain intact as a body without significant material support from its members. From its very beginnings the Free Church went on from strength to strength. Buildings were erected, ministers were supported, numbers increased and souls were saved. In short, the Free Church saw the goodness of the Lord in meeting their every need both materially and ministerially. As Chalmers himself could say, 'The Church is finished, the schools are flourishing, our ecclesiastical machinery is about as complete, and all in good working order. God has indeed heard my prayer, and I would now lay down my head in peace and die.'

The following year, Free Church College was opened with Chalmers as its head. He also began his Territorial Scheme. This was an experiment he had long cherished but had never had the opportunity of trying it. It was aimed at winning the careless, poor and downtrodden people of Edinburgh to Christ. To help facilitate this he took upon himself one of the poorest areas in Edinburgh and looked for God's blessing upon his efforts. He said:

> I have determined to assume a poor district of two thousand people and superintend it myself, though it be a work greatly too much for my declining strength and means. Yet such do I hold to be the efficiency of the method with the Divine blessing, that perhaps, as the concluding act of my public life, I shall make the effort to exemplify what as yet I have only expounded. (Mrs Oliphant, *Thomas Chalmers,* p. 243)

This new scheme at West Port in Edinburgh was to become the chief joy of his life. It thrilled him to see it progressing even though it called for tremendous exertion on his part. However, it was to be his last major contribution to the Church. After a somewhat turbulent career Chalmers died at home in his sleep. The day before he had gone to church with his friend William Cunningham, had come home and after lunch was heard to say as he walked in the garden, 'O Father, my Heavenly Father!' Like Enoch of old he knew what it was to walk with God. The company and fellowship he enjoyed was the result of the new life he had received. When his family found him on the morning of 1 June 1847, he appeared as one in complete rest. The day before he had said, 'I'm fond of the Sabbath. Hail sacred Sabbath Morn!' It was his last Sabbath in this world. The following day he was to enter that eternal Sabbath where the souls of Christians rest and their works do follow them.

24
John Elias
(1774-1841)

John Elias, like his Old Testament namesake Elijah, was an exceptionally powerful figure. He feared and favoured no one, speaking with such authority that people were known to cry out under his preaching. His sermons made such an impression on them that it became impossible to contain their emotions. It was as if fire fell from heaven at his behest. His logical and oratorical style of preaching was so impressive and effective that many considered him the greatest preacher Wales ever produced, greater even than Daniel Rowland of Llangeitho.

He was christened John Jones and was the son of Elias Jones. It is said that when John Jones of Edern, one of his ministerial examiners, heard he was also called John Jones, he enquired as to his father's name, and he was told, 'Elias Jones'. 'Good gracious!' he exclaimed, 'call the boy John *Elias,* or else we shall be all John Joneses before long.' John Elias belongs to the second generation of Methodist leaders in Wales, the leaders of the Evangelical Awakening – Howel Harris, Daniel Rowland and William Williams, Pantycelyn – having passed on before Elias emerged as a preacher.

Elias was born in the hamlet of Aber-erch, near Pwllheli, North Wales in May 1774. It was not until he was married that he ferried across the Menai Strait to live in Anglesey, where he lived with his wife and family for the remainder of his life. Anglesey became not only his home but the scene of his greatest exploits.

Elias was remarkable in many ways. He was brought up under the caring eye of his grandfather and attended the local parish church. Their attachment to one another was forged early on. His grandfather doted on him and took tremendous interest in his development. He taught Elias to read before his fourth birthday and by the time he was six he could read his Welsh Bible without any difficulty or help.

His ability to read, which was very unusual at the time, was used to good effect by his grandfather. If a preacher was late for some reason he would get John to read a passage from the Bible. When the people saw him standing and reading they soon became very attentive. They were not accustomed to hearing such a young boy read from the Bible. Once, when a preacher was late, his grandfather put him into the pulpit to read. As he began to read the restless and agitated congregation soon became quiet. After reading a few verses from the Sermon on the Mount, he suddenly stopped, looked round, and found to his consternation the preacher waiting at the pulpit door for him to finish. It was his first time in the pulpit and one he was only too glad to vacate.

His grandfather often warned him about swearing, lying and Sabbath-breaking. He was also keen to take him to church with him. On Sundays they could be seen walking together, hand in hand, to the church. Elias was always very serious. Perhaps it was due to the amount of time he spent with his grandfather. As a young boy he had an unusual sense of eternity. The impression of heaven, hell and judgment were often uppermost in his mind. These were not figments of an over-active imagination, but the start of a spiritual awareness rarely found in children so young. Before his seventh birthday he had read from Genesis to the middle of Jeremiah. Every day he read a small portion from his Bible. When he contracted smallpox and became delirious his family thought he was going to die. After several trying days he opened his eyes, though temporarily blind, and found his grandfather sitting by his bedside. The tearful old man asked, if he could remember his Bible lesson? 'Yes', he said, and began quoting a chapter from Jeremiah.

Elias never went to school, and all he learnt was from his grandfather. His own father was a weaver and smallholder which meant there was little chance of him going to school. Since he could read he was able to read several religious books. These made an indelible impression on him. As he grew up he longed to join the Welsh Calvinistic Methodists but was afraid because he thought he was not really converted.

As a young man his one ambition was to hear Daniel Rowland of Llangeitho preach. Rowland was now an old man, and the likelihood of him preaching again in North Wales was remote. While Elias was making plans to visit Llangeitho he heard of Rowland's death. When he heard the news, he wept, because he thought that he had missed his opportunity of great spiritual benefit from his ministry.

At what time Elias was actually converted is uncertain. Though he had been helped by a sermon of Robert Roberts of Clynnog, it was more in the way of assurance than conversion. On his way home from Bala, after attending his first Calvinistic Methodist Association Meeting, he was gripped by Paul's words in 2 Corinthians 5:18,19, 'the ministry of reconciliation'. They began to take on an entirely new meaning to him. He saw, as if written by a sunbeam, the doctrine of a dual imputation, how that God in a moment can transfer the righteousness of Christ to a sinner and the sinner's guilt to Christ. This sudden and powerful impression came as a summons from God to preach.

Because of the ungodliness that surrounded him at home Elias felt the need to leave and live with a godly family. He went to work for Griffith Jones, a Methodist exhorter in Penmorfa, near Portmadoc. Once, when a visiting preacher called at Jones' house, the whole family, labourers and neighbours, were called to hear him. Afterwards a communion service was to take place but Elias was sent to go and turn the hay. Later, he was found in the field unable to work. As the tears rolled down his cheeks, Griffith Jones asked him what was the matter. Elias replied, 'Oh my dear uncle, that word broke my heart, *And those that were ready went in, and the door was shut*; you shut the door today and I was out.' Elias was as sensitive as he was serious. He thought the door of mercy had been closed and there was now no hope for him. It was not until he was received into fellowship with the Welsh Calvinistic Methodists that he really believed he was saved. Even then he felt he might draw back and become engrossed in the world, and the sense of his own weakness made him tread carefully.

While Elias was living with Griffith Jones in Penmorfa he was encouraged to read and pray during family devotions. He was so good at it that Jones asked him to alternate with him. His proficiency as a speaker meant that he was often asked to read the Bible after a night school he attended. Later, the other students encouraged him to speak a few words of exhortation. Without realising it his life as a preacher had now begun. Sometimes, if a visiting preacher was unable to fulfil an engagement, he was asked to lead the meeting. Suddenly, and unintentionally, he began to be hailed as a rising Methodist preacher.

When his ministry began to mushroom people's opinions of him differed. Many admired his gifts but some were sceptical of the young upstart. Elias was not officially recognised as an 'exhorter' or preacher until Christmas Day 1794. He was still not quite twenty-one years old. In 1811, when the Methodists seceded from the Church of England to form the Welsh Calvinistic Methodist denomination, he was one of its first candidates for ordination. His preaching itineracy took him throughout much of North Wales and to several Welsh congregations meeting in Liverpool and Manchester. As people thronged to hear him he thought it was due to the novelty of his youth. But there was something unusual about his preaching, a power which had not been seen in Wales for a long time. There was steel in his words and God was with him as he was with Elijah of old.

As is often the case comparisons are made between preachers. When Elias first started to preach some of the older people began comparing him with Howell Harris. Rarely did they compare him with Daniel Rowland because they considered him '*the* Prince of Preachers.' Some thought he was at least Harris' equal if not his superior in preaching. But natural preferences often affect a person's judgment and no two people always agree in every point. Owen Thomas, a younger Welsh preacher of the day, living in Liverpool, wrote of him:

> As a preacher, we feel that John Elias is altogether indescribable. There was something in him that makes it impossible, we think, to convey an adequate conception of him to those who never heard him; and there was something in him that made his influence over his hearers incomparably great. In those special qualities in which he excelled, he was, in our estimation, so much superior to all others that not only was there no one like him, but no one came near enough to be within the scope of comparison with him. He was, without a doubt, the most popular preacher, taking the whole Principality, that ever rose in Wales. (Owen Jones, *Some of the Great Preachers of Wales,* p. 224)

This assessment was made by someone who had often heard him. Yet William Roberts of Amlwch told Owen Thomas, 'You have never heard John Elias'. 'Of course', Dr Thomas replied, 'I have heard him preaching hundreds of times.' 'No, never,' Roberts countered, 'you heard *Mr* Elias – you never heard *John* Elias!'

The difference was one of chronology. Roberts had known Elias much earlier than Thomas and had seen him in his raw, unpolished state. Thomas had seen the finished stone, shining in all its glory. Under Evan Richardson's tuition at his school in Caernarfon, Elias had lost much of his initial rawness. In his early days Elias had a very awkward style and was far too demonstrative in his delivery. Richardson made several suggestions to help him overcome these weaknesses. For William Roberts Elias never excelled those early days for force, warmth and originality. To him, they were his best days. Yet both, Roberts and Thomas, agreed that they had never heard anyone quite like him.

Elias had come into contact with Evan Richardson due to his desire to improve himself. He realised his own shortcomings as a preacher because of his limited education. When he approached the elders at their monthly meeting to ask their permission to study English in Manchester for a year, he was refused. Instead of encouraging him they rebuked him for his pride and egotism. They thought he wanted to gain some advantage and become a popular preacher. Little did they know him or the purity of his motives. This

240

rebuff acts as an example of how wrong actions can be carried out by right motives. They were sincere men, yet obviously wrong. Elias' only reason for wanting to learn English was in order to preach better. It was purely functional, not personal. English allowed him greater access to many books still unavailable to non-English speakers. Later however, when he requested to study English at Richardson's home nobody opposed it.

After a few months with Richardson at Caernarfon Elias resumed his itinerant ministry. He was an astute scholar and soon grasped the elements of English grammar which enabled him to preach both in English and Welsh. During his stay with Richardson Elias was highly regarded by his fellow students. Indeed the younger of these were awestruck by him. Two of them returning from one of his services were discussing his preaching. 'Why does John Elias accompany his words with such motions, and why does he stretch forth his arm?' said one. 'O,' said the other, 'it is to point out the way to heaven.' 'Does he know the road there?' 'Yes, and all the people says he does uncommonly well.'

After his marriage in February 1799, he went to live in Llanfechell, near Cemaes, Anglesey. This island, now linked to the mainland by two bridges over the Menai Strait, was extremely irreligious and immoral, and underwent an unprecedented transformation. Drunkenness, sexual laxity and the plundering of wrecked ships were habitual practices among them. Shortly they were to be replaced by sobriety, morality and benevolence. This moral revolution was the result of a spiritual revival. It is true to say that there is no such thing as a 'Christian society', only a society touched by the Christian ethic. Before this every effort to convert the people of Anglesey had failed. What Julius Caesar once said of Britain, Elias could well have said of Anglesey, 'I came, I saw, I conquered.' This was achieved not by his own power but by God's power. He wielded the Spirit's sword in such a way that very few of his sermons failed to convert. Once he preached to an estimated 10,000 people, a quarter of the island's population. The spiritual transformation was phenomenal.

This moral change came about through Elias' defiance of all ungodliness. Wherever it appeared Elias challenged it. He was a fearless evangelist. Nothing could deter or daunt him. He attacked the very heart of Satan's strongholds. Through his exertions he managed

241

to bring to a final end the annual fair at Rhuddlan, in Denbighshire. This was held on Sundays and was used by the farmers for hiring labourers to reap the harvest. They would come to the fair with their scythes ready for work. Drink and drunkenness was a traditional part of the proceedings. When Elias stood on the steps of the local Inn to preach on, 'Six days thou shalt work, but on the seventh day thou shalt rest: in earing time and in harvest thou shalt rest' (Exod. 34:21), thousands heard him. Before he had finished praying, men began to hide their scythes and sickles. They were so overcome by what he said they became fearful of God.

It is generally accepted that behind every great man there is a great woman, and this was true of Elias. His first wife ran a shop in Llanfechell in order to support him preaching. She refused to bother him with any material concerns because she considered him engaged in something far too important to distract him with such mundane matters. It would be hard to find a wife more self-sacrificing than she. Everything she did was to set him free to preach whenever and wherever it was necessary. She died in 1828 and in 1830 Elias married the widow of Sir John Bulkeley of Bodedern and moved to Llangefni, where he remained for the rest of his life.

Elias' sermon construction was quite simple. The first twenty minutes were spent expounding the text and explaining what the various commentators had said. Then he drew out its implications and applied them to every kind of person imaginable. He always preached extemporarily. 'Paper', he said, 'is a very poor thing in which to carry fire.' And he always seemed to be ablaze with his subject. His fire was often fuelled by his tears, which he shed profusely in prayer. His pulpit prayers often reflected his private prayers. Sometimes, when his wife called him for a meal he would appear with his cheeks still wet with tears from prayer. His daughter wrote:

> To live in his family was to a great degree heaven upon earth. I can never forget the light that followed our family worship, and the pleasure and edification we found in conversations. And never can I forget the tears I saw on the chair in his study by which he bent his knees; though nothing was heard, we were well aware that he was pouring out a profusion of tears in his secret prayers. Many times did I observe him coming out of his chamber, like Moses coming down from the mountain, with so much

of the image of God upon his countenance that no one could look him in the face. (Owen Jones, *Some of the Great Preachers of Wales,* p.275)

There was nothing of the exhibitionist in him. He was a humble, prayerful man. When a roofer came to mend his leaking roof, he climbed past Elias' study window. As he looked in, he saw him lying prostrate on the floor. At first, he thought nothing of it and carried on working. Afterwards, he again happened to look into the study. Much to his surprise, he saw Elias still lying there. He was so shocked at this that he thought he must either be ill or dead. He rushed to tell a servant girl who calmly told him that he was praying.

It is impossible to think of Elias without thinking of passion. Every sermon was a passionate appeal to sinners. His intense feeling often made him very dramatic in the pulpit and won him universal acclaim. This theatrical gift, and especially his commanding eye, pointing forefinger and tense silences, was often used to great advantage. He could hold congregations spellbound as he lived out his message before their very eyes.

However, not everyone admired this ability. One of his critics, Dr. Lewis Edwards, principal of the Welsh Calvinistic Methodist College at Bala from 1837 until his death some fifty years later wrote, 'Perhaps he would have been more acceptable to the learned if he had not acted so much.'

It should be noted that Elias never planned to be dramatic. It was just a part of his make-up. As he warmed to his subject he found it irrepressible. With huge delineative strokes he painted the most dramatic scenes imaginable before his congregation. There was no prior thought or rehearsal beforehand. He simply gave vent to his feelings in this way at the time. Towards the end of an Association meeting held in Bala, Elias preached from Isaiah 49:24:

'Shall the prey be taken from the mighty, or the lawful captive be delivered?' As he was preaching his feelings intensified until he cried out, 'Satan, what sayest thou? Shall the prey be taken from the mighty?' 'Never! I will intensify the darkness of their minds, the hardness of their hearts, the power of their sins, and the strength of their chains. Never shall the prisoners be delivered. The feeble effort of these preachers I scorn and despise.'

'Gabriel, Gabriel, messenger of the Most High God, shall the prey be taken from the mighty?' 'I am afraid not. For two days have I been hovering over this great multitude, while they hear the words of everlasting life; but I have not yet seen the chains knocked off, and the prisoners set free. And now, the meetings are nearly over, and I cannot carry the tidings home of the repentance of a single sinner.'

He then turned to the preachers upon the stage, 'What think you, ministers of the living God? Shall the prey be taken from the mighty?' 'Alas, who hath believed our report, and to whom is the arm of the Lord revealed? We have laboured in vain, and have spent our strength for nought. The Lord is as if he is hiding his face from us. We are afraid there is but poor hope of deliverance.' . . .

'Ye men of prayer, what say you? Shall the prey be taken from the mighty?' 'Lord God, *Thou* knowest. High is thy hand, and strong is Thy right hand. Oh, that Thou wouldst put forth Thy mighty power and overcome. . . '

Then looking up towards heaven he said, 'And what is the mind of the Lord respecting these captives?' 'Thus saith the Lord, even the captives of the mighty shall be taken away, and the prey of the terrible shall be delivered.' Blessed be God in heaven, there is not the slightest shadow of a doubt about the question, but everlasting certainty. The ransomed of the Lord shall return, and come to Zion, with songs and everlasting joy upon their heads. (Owen Jones, *Some of the Great Preachers of Wales,* pp.248-49)

We can only imagine the effect this kind of preaching had upon the people as they visualised the scene. His style was unmistakable. It was as if he saw every party in the drama of his sermon. Yet his preaching was not play-acting but extremely serious. Preaching on the judgment of Paul before Agrippa, Elias described him, his condition, his circumstances and his audience in such a way that one sailor shouted out, 'Shame, shame, strike off those chains from the man's hands!'

Though his unorthodox style of preaching proved exceptionally effective it needs to be remembered that Elias' only intention was to convey the gospel. It was no gimmick. Rather, he brought the gospel to the people in a way they could understand. He never aimed to impress the intelligent and learned among his congregation, but ignorant and uneducated people. Neither was it in a language unintelligible to them. His method and style was adapted to their capacity. His critic, Lewis Edwards, pandered too much to the whims of the purist and failed to see that language is only the medium and not the essence of the message.

Elias died on 8 June 1841, after several months of suffering, and was buried amidst an immense gathering at Llanfaes, near Beaumaris. As death approached he expressed a wonderful sense of peace within. One of his ministerial friends who often visited him wrote:

> The state of Elias' mind is very comfortable, and at times ecstatic. One night when in great pain, he felt so happy, that he thought he was in heaven. But he does not like to say much on this head, lest he should appear to boast. His own expressions are: 'I am as happy as to the frame of my mind as a person can be under such pain as I suffer. There is *no* cloud intercepting between my soul and my God; those comforts I used to enjoy in the means of grace and in the ministry are still flowing freely into my soul: I think they are sometimes more strong and lively in their effects now than formerly.' (Edward Morgan, *John Elias: Life, Letters and Essays,* pp.180-81)

Elias died, a man full of the Holy Spirit and the knowledge of God. He played a prominent part in drawing up the Confession of Faith of the new Welsh Calvinistic Methodist denomination in 1823 and was a keen supporter of the Bible Society and the London Missionary Society. But above all he was Wales' greatest preacher of the first half of the nineteenth century.

25
Christmas Evans
(1766-1838)

There have been many great preachers in Wales over the years but none have ever cultivated the allegorical style of preaching to such perfection as did Christmas Evans. In this respect he is often thought of and described as the John Bunyan of Wales. However, his presentation was not original: there were other Welsh preachers who utilised it. His adoption of it came after hearing the unique and seraphic Robert Roberts of Clynnog. As a young man, he probably realised that this was the best method of preaching for himself. Some preachers naturally turn everything into alliteration. Christmas Evans tended to turn everything into allegory.

His unusual name was the result of being born on Christmas day 1766, in Esgair-wen, near Llandysul, Dyfed. His father was a shoemaker who died when Christmas was still a boy. This left the family almost destitute. When his maternal uncle offered to take him home with him his mother jumped at the opportunity. This may have alleviated her immediate situation slightly but it placed Christmas in a very unhappy position. It was not from any kindred feeling that James Lewis had suggested this. Christmas was expected to earn his keep. Under his roof he received nothing but harm from this hard and often merciless man. 'It would be difficult', he later wrote, 'to find a more unconscionable man than James Lewis in the whole course of a wicked world.'

After enduring six years of abuse Christmas decided to leave his uncle's farm. He continued working as a farm labourer simply because he knew nothing else. Educationally, he had been neglected and was totally illiterate at the age of seventeen. It was not until his conversion that he finally learnt to read.

Christmas' work took him to a farm near Llwynrhydowen where the Arminian Presbyterians had a chapel. The minister, David Davies, was also a Welsh poet and literary man. Under his ministry a revival broke out and Christmas, along with several other young people, was converted. From then on he possessed an insatiable thirst for knowledge. Still more important, as he was learning to read he was also learning to pray.

About this time Christmas lost his right eye. There are several accounts of this tragedy. It is generally agreed that it was caused through a fight when six of his former friends attacked him and beat him mercilessly after his conversion. One of these struck him with a stick which resulted in the loss of his eye. He became known as the 'one-eyed preacher from Wales'.

David Davies employed Christmas on his farm as a labourer. But his unusual behaviour soon attracted his attention. After enquiring from his chief hand about him, Davies was led into the fields where Christmas was found preaching his morning sermon to the animals. In the evening he was told that his services were no longer required on the farm and that someone else would be taking his place. As Christmas thought of what he had done to merit his dismissal, Davies said, 'You are to come to my school. You shall be educated free of charge.'

For the next six months he was taught Latin Grammar. Throughout this time he cherished the hope of becoming a preacher. He thought of it, even dreamt of it, but it seemed very unlikely. The Presbyterians had a strict code of conduct debarring all ministerial candidates who did not have a college education. As a result, he left the Presbyterians and joined the Baptists. This change was not simply an act of convenience but a matter of conscience. He was already a Baptist by conviction if not in practice.

His first sermon was preached in a small country cottage. He later confessed that he had borrowed it. Unfortunately, one of his hearers, a discerning farmer, found it the following week in Beveridge's *Thesaurus Theologicus*. As a preacher it seemed that Evans' credibility had suffered a serious setback. However, the farmer was just as much impressed with Evans' prayer as he had been with his sermon. 'Still,' he said, 'I have some hope of the son of Samuel the shoemaker because the prayer was as good as the sermon.' Little did he realise that the prayer was also borrowed, culled from a book of prayers by Griffith Jones of Llanddowror.

Like most aspiring preachers Evans struggled to realise what

Christmas Evans

would be the best method of preaching. He felt that memorising sermons inhibited the Holy Spirit's freedom. He also had such a low opinion of his ability and vocabulary that he decided to give the Spirit a free rein and not prepare at all. This experiment proved a complete disaster. Yet for all that he did not give up. The preacher in him was still in his formative years.

In 1789 he attended the Baptist Association held in Maesyberllan where he was persuaded to go to the Lleyn Peninsula in North Wales as an evangelist. This obscure place soon became the training ground for his future usefulness. Here God first began to bless his public ministry. A constant flow of people kept coming to him requesting baptism. At first he found it hard to believe that they had been converted under his ministry, but their lives soon gave eloquent testimony to the reality of their regeneration. Revival also became a marked feature of his ministry. Wherever he went blessing seemed to attend his preaching. He saw the boundaries of God's kingdom extended. 'Righteousness, peace and joy in the Holy Spirit,' abounded throughout the district. The people were joyful, happy and holy as the churches continued to flourish under his exertions.

During his time in Lleyn, in the North, he married and made his first visit as a preacher to the more prosperous South. Because of his extreme poverty he had to walk the whole way. He was so poor that he could not afford to buy a horse, even an old nag. However, he was strong and fit and returned none the worse for wear. His popularity in South Wales was instantaneous. Just the mention of his name was enough to draw a crowd. When they heard that the one-eyed preacher from the North was to preach they left everything they were doing to hear him. His eloquent portrayal of the gospel in allegories captured the Welsh imagination. Under his preaching tears flowed profusely and praise ascended triumphantly. The unsuppressed 'Amens' of the congregation often resounded throughout the building or in the open air. He wrote at this time:

> The chapels and burying-grounds were filled with people who crowded to hear me in the middle of harvest time. In the evening I frequently preached in the open air, and the singing and rejoicing continued till broad daylight. Such a spirit of tenderness descended upon the hearers that they wept floods of tears and cried aloud. Whole multitudes, men and women, seemed melted by the power of the Word . . . I continued to be thus inspired wherever I went, so that preaching was a delight to me. The same people would gather to hear me fifteen or twenty times in the counties of Cardigan, Pembroke, Carmarthen, Glamorgan, Monmouth and Brecon. And the excitement then produced, especially in the districts of Cardigan and Pembrokeshire, inclined the whole country to think more favourably of religion.

It was also in South Wales that he first preached at a Baptist Association Meeting held in Felin-foel, near Llanelli. This incident was to make him a much sought-after preacher. The congregation had gathered to hear two of Wales' most renowned preachers, but something had delayed them. The organizers decided to have a preliminary sermon while they waited and sought an appropriate preacher. Due to the occasion there was a marked reluctance on the part of the other preachers to actually preach. Eventually, Timothy Thomas, Evans' first Baptist minister, who always liked to boast that he had 'baptised Christmas Evans', suggested to the master of ceremonies, 'Why not ask the one-eyed lad from the North? I hear that he preaches quite wonderfully.' Some thought it was preposterous, others were sceptical and derisory. 'Surely,' they said, 'he can never ask that absurdity to preach!' But he did preach and with what power! As he began to preach those on the fringe of the meeting began to close in until the whole assembly was tightly grouped

Cil-dwrn Meeting Place, Llangefni, Anglesey

together. He preached from Colossians 1:21,22: 'And you, who once were alienated and enemies in your mind by wicked works, yet now he has reconciled in the body of his flesh through death, to present you holy and blameless, and irreproachable in his sight.' He began slowly, which at first seemed to justify his critics' assertions. Then as he warmed to the task there were shouts of praise as all misgivings evaporated. This one sermon elevated Christmas Evans in the esteem of the people to become one of Wales' most influential and sought-after preachers.

In 1791, after only two years in Lleyn, he moved to the isle of Anglesey to oversee the interests of the Baptist Association's ten societies there. He and his wife, Catherine Jones, moved to Llangefni in 1792. His stipend was a mere seventeen pounds a year which he received for the next twenty years without asking for more.

The Baptist cause in Anglesey had for some time suffered due to an internal dispute. When Evans came and saw the condition of the societies he immediately called for a day of prayer and fasting. Not long after a revival was under way. God saw fit to bless his labours, and those areas of the work which had so long languished now began to flourish. For a while the life and vitality of the church had returned as many souls were converted.

This turn of events continued for several years until the blight of Sandemanianism struck North Wales. This debilitating teaching was named after Robert Sandeman, a Scotsman. He taught that the essence of faith was found in a mental assent to truth, and nothing more. This effectively meant that faith was an act of the mind and not of the heart. The result of this was to turn the rivers of God's blessing into a drought and his fields into a desert. Faith became a dry intellectualism devoid of emotion, and its effect on preaching was devastating.

Had Christmas Evans remained firm to the old ways he might have been able to stem its tide. Unfortunately, he himself was affected and for the next twelve to eighteen months he propagated it. With such a cold wind blowing upon the Lord's vineyard nothing grew. The Baptist societies which had been rapidly progressing under his ministry suddenly lost their spiritual vitality. The chill was too much for the young seedlings and there was a dramatic dropping off in attendance. Evans was far too spiritually sensitive not to have noticed this change. He had sufficient discernment to see that something had gone terribly wrong. If he failed to understand it intellectually he felt it in his heart. He knew there was a loss, a dreadful loss, which he longed to see restored. He later wrote:

> The Sandemanian heresy affected me so much as to drive away the spirit of prayer for the salvation of sinners . . . The power that gave me zeal and confidence and earnestness in the pulpit for the conversion of souls to Christ was lost. My heart sank within me, and I lost the witness of a

251

good conscience. On Sunday night, after I had been fiercely and violently condemning errors, my conscience felt ill at ease, and rebuked me because I had lost communion and fellowship with God, and made me feel that something invaluable was now lost and wanting. I would reply that I acted according to the Word. Still it rebuked me, saying that there was something of inestimable value gone. To a very great degree had I lost the spirit of prayer, and the spirit of preaching. (Owen Jones, *Some of the Great Preachers of Wales,* p.170-71)

Poor Evans was at a loss to know what to do. This condition was slowly but surely sapping the very life out of him, and his fire and fervour were fast becoming a distant memory. But God, who is faithful, would not allow his servant to wander endlessly in these barren paths. His time to restore the wanderer had come and Evans would again feel the presence of the Lord within. God met him and restored him in that never-to-be-forgotten event on his journey over Cader Idris. This is how he wrote of that experience:

My coldness of heart towards Christ, His atonement, and the work of His Spirit – coldness of heart in the pulpit, in my secret chamber and study – pained me; especially when I remembered that that heart for fifteen years before had been burning within me . . . A day came at last, a day ever memorable in my life, when I was on my way from Dolgelly to Machynlleth. As I was climbing up towards Cader Idris, I felt it my duty to pray; though my heart was hard enough, and my spirit worldly. After I had commenced praying in the name of Jesus Christ, I could soon feel as if my shackles were falling off, and as if the mountains of snow and ice were quickly melting away. This engendered a hope in my mind for the promise of the Holy Ghost. I felt as if my whole spirit was liberating itself from some great bondage, and as if it were rising up from the grave of a hard winter. My tears profusely flowed, and I was compelled to cry out aloud, and pray for the gracious visitations of God, for the joy of His salvation, and for the Divine presence once more in the churches of Anglesey that were under my care. I prayed for all the churches, and for almost all the preachers of Wales by name. The struggle lasted for three hours. It would come over me again and again, like waves of the sea, like a tide and a strong wind, until my physical power was greatly weakened by weeping and crying. I gave myself up altogether to Christ, body and soul, talents and labour; my life, every day and every hour, and all my cares, I entrusted into the hands of Christ. In the first services I held after this event, I felt as if I had been removed from the cold regions of spiritual ice, into the pleasant lands of the promises of God. (Owen Jones, *Some of the Great Preachers of Wales*, pp.170-72)

After this he drew up a covenant with God (an exercise which he repeated often during his life) owning Christ as his only, all-sufficient Saviour and casting himself entirely upon him alone for salvation. There was also a dramatic change in his feelings. Joy and peace came flooding in and reversed the leanness of the previous year. The churches were also affected by his renewal. There was a sudden upsurge in those seeking after God. Within two short years the Baptist societies had doubled from ten to twenty.

With the increase in numbers there came a corresponding increase in responsibilities and needs. There was an acute shortage of space to accommodate the new converts. This meant that a new building programme had to be put into operation. These new churches were built on borrowed money with Evans himself becoming guarantor for the necessary loans. Not that he possessed any money or assets: it was his name alone which stood him in good stead with the creditors. In order to pay off these debts he had to make several trips to South Wales to plead the cause of the poor northern brethren. It was a humiliating experience. After preaching he would stand at the door, cap in hand, to receive gifts from the departing congregation. His frequent visits often stretched the patience of the ministers in South Wales who complained that he came there far too often. But what else could he do when the burden of these debts weighed so heavily upon him. On one occasion he was even threatened with a court action. However, after pleading with God time and again he finally knew peace within and heard nothing more of it.

To a rising generation of young ministers Christmas Evans had seemed like a father figure. He chaired their Association meetings in Anglesey, not as a superior, but as the first among equals. They respected and admired the ageing warrior. For a long time his position among them had seemed unassailable. However, sadly, situations and circumstances change, and when he should have been preparing to spend his remaining days there in Anglesey in peace he was suddenly forced to leave.

The developing situation in the societies meant that the new

253

ministers and people alike had become less and less dependent upon him. When they began to question his decisions and refused to endorse his suggested ministerial candidates, tensions between them inevitably arose. Everything now became highly emotive as the complexion of things changed. It seemed that the old man was losing his grip of things and that a change would be beneficial.

Thus in 1826, as Evans approached his sixtieth birthday and should have been thinking of easing up in his strenuous exertions, he left his beloved Anglesey for Caerphilly, near Cardiff, in the South. It was a sad day when this lone figure left the island never to return. Behind was the grave of his wife who had died only a few years earlier in 1823. Her death together with these events must have helped to precipitate his move.

When Evans came to South Wales his appeal as a preacher was as intense as ever. The shout went up, '*Christmas Evans is come!*' 'Are you sure of it?' someone replied. '*Yes,* quite sure of it; he preached at Caerphilly last Sunday.' The church in Caerphilly, like his former churches in the Lleyn peninsula and Anglesey, experienced something of God's renewed blessing after his coming. It was as if he had brought the Spirit of God with him and he wrote, 'The Spirit descended upon the church at Caerphilly, and we united to seek in the name of Christ an outpouring of divine influence.' Within a short two years a hundred and forty were added to the church by baptism. Had Christmas Evans needed any endorsement of his decision to leave Anglesey, God had given it.

His sermons in Caerphilly made such an impression on the common people that they even began measuring time by them. Because of their uniqueness they were unforgettable. They were used like hooks on which to hang memorable events. If something unusual took place it was dated as at the time of one or other of his famous sermons. They were like living coals from off the altar and were stamped in the people's memory. If there was any fault to be found in his sermons it was probably in his overstretching a point. At times he would be so carried away with his picture that sometimes he would slip from the sublime to the ridiculous. It was hard, even for this master of illustrative preaching, to hold the reins of his imagination as firmly as he would have liked. But more often than not he excelled in his delivery, his congregations gripped by his vivid descriptions.

Not long after coming to Caerphilly he remarried. Instead of marrying someone with money, as was suggested by some of his friends, he sent for his former housekeeper to come and look after him. Soon after her arrival they were married.

In 1828, after only a short time in Caerphilly, Evans moved to Cardiff. This new situation was blessed with the same old power. God was still with him. 'The divine power,' he wrote, 'upon which the old field-marshal relies, took here again some scores of prisoners of war, and I trust they will be sustained in the new army to the end.' His Cardiff ministry was short-lived and by 1832 he was again on the move.

North Wales, which had so harshly treated him only a few years before, was now beckoning him to return. Though he was happy in his new church in Caernarfon some old problems came back to haunt him. The church had a debt of eight hundred pounds, four hundred of which he had already managed to raise, but the rest remained outstanding. As the church had no funds and no possibility of raising any, there was no alternative but to go to South Wales with his begging bowl. This journey was to be his last on behalf of his Master. When he left the shires of the North it was to leave them, never to return.

On 16 July 1838, at Swansea, he preached his last sermon. It was typical of the man. His text was on Jesus' last words to his disciples in the Acts of the Apostles, chapter one, to begin preaching the gospel at Jerusalem. '"At Jerusalem, Lord?"' he said, "Yes." "Why, Lord, these are the men who crucified Thee; we are not to preach it to *them?*" "Yes, preach it to all" . . . "Suppose we meet the very man that nailed Thy hands and feet to the cross, the very man that pierced Thy side, that spat in Thy face?" "Preach the gospel to them all: tell them all that I am the Saviour; I am the same Lord over all, and rich unto all that call upon me."' As he descended from the pulpit Evans said, 'This is my last sermon.' He was taken ill and died a few days later on 19 July. As he lay dying he waved his hand and cried, 'Goodbye! Drive on!' It was his last dramatic scene and final exit, almost as if the chariot of the Lord had been sent to transport this servant of God on his last trip through the valley of the shadow of death to the gates of the celestial city.

26
Robert Murray McCheyne
(1813-43)

Robert Murray McCheyne often prayed, 'Lord, make me as holy as a pardoned sinner can be made.' In his case this seems to have come true. As a young man he was highly regarded by his peers for his godliness. It was this quality more than anything else which made him stand out amidst a generation full of rising lights. For him to have made such a universal impression also on his seniors indicates true greatness.

McCheyne was born on 21 May 1813, and died on 25 March 1843 before reaching his thirtieth birthday. Humanly speaking, he was just entering his prime when God took him. Yet the overall impression he left behind was quite amazing. His death was mourned not only by his own church in Dundee, but by the whole Church in Scotland. He died as he had lived, serving the God he loved. While visiting the sick and dying in Dundee, during an epidemic, he contracted typhus fever and after a short struggle he died.

This young man of exceptional holiness, before his premature death, was instrumental in saving many souls through his preaching. What made it so unusual was the very real sense of God which accompanied him. He gave the impression of one in constant fellowship with God. His whole demeanour acted as a reminder of Christ. What he once wrote to an aspiring preacher he himself embodied.

> Remember you are God's sword – His instrument – I trust a chosen vessel unto Him to bear His name. In great measure, according to the purity and perfections of the instrument, will be the success. It is not great talents God blesses so much as great likeness to Jesus. A holy minister is an awful weapon in the hand of God. (Andrew Bonar, *Memoir and Remains of R.M.M'Cheyne,* p.282)

Godliness was so conspicuous in him that holiness appeared like a natural endowment rather than the implantation of grace. But like every truly saved sinner, McCheyne's holiness was infused by regeneration. What differentiated him from others was that the remnants of the old nature, which often appear so dominant in others, seemed to have been wholly overcome in him.

Though he had lived a comparatively moral life before his conversion he was just as sinful as other young men. He had lived carelessly and without thought of God until his brother, David, tragically died on 8 July 1831. His close attachment to him caused him to consider his spiritual condition. His brother had often spoken to him about salvation but it had had no effect. Struck with the reality of death McCheyne now became far more serious about his soul.

From the moment of his conversion one thing seemed to dominate him, the desire to be like Christ. He longed for holiness above everything. His heart craved for it just as much as his lungs craved for air. It became his all-consuming passion. He seized every opportunity to foster his sanctification and avoided anything which tended to threaten it. His insight into man's innate depravity reveals his acquaintance with a 'heart which is deceitful above all things, and desperately wicked' (Jer. 17:9). Due to his natural introspection sin was unable to hide or camouflage itself with plausible arguments. He knew the need for vigilance because sin was always lurking in the shadows waiting to reassert itself. His diary reveals the intensity of his aspirations for holiness. He often felt a sense of his own failings which spurred him on to renewed endeavour. Christ became the end of life. Sin was considered hateful, holiness desirable, with heaven as its fulfilment.

In his preparation for preaching he often bemoaned the fact that he was better prepared in his head than in his heart. His ambition and prayer soon began to reverse this trend. 'In the morning', he wrote, 'was more engaged in preparing the head than the heart. This has been frequently my error, and I have always felt the evil of it, especially in prayer. Reform it, then, O Lord.' McCheyne knew that for his work to be really effective he needed his heart as well as his head to be right. In preaching people needed to feel the fire as well as see the light, and the need for a tender and sympathetic frame was of the highest importance. The gospel is a gentle message which needs to be preached in a gentle way.

After preaching to a very large congregation in Carron-shore, on Judas' betrayal of Christ, he wrote:

Much more tenderness than ever I felt before. Oh that I might abide in the bosom of him who washed Judas' feet, and dipped his hand in the same dish with him, and warned him, and grieved over him – that I might catch the infection of his love, of his tenderness, so wonderful, so unfathomable. (Andrew Bonar, *Memoir and Remains of R.M.M'Cheyne*, p.45)

Like many of his Scottish brethren, he possessed a very high regard for Sundays. He saw it as 'the Lord's Day', established and set aside by God from the creation for man's physical and spiritual refreshment. His personal feeling was that because it was the Lord's Day, and wholly his, that nothing should be allowed to interfere with its sanctity.

When news broke in Scotland that some of the Edinburgh and Glasgow Railway directors were about to propose to its shareholders the use of trains on Sunday, McCheyne was outraged. He saw it as a clear affront to God, an act of open rebellion against his regal rights. In response, he vehemently attacked it and wrote a tract entitled, *I Love the Lord's Day*. Here he reproved their intentions and outlined his own thinking. Today, in our modern society, the chief reasons presented against Sunday trading are more social and economic than spiritual. For McCheyne, the reverse was true; it was primarily and essentially spiritual. He wrote, 'We love to rise early on that morning, and to sit up late, that we may have a long day with God.' Sundays were like foretastes of that 'rest that remains for the people of God'. They illustrate that eternal day when God's curse is removed and he himself is praised and worshipped forever. McCheyne saw this proposal as an evidence of increasing ungodliness in the land.

What lay behind this proposal was not the people's spiritual or even their social well-being but the Company's balance sheet. His clarion call resounded:

How many may know from this that they will never be in heaven! A straw on the surface can tell which way the stream is flowing. Do you abhor a holy Sabbath? Is it a kind of hell to you to be with those who are strict in keeping the Lord's Day? The writer of these lines once felt as you do. You are restless and uneasy. You say, 'Behold what a weariness is it!' 'When will the Sabbath be gone, that we may sell corn?' Ah! soon, very soon, and you will be in hell. Hell is the only place for you. Heaven is one long, never-ending, holy Sabbath-day. There are no Sabbaths in hell. (A.Bonar, *Memoir and Remains of R.M. M'Cheyne*, p.597)

Communion services also lay very close to his heart. It was customary in the church to hold these twice a year. Though he never felt restricted by this he extended it to four. These refreshing times began on the Thursday and continued through to Monday. To those in attendance they were precious, memorable times.

For all his seriousness and strong views, McCheyne possessed a winsome personality. It would be wrong to think of him simply as a dour young Scotsman. He was often serious because of his calling and the heavy responsibilities he felt laid upon him. He was aware that if humour had not been a natural part of man's make-up he would never possess it in such abundance. His friend, John Milne of Perth, once wrote to Andrew Bonar, 'I still remember our first meeting in the Old Presbytery, and where I was sitting when you came in and shook hands; and then R. McCheyne and you coming in to me at 14 Rose Terrace, and laughing at my carte blanche to Miss – to collect a staff of lady Sabbath school teachers.' Somebody else also wrote, 'I remember Robert McCheyne coming in one morning to a private prophetical reading which some of us had, before he went to Dundee, and saying, "I felt so happy this morning that I could not refrain from skipping as I came along."' Not quite the picture we sometimes have of a dour Scotsman.

For him, holiness and happiness were not exclusive to one another. Rather, they complimented each other. Because of his impeccable character McCheyne stood out. There was something about him that made people feel he was different. His standard of holiness was so high that anyone meeting him realised that he was 'a man of God.' On his delegation work to Palestine he stayed in Alexandria in Egypt. A belligerent woman staying at his hotel often attacked Christians as being nothing more than hypocrites. 'I would not believe any of them,' she would say. 'They would cheat whenever and wherever they could.' 'Well,' said one who was patiently listening to this tirade, 'did you never in all your life see one Christian, *one* follower of the Lord Jesus Christ you believed in?' After a short pause she said, 'Yes, I saw one – a man – a minister, in this hotel, a tall, spare man, from Scotland. He was a man of God. I watched him and felt he was a genuine Christian. His very look did me good.'

It may be thought that her distant appraisal of him may have been different had she known him better. It is a fact that the hardest place for godliness to shine is at home. There, if anywhere, a person's true character will be seen. Impressing the family is the most difficult thing to do. Jesus said that, 'A prophet is not without honour except among his own people.' Yet, even here, he passed the test. On a visit to Dumfries-shire, in August 1842, he met three of his cousins. All three sisters were young and worldly-minded and thought that religion was very miserable. However when they saw how pleasant and happy he was they were surprised. As he visited the sick they accompanied him. His godliness was so infectious that before he returned back to Dundee all three were converted. Each one was gradually broken down by a sense of their own sin and pride. Later they acknowledged that it was due to the tenderness of his prayers for the sick, and his look, that had convinced them of the reality of Christianity. Initially, he was introduced as their 'clerical friend'; afterwards, as their spiritual father.

The secret of McCheyne's godliness was his prayer life. For those who commune often with God retain something of a mysterious aura. That interchange of thought and feeling, which takes place in prayer, affects the person and instils fresh supplies of grace. When the holiness of God is felt and savoured, then conformity to Christ becomes its natural consequence. Afterwards the fragrance of Christ's presence lingers, and those who know him best sense it most. When Paul instructed the church in Thessalonica to pray without ceasing he wanted them to be always in an attitude of prayer. When this is practised regularly turning to God becomes as natural as talking to a close friend. McCheyne's closest friends were often left with the distinct impression that his heart was fixed on God. Everything he did was done for God, and prayer was as natural to him as breathing.

While visiting his friend, Andrew Bonar, at Collace, a servant said, 'Oh, to hear Mr McCheyne at prayers in the mornin'! It was as if he would never gi'e ower; he had sae muckle to ask. Ye would ha'e thocht the very walls would speak again.' Even his letters breathe the air of prayer. He longed for greater prayerfulness in himself and for all God's people that they would be more earnest for revival and for his servants. In a letter to Horatius Bonar, he pleaded, 'Meet with me as we did before your communion, every night for a little, about half-past ten, at our Father's footstool, praying for a blessing from on high.'

In October 1841 special prayer unions were established throughout Scotland for God's people to meet on ten successive days to ask God's special blessing upon his work. McCheyne entered wholeheartedly into this concert of prayer and felt it was an omen of better and greater things to come. Writing to Horatius Bonar in 1842, inviting him to preach in Dundee the following October, McCheyne said:

> I expect a time of remarkable blessing. This concert for prayer has taken hold of the people, and I think God is opening the windows of heaven. We have met in the church every morning at eight, eight or nine hundred people, and on Sabbath about a thousand. We are waiting for an answer, and I believe it will come. Some drops have fallen. One soul, weary and heavy-laden for four years, was brought, I trust, to a saving rest in Jesus on the first evening during the hour of prayer, and in secret. (Horatius Bonar, *Life of John Milne,* p.37)

McCheyne had begun his ministry in St Peter's, Dundee in November 1836. Except for ten months spent in Larbert and Dunipace as John Bonar's assistant, it was his only church. With such a pastor at its helm it is not surprising to learn that St Peter's experienced a time of revival. Yet for some strange reason he was not to be God's instrument in it. When revival came he was far away in Palestine. But God had heard his prayers for the church and Scotland and had blessed them in his absence. Before leaving for Palestine, McCheyne had written to William Chalmers Burns, just out of university, to take his place in St Peter's. It was under Burns' preaching that revival came. McCheyne, true to form, prayed before going that Burns would receive a thousand times as much blessing upon his ministry as he had known. God obviously heard him! When he found out that revival had come during his absence there was never a hint of peevishness or resentment because God had overlooked him in favour of another. He simply revelled in what God was doing irrespective of the instrument. His sentiment was always, 'To God be the glory, / Great things he hath done!'

It was not until he was returning from Palestine that he heard anything of what God was doing in Scotland. In eager anticipation he longed to be back at home to see if what he had heard was true and that God had again in mercy visited his people. As soon as he arrived in Dundee, Thursday afternoon, prayer meeting day, he went straight to the church to find out what had been happening. What he encountered almost overwhelmed him. As he entered the building and saw the congregation he was deeply moved and affected. He had never seen such a sight, though he had often prayed for it. The church was full to bursting. Old men and young children were sitting on both stairways leading up to the pulpit. How well he entered into this new situation. His heart's desire for the church's awakening had now been fulfilled. The only thing remaining was to see the whole and not just a part of the Church in Scotland revived.

When he wrote to Horatius Bonar on 25 December 1839, the year revival started, he said:

> Oh, let us pray that what is past is but the beginning of days to our thirsty land! Let us stretch out our souls for more. Anderston, Kirkfield, and Wellpark are decidedly quickened from on high. I also visited a school in St George's parish, and preached to many weeping children. . . I have also hopes of Perth. It is a very dead place; but the people in Mr Gray's church are stilled as if waiting for something. The attendance at his week meeting has doubled . . . Would it not be greatly for Immanuel's honour to come and reveal Himself in such a way that no man could take any of the praise? Oh to be humble and believing and expecting! (H.Bonar, *Life of John Milne*, p.33)

Every revival has its blemishes and that in St Peter's was no exception. Though the quantity and quality of Christians increased dramatically there were some discordant elements. Churches, even in the midst of revival, can never attain to the Church in glory. When he returned to St Peter's not everyone greeted him with open arms. Those who were saved under Burns' ministry wanted him to continue with them. Again, the Corinthian cry was heard, 'I am of McCheyne', 'I am of Burns'. If it had not been for the depth of their spirituality the revival could easily have been irreparably damaged.

McCheyne, magnanimous as ever, encouraged Burns to stay in the belief that his work was not yet finished. Burns, who only saw himself as a stand-in for McCheyne, was adamant that his time to leave had come. To those who sometimes attended St Peter's the whole atmosphere seemed permeated with God. McCheyne's very presence seemed to carry a sense of God into the building. It was unmistakeable: God was with him both in private and in public, both at home and in the church. Nobody entering St Peter's could deny that God was there. Being there was like going into the very throne-room of God himself! It was God the people sought and they were rarely disappointed. Visiting preachers were also conscious of this. It was not unusual to find them exhilerated by a sense of God. James Hamilton wrote to Andrew Bonar:

> It was pleasant to preach at St Peter's Church. The children on the pulpit stairs, the prayers in the vestry, the solemn and often crowded auditory, the sincerity of all the worship, and the often-felt presence of God, made it like few other sanctuaries. It was only on week-evenings that I was there, but perhaps they were more remarkable than even the Sabbaths . . . One reason for the peculiar blessing which rested on them was the happy freedom which they gave the minister. He could descend from the stateliness of sermons to the most familiar and affectionate and varied addresses; and as members of other congregations could attend them, the benefit was widely diffused. So sensible was Mr M'Cheyne of the special presence of the Spirit in his ministry in St Peter's, that I remember, when leaving Abertyne, he said to me, 'I would beg my bread to get preaching at Dundee.' (William Arnot, *Biography of James Hamilton*, pp.238-39)

There are few recorded examples in church history to compare with McCheyne for holiness. His great strength was not in his oratory or in any other natural endowment. Rather, it lay in his great likeness to Christ, that quality of character which longs to give everything, unreservedly to him. His place within the Church is identical to that of Enoch, that he was a man who 'walked with God'. Someone once wrote, 'McCheyne was not an orator like Chalmers or Guthrie, nor – though he was a scholarly man – was there any parade of learning in his sermons. He preached in fact with remarkable simplicity, and yet perhaps there was no preaching in Scotland at that time which so *told.'* What Andrew Bonar once said of McCheyne's tomb is as true today of his memory. 'There is still some peculiar fragrance in the air round Robert McCheyne's tomb.' As long as the Church maintains an interest in the lives of its great preachers, McCheyne's memory will always hold a special place in the heart of God's people. Truly he was a man after God's own heart.

27
William Chalmers Burns
(1815-68)

William Chalmers Burns is best remembered as a pioneer missionary to China and a close friend of Hudson Taylor, the founder of the China Inland Mission. However, before going to China Burns made an indelible impression on Scotland as a preacher. Unfortunately, like many of his contemporaries, Burns has been hidden behind the aura of Robert Murray McCheyne. If McCheyne is best remembered for his godliness, Burns should be remembered for his zeal; in everything, he tried to make Christ known. To extend the boundary of Christ's kingdom was with Burns an all-consuming passion.

Unlike McCheyne, Burns was an evangelist. He was ordained as a preacher but never inducted into a pastorate. He lived as an itinerant preacher and travelled extensively. His preaching career began in 1839 when he was twenty-four years old in St Peter's, Dundee. This was due to McCheyne's appointment, by the Church of Scotland, as a delegate to Palestine. Burns, who was waiting to go as a missionary, possibly to India, was invited by McCheyne to occupy his pulpit in his absence. This resulted in a nine-year suspension of his missionary plans. It was not by design but controlled by a higher power. God, it seems, had other work for Burns to do before embarking on his missionary life.

Burns was born on 1 April 1815. He was the third son in a family of ten children. His father, William Hamilton Burns, was a Church of Scotland minister in the country parish of Dun in Angus. Unlike many of his contemporaries Burns was an ardent supporter of the traditional Reformed theology as defined by John Calvin. While studying at Edinburgh University with the celebrated Thomas Chalmers, he was invited to spend the weekend with him at his parents' home in Anstruther. Chalmers explained that his only reason for asking him was because 'he was the only Calvinist in their class', a sad reflection on the spiritual climate of the day.

Burns' father was a quiet, withdrawn man who exerted a profound influence on him. He maintained such a close walk with God that it inevitably affected his son's outlook on life and death. After being away from home for a while he and his brother, Islay, lay in bed talking of their future. They were deep in conversation when they were struck by the sound of their father's voice downstairs. He was praying. William suddenly became serious for a moment and said, 'There can be no doubt where *his* heart is, and where he is going.'

When he was six years old the family moved from Dun to Kilsyth, about twelve miles east of Glasgow. This little town had been made famous a century before by a revival in 1742, under the ministry of James Robe. Burns' father, always keen to learn of such events, read and prayed for a similar work of God. William was too preoccupied with physical pursuits to be concerned about such things; he was a strong, sturdy boy and always wanted to be a farmer. Later, he changed his mind and wanted to be a lawyer. But unknown to him, God had already earmarked him for a preacher. His friends had influenced his first choice, materialism his second and conversion his third.

When William returned home in 1831, after finishing a course of study in Aberdeen, he thought his student days were over. However, as he considered his future and saw 'that lawyers were always wealthy and lived in fine houses', he set his sights in that direction. Materialism had laid siege to his heart and there was little real defence against it. When he asked his father's permission to study law, his father was extremely unhappy. His parents had always hoped he would enter the ministry. But when his father saw how determined he was, he reluctantly consented, and the young Burns began his training with his uncle, Alexander Burns, a lawyer in Edinburgh.

When the time came for him to leave home for Edinburgh, both parents were heavy-hearted. They feared he would become so entwined in this world that he would loss all sense of the next. As he was leaving, his father gave him Pike's *Early Piety*. This was to become the chief instrument in his salvation.

It was some time before the family had any real hope concerning his spiritual condition. They had written to him expressing their concern for his soul and their fear that he might become too worldly and forget God. He wrote back asking them to send him some good Christian literature. They sent him Thomas Boston's *Fourfold State of*

Man. This was the turning point in his life. One evening, soon after this, he unexpectedly walked into the dining-room of the old manse. His startled mother asked him, 'Oh, Willie, where have you come from?' 'From Edinburgh,' he replied. 'How did you come?' she said. 'I walked.'[a distance of thirty-six miles] Everything went silent for a moment until he said, 'What would you think, mamma, if I should be a minister after all?' Much to the surprise and delight of the family he explained how the Lord had dealt with him and that he could have no peace in his heart until he found out if they would mind. This change of heart was almost too wonderful to believe. Had the family not believed in the God of wonders they may have thought it was impossible! Humanly speaking, the world had taken possession of his heart, but God was able to expel it.

He recorded what had led up to that decisive event. Not one thing but a combination of several things brought about this change: the preaching of God's Word, the reading of Christian books, the fear of death at the outbreak of cholera and a very affecting letter from his sisters.

> I could not think of my Christian parents and my godly home with all its sweet and solemn privileges, without an awful conflict of soul at the thought of parting with them for ever. I could think of parting with Christ, for I knew him not . . . but to part with them was too much for me to bear. In this way the way was prepared, but as yet I am fully conscious that my heart was spiritually dead. However the set time came. I sat down, with solemn impressions arising from the causes now mentioned, to read a part of Pike's *Early Piety* . . . and in one moment, while gazing on a solemn passage in it, my inmost soul was in one instant pierced as with a dart. God had apprehended me. I felt the conviction of my lost estate rushing through me with resistless power; I left the room and retired to a bedroom, there to pour out my heart for the first time with many tears in a genuine heart-rending cry for mercy. From the first moment . . . I had the inspiring hope of being saved by a sovereign and infinitely gracious God; and in the same instant almost I felt that I *must* leave my present occupation, and devote myself to Jesus in the ministry of that glorious gospel by which I had been saved. (Islay Burns, *Memoir of Rev. Wm. C. Burns*, pp.26-27)

In 1834 he received his degree and went on to further studies in

Glasgow University – an unusual decision considering the fame and popularity of Thomas Chalmers in Edinburgh. This transition brought him under two major influences which were to affect the rest of his life. One affected his character, the other his future.

Firstly, he joined Milton Church, Glasgow where he came under the influence of the Rev. John Duncan (Rabbi Duncan), whose penetrating preaching made Burns re-evaluate his Christian life and commitment, resulting in a deepening of his spiritual awareness. Secondly, he had joined the Students Missionary Society. This opened his eyes to the wider horizons of the work of the Church. After listening to Dr James Kalley, who was about to embark for China, Burns dedicated himself to missionary work. 'It was here,' wrote his brother, 'that he first rose to the full idea of that entire and absolute consecration of his whole being and life to the service of Christ, which in his subsequent ministry so remarkably distinguished him.'

Burns possessed the heart of an evangelist with his passion for souls. One day, as he was walking through Glasgow, he was so overcome by the thought of perishing souls that he did not notice his mother coming up to him until she spoke. With a surprised look he said, 'O mother, I did not see you: for when walking along Argyle Street just now, I was so overcome with the sight of the countless crowds of immortal beings eagerly hasting hither and thither, but all posting onwards towards the eternal world, that I could bear it no longer, and turned in here to seek relief in quiet thought.'

After finishing his university course Burns waited on the Lord to know his next move. It was then, in April 1839, that he received the invitation to fill the pulpit of St Peter's, Dundee. Within a short time his preaching met with tremendous results. One of McCheyne's church officers made the following comparison between Burns and his beloved pastor:

Gifted with a solid and vigorous understanding, possessed of a voice of vast compass and power – unsurpassed even by that of Mr. Spurgeon – and withal fired with an ardour so intense and an energy so exhaustless that nothing could damp or resist it, Mr. Burns wielded an influence over the masses whom he addressed which was almost without parallel since the days of Wesley and Whitefield. Crowds flocked to St Peter's from all the country round; and the strength of the preacher seemed to grow with the incessant demands made upon it. Whenever Mr. Burns preached a deep impression was produced on his audience, and it was felt to be impossible to remain unconcerned under the impassioned earnestness of his appeals. With him there was no effort at oratorical display, but there was true eloquence; and instances are on record of persons, strong in their self-confidence and enmity to the truth, who fell before its power. (Islay Burns, *Memoir of the Rev. William C. Burns,* pp.61-62)

Although his preaching was powerful it had the tendency to fluctuate. This was due, in part, to his insistence on being moved by impulse at the time of delivery. He considered this of primary importance, a sign of the Spirit's presence. Still, he was a much sought-after preacher, especially when revival broke out under his ministry.

When revival came, in July of 1839, it was in his father's parish of Kilsyth. For a long time the thought of revival had dominated the minds of the people. His father, who had often read and reflected on the Kilsyth revival of almost a century before, longed and prayed for a similar outpouring of the Spirit. What a day it must have been for him when revival came, especially, under the preaching of his own son! Burns' own account of this remarkable event gives us an insight into the processes at work in his own heart as he surveyed what was happening among the congregation. It is a fascinating account for those interested in the doctrine of revival as it takes us into the very heart of the preacher.

When I entered the pulpit, I saw before me an immense multitude from the town and neighbourhood filling the seats, stairs, passages, and porches, all in their ordinary clothes, and including many of the most abandoned of our population . . . . When we had prayed a second time, specially imploring that the Lord would open on us the windows of heaven, I preached from the words (Psalm 110:3): 'Thy people shall be willing in the day of thy power.' *(Memoir,* pp.93-94)

After stating his plan he went on to say:

I was led under this last particular [4. It is the day of the outpouring of the Holy Spirit] . . . to allude to some of the most remarkable outpourings of the Spirit that have been granted to the Church . . . I had come to notice the glorious revelation of Jehovah's right hand which was given at the Kirk of Shotts in 1630, while John Livingstone was preaching from Ezekiel 36:26, 27 . . . In refering to this wonderful work of the Spirit, I mentioned the fact that when Mr. Livingstone was on the point of closing his discourse a few drops of rain began to fall, and that when the people began to put on their coverings, he asked them if they had any shelter from the drops of Divine wrath, and was thus led to enlarge for nearly another hour in exhorting them to flee to Christ, with so much of the power of God, that about five hundred persons were converted. And just when I was speaking of the occasion and the nature of this wonderful address, I felt my own soul moved in a manner so remarkable that I was led, like Mr. Livingstone, to plead with the unconverted before me *instantly* to close with God's offer of mercy, and continued to do so until the power of the Lord's Spirit became so mighty upon their souls as to carry all before it, like the rushing mighty wind of Pentecost! During the whole of the time that I was speaking, the people listened with the most riveted and solemn attention . . . but at the last their feelings became too strong for all ordinary restraints, and broke forth simultaneously in weeping and wailing, tears and groans, intermingled with shouts of joy and praise from some of the people of God. The appearance of a great part of the people from the pulpit gave me an awfully vivid picture of the state of the ungodly in the day of Christ's coming and judgment. Some were screaming out in agony; others, and among these strong men, fell to the ground as if they had been dead; and such was the general commotion, that after repeating for some time the most free and urgent invitations of the Lord to sinners . . . I was obliged to give out a psalm . . .

To my own astonishment during the progress of this wonderful scene, when almost all present were overpowered, it pleased the Lord to keep my soul perfectly calm. Along with the awful and affecting realisation which I obtained of the state of the unconverted, I had such a view of the glory redounding to God, and the blessings conferred on poor sinners, by the work that was advancing, as to fill my soul with tranquill joy and praise. (Islay Burns, *Memoir*, pp.93-94)

Events similar to this were repeated in other places, such as St Peter's, Dundee, on his return there in August of the same year. His lifelong friend, James Hamilton, who was also at university with him, wrote of the effects of this revival in Kilsyth and Dundee. In a letter to the Rev. J.Willis on 27 August 1839, he wrote:

I would say he is more distinguished (prima facia) by zeal for the glory of Christ than, as I have noticed that many are, by mere concern for perishing sinners. This gives a lofty bearing and an apostolical character to his ministrations, and keeps him from many sources of vexation to which others not so actuated are liable. I do not say that he wants the other motives of ministerial fidelity, but I do say that every other is with him subordinate to that noblest of all, the exalting of Christ in the salvation of souls. He speaks, too, with such warmth and solemnity, such empressment, that his hearers cannot for a moment forget his earnestness and sincerity. (William Arnot, *Biography of James Hamilton*, pp.142-44)

One of the many changes that takes place in the Church when revival comes is the amazing elevation of Christian character. There is such a sense of the all-pervading presence of God that the standard of true spirituality is immeasurably enhanced. It seems that the world is suddenly expelled from the Church. When James Hamilton wrote to his uncle about the revival he said:

Since I wrote to you I have been once at Kilsyth, and often at Dundee, and I must say that I have nowhere felt the reality of religion more irresistably; nor did I know till then the efficacy of the prayer of faith, that power which asks of God, 'believing that it shall have them'. The converts in these places are Christians of a superior style to the professors who have long filled the Church. Religion is all in all with them, and sits so naturally upon them, that even worldly men can hardly call them either hypocrites or enthusiasts. They have exemplified nobly the rare virtue of making sacrifices for the sake of Christ, and the consequence of having identified themselves so completely with him is that they are joyful and assured believers. (Arnot, *Biography of James Hamilton,* pp.152-53)

When McCheyne returned to Dundee in November 1839, Burns embarked on an itinerant ministry. He travelled throughout Scotland preaching and many were converted. As he journeyed along revival seemed to follow him. He also preached in the North of England but with limited success.

In 1843, after the Disruption, Burns left Scotland for Northern Ireland and later Canada, preaching there not only to the English-speaking population, but also to the French inhabitants and to the

Gaelic-speaking Highlanders from Scotland. His departure to Canada was not due primarily to the Disruption (which he supported), but because he felt a change in the spiritual climate of Scotland. Burns was an evangelist and looked for opportunities to preach the gospel. He always aimed at the salvation of souls, more so than at the edifying of the Church. He felt that the Disruption tended to cause people to be more concerned about the doctrine of the Church and related matters than to the primacy of seeking the salvation of the lost. The winds of change had come and he was first to discern it.

His friend John Milne of Perth, who also witnessed revival under Burns' preaching, was of a different opinion. He saw the new development of 1843 and the founding of the Free Church of Scotland as a golden opportunity for evangelism. Those boundaries established under the parochial system were now removed and the Evangelical party was free to preach anywhere. There was no longer any need for ministerial etiquette, and those parched areas previously controlled by the Moderates were now thrown open to evangelicals.

When Burns returned to Scotland in 1846, the strain of his exertions was evident. His brother wrote:

> Mr Burns returned to Scotland after about two years of incessant labour in Canada in the same vessel in which he had before sailed for the West, arriving in Glasgow on the 15 September 1846. He was still in vigorous health, yet showing but too evident traces of the exhausting and and peculiarly trying scenes which he had passed through. The clear tones of a voice of more than ordinary compass and power were gone; his mind and spirit were worn and jaded; and he had already begun to acquire a certain *aged* look which he never afterwards wholly lost. He had indeed emphatically 'endured hardness as a good soldier of Jesus Christ,' and he bore the marks of it more or less to his grave. (Islay Burns, *Memoir,* p.288)

In 1847, Burns felt called to China. In the nine preceding years, since he had first offered himself for missionary work, he had never once lost the vision. He always felt that becoming a missionary was what God intended for him. His summons to go to China came not through his own denomination but through the Presbyterian Church in England. They had given him an unsolicited invitation to go as their representative to China. His determination to go into comparative obscurity in China highlights his overriding zeal for the Lord. It could be said of him as it was of his Saviour, 'zeal for your house has eaten me up.' True to form, Burns when he was asked when he would be ready to go to China replied, 'Tomorrow. I have all my things with me, and would rather go at once.'

In June 1847, Burns sailed from Portsmouth, to see his native Scotland again only once, and that was not through any desire of his own, but because no one else could be found to accompany a sick missionary on the six-month sea voyage it took to get home. For twenty years he evangelized in China, clad in Chinese dress, labouring to share the gospel with the ignorant masses who had never heard of a Saviour who had died for them. Only once did he see anything reminiscent of those early years in Scotland. He died as he had lived, for the Lord. It had been costly for him to leave the land of his birth and the popularity he enjoyed as a preacher there, but he left all to follow Christ. He died in Nieu-chwang on 4 April 1868.

No better tribute can be found of his power as a preacher than that given by McCheyne, who knew and loved him.

> He is certainly a very remarkable preacher. The plainness and force of his statements, and his urgency, I never saw equalled. He has a very clear view of divine things, and an amazing power of voice and body. But, above all, God seems really to accompany his preaching with demonstrations of the Spirit . . . His manner is very powerful – so much so that he made me tremble.

28

Charles Haddon Spurgeon

(1834-92)

The name of Charles Haddon Spurgeon conjures up different pictures to different people. To those who hold the evangelical faith precious, he exhibits in himself everything a true servant of God should be. He was faithful, fervent, diligent, possessing great faith and vision, and a lover of souls. If anyone could be called Mr Great-heart, it was Spurgeon. He once told his friend William Williams, minister of Upton Chapel, Lambeth Road, 'If you receive the heart of a friend, mind you give him back your own.' Spurgeon suffered much

C. H. Spurgeon in 1857

heartache towards the end of his life because of this sensitivity, in connection with what has been described as 'The Downgrade Controversy'.

Reading his sermons, sixty-six volumes in all, you gain some impression of the life and vigour that characterized his preaching. They are bristling with spiritual vitality and remain a glorious memorial to his ability and industry. Every Monday morning he would edit one of his Sunday sermons which was published on Thursday. These were in such demand that they were sent throughout the British Empire and America and also translated into many languages. This made Spurgeon a truly international figure.

Spurgeon was born on 19 June 1834 in the small village of Kelvedon in the County of Essex. His lineage was well-known for its preachers but none ever reached the standard of Charles Haddon. When he was fourteen months old he went to live with his grandparents in Stambourne. He remained there for five years and was a constant companion to his grandfather. The old man, James Spurgeon, loved nothing more than walking and talking with his little grandson, and he noticed that the boy had a real fascination for books. When young Charles looked at the drawings in Bunyan's *Pilgrim's Progress*, he said, 'When I first saw in it the woodcut of Christian carrying the burden on his back I felt so interested in the poor fellow that I thought I should jump for joy when, after he had carried it so long, he at last got rid of it.' Later, when he came on his summer holidays to Stambourne, he would wend his way to the attic of the old manse where his grandfather kept his stock of Puritan literature. To Spurgeon it was a real Alladin's cave, full of great treasures. 'Out of that darkened room', he said, 'I fetched those old authors . . . and never was I happier than when in their company.'

The influence of his grandfather played a large part in his upbringing. He was a man of principle and sought to impress it upon the young Spurgeon. This early lesson was to be enduring, though it sometimes got him into hot water at home.

The Stambourne style of singing led me into trouble when I returned to my home. The notion had somehow entered my little head that the last line of the hymn must always be repeated, and grandfather had instilled into me as a safe rule that I must never be afraid to do what I believed to be right; so, when I went to the chapel where my parents attended, I repeated the last line whether the congregation did so or not. It required a great deal of punishment to convince me that a little boy must do what his parents think to be right; and though my grandfather made a mistake in that particular instance, I have always been grateful to him for teaching me to act according to my belief whatever the consequences might be. (Autobiography, Vol.1, *The Early Years*, p.18)

One remarkable event which happened to him as a boy was the prophecy of Richard Knill. This was often thought spurious but Spurgeon maintained that it was true. William Williams also, quoting from Knill's biography, gives this concise picture of what happened.

When walking and conversing with the boy in the garden Mr. Knill became pervaded by a deep concern for him, and, turning aside into an arbour formed by an old yew-tree, he placed his hands upon his head and invoked the Divine blessing upon him, saying at the close that he believed that he would live to love Jesus Christ, and preach His Gospel to the largest congregation in the world.

Even before his conversion Spurgeon was steeped in Puritan theology. This had made an obvious impression on his mind. He knew that 'unless a man is born of water and the Spirit, he cannot enter the kingdom of God' (John 3:5). The awareness of his sin and need intensified as he entered mid-teens. His one desire was to know how to have his sins forgiven. As he struggled along God was preparing the way for his entrance into his kingdom. There was no sudden flash from heaven, no moving oratory, no emotional music, just the simple unadorned gospel presented in the most simple fashion imaginable. His written testimony is long but uncondensable.

I sometimes think I might have been in darkness and despair until now had it not been for the goodness of God in sending a snowstorm, one Sunday morning, while I was going to a certain place of worship. When I could go no further, I turned down a side street, and came to a little Primitive Methodist Chapel. In that chapel there may have been a dozen or fifteen people. . . The minister did not come that morning; he was snowed up, I suppose. At last, a very thin-looking man, a shoemaker, or tailor, or something of that sort, went up into the pulpit to preach . . . The text was – *'Look unto me, and be ye saved, all the ends of the earth.'* . . . The preacher began thus: 'My dear friends, this is a very simple text indeed. It says "Look". Now lookin' don't make a deal of pain. It ain't liftin' your foot or finger; it is just, "Look". Well, a man needn't go to

College to learn to look. You may be the biggest fool, and yet you can look. A man needn't be worth a thousand a year to be able to look. Anyone can look; even a child can look. But then the text says, "Look unto *Me*"'. 'Ay!' said he, in broad Sussex, 'many on ye are lookin to yourselves, but it's no use lookin' there. You'll never find any comfort in yourselves. Some look to God the Father. No, look to Him by-and-by. Jesus Christ says, "Look unto *Me*". Some on ye say, "We must wait for the Spirit's workin". You have no business with that just now. Look to *Christ*. The text says, "Look unto *Me*"'.

Then the good man followed up his text in this way: 'Look unto Me; I am sweatin' great drops of blood. Look unto Me; I am hangin' on the cross. Look unto Me; I am dead and buried. Look unto Me; I rise again. Look unto Me; I ascend to Heaven. Look unto Me; I am sittin' at the Father's right hand. O poor sinner, look unto Me! Look unto Me.'

When he had gone to about that length, and managed to spin out ten minutes or so, he was at the end of his tether. Then he looked at me under the gallery, and I daresay, with so few present, he knew me to be a stranger. Just fixing his eyes on me, as if he knew all my heart, he said, 'Young man, you look very miserable . . . and you always will be miserable – miserable in life, and miserable in death – if you don't obey my text; but if you obey now, this moment, you will be saved.' Then, lifting up his hands, he shouted . . . 'Young man, look to Jesus Christ. Look! Look! Look! You have nothin' to do but look and live.' I saw at once the way of salvation . . . I had been waiting to do fifty things, but when I heard that word, 'Look!' what a charming word it seemed to me! Oh! I looked until I could almost have looked my eyes away. There and then the cloud was gone, the darkness had rolled away, and that moment I saw the sun; and I could have risen that instant, and sung with the most enthusiastic of them, of the precious blood of Christ, and the simple faith that looks alone to Him. (*The Early Years*, pp.87-88)

Young Spurgeon was a very good, moral, religious and sensitive teenager, yet still unsaved. By faith, he saw the Saviour and by faith he trusted in the Saviour. One look caused his burden to roll away, never to return. His desire to preach almost coincided with his conversion. Soon after that momentous Sunday morning he felt the urge to preach the gospel. His previous sadness was replaced by 'joy unspeakable and full of glory.'

His family were Congregationalists and as such paedo-baptists, that is, they baptized children. His father and grandfather were Congregational ministers. Yet Spurgeon became a Baptist and believed that only believers should be baptized. Even before his conversion, after a study of the New Testament, he had argued for the Baptist cause. After his conversion and in compliance with his conscience and belief he was baptized. After his baptism, his mother said, 'Ah, Charles! I often prayed the Lord to make you a Christian, but I never asked that you might become a Baptist.' Spurgeon said in his normal humorous way: 'Ah, mother! the Lord has answered your prayer with his usual bounty, and given you exceeding abundantly above what you asked or thought.'

Spurgeon began his ministry as a Sunday school teacher. In 1850, he had come to Cambridge as an assistant teacher. He was still only a lad of sixteen but his gifts and abilities shone out. At first he was tricked into preaching. James Vinter, who was in charge of a lay preachers association, asked Spurgeon to accompany a young man to a preaching centre where he was to preach. As they walked along Spurgeon asked him where he was going to preach from. The startled young man replied that he was only accompanying Spurgeon at the request of Vinter and had never preached a sermon in his life. Before reaching their destination Spurgeon knew what his text would be.

Waterbeach Chapel before 1863

278

Afterwards, the congregation could hardly contain their enthusiasm. Before long he was preaching in cottages and barns, and walked miles every evening to preach in the surrounding villages.

When he was still only sixteen he received a call to a small Baptist church in Waterbeach, some six miles east of Cambridge. The effect of his ministry there was tremendous. The transformation which resulted was similar to that which had taken place under Richard Baxter in Kidderminster.

> There went into that village a lad, who had no great scholarship, but who was earnest in seeking the souls of men. He began to preach there and it pleased God to turn the whole place upside down. In a short time the little thatched chapel was crammed, the biggest vagabonds in the village were weeping floods of tears, and those who had been the curse of the parish became a blessing. Where there had been robberies and villanies of every kind all round the neighbourhood, there were none, because the men who used to do the mischief were themselves in the house of God, rejoicing to hear of Jesus crucified. (Arnold Dallimore, *Spurgeon: A New Biography*, pp.35-36)

For three years he continued preaching in Waterbeach. However, a small village like Waterbeach could not hope to retain such a great preacher. In 1853 he received an invitation to preach in New Park Street Chapel, London. Spurgeon wrote back convinced that they had made some mistake and that another Spurgeon must have been meant. They assured him they had not made a mistake and a date was fixed in December.

Sunday 18 December arrived and Spurgeon found himself in New Park Street's imposing chapel. At first he felt quite fearful until he entered the pulpit. There the sense of his commission caused all fear to evaporate. He had come not to impress but to express the Word of God. Afterwards, many of the congregation did not know what to make of him. The evening service saw a much larger congregation gathered. This was due to the reports many had taken home to their friends and absent members. Before this, nobody had been invited back to preach. Immediately the people began pressing the deacons to arrange another date or even more than one. He returned in January and preached on several successive Sundays. Soon after the call came and Spurgeon found himself the new minister of what had been one of the most famous Baptist churches in the land.

From the moment he came to New Park Street, he had an immediate appeal. The church soon became too small to hold the growing congregations which came to hear him. To help facilitate this sudden development a new building project was set in motion. This increased the seating capacity to 1,500. While the building was in progress the church met at Exeter Hall. This spacious building could seat 4,000 with room for another 1,000 standing. Again, it proved too small. Both morning and evening services were packed to capacity.

This changing situation meant that the church had to move again, this time to the Surrey Garden Music Hall. This immense auditorium could hold 10,000 people. Unfortunately, the first night was to end in tragedy. Spurgeon, still only twenty-two years old, had just began to pray when someone cried out 'Fire'. Other warnings were heard which resulted in mass confusion and a stampede for the doors. In the ensuing upheaval seven people were killed as parts of the building collapsed through the force of the crowd. For days Spurgeon lived under a cloud. Sadly for him, what should have been a highlight in his career was turned into an ordeal. Whether or not the incident had been maliciously prearranged was never proved.

For three years the congregation continued to use the Hall in the morning and the chapel in the evening even though it was too small to host the huge crowds Spurgeon attracted. Eventually another church project was set in motion in an attempt to house the growing church. This new building was called 'The Metropolitan Tabernacle'. It was designed to seat 3,600 with standing room for a further 2,000. His popularity as a preacher was so great that attendance was generally by ticket only.

In 1859, revival was spreading throughout the country, especially in Northern Ireland and Wales. This period was arguably the richest time for Spurgeon. The church, already bursting at the seams, experienced a new impetus. The wind of heaven blew upon them, souls were saved, the church was refreshed and Spurgeon was still in his prime.

What prayer meetings we have had! Shall we ever forget Park Street, those prayer meetings, when I felt compelled to let you go without a word from my lips, because the Spirit of God was so awfully present that we felt bowed to the dust.. . . And what listening there was at Park Street, where we scarcely had air enough to breathe! The Holy Spirit came down like showers which saturate the soil till the clods are ready for the breaking; and then it was not long before we heard on the right and on the left the cry, 'What must I do to be saved?' (Iain Murray, *The Forgotten Spurgeon,* p.35)

For Spurgeon his oratorical gifts were no compensation for the lack of the presence of God by his Spirit. He did not aim to amuse but to glorify Jesus Christ. This was always his goal and ambition in preaching. During the revival three hundred people were converted under his sermon, 'Compel them to come in'. Even in its written form Spurgeon could testify, 'It has been signally owned of God, that scarcely a week occurs without some case of its usefulness coming to light.' Numerous examples could be taken to highlight Spurgeon's zeal to exalt Christ in his sermons. His wife speaks of his near exhaustion while preaching on 'The Eternal Name'. 'Let my name perish,' he cried, 'but let Christ's Name last forever! Jesus! Jesus! Jesus! Crown Him Lord of all.'

An interesting comparison was made, by several American preachers visiting Britain, between Spurgeon and Joseph Parker, another famous London preacher.

On Sunday morning they attended the City Temple where Dr Joseph Parker was the pastor. Some 2000 people filled the building, and Parker's forceful personality dominated the service. His voice was commanding, his language descriptive, his imagination lively, and his manner animated. The sermon was scriptural, the congregation hung upon his words, and the Americans came away saying, 'What a wonderful preacher is Joseph Parker!' In the evening they went to hear Spurgeon at the Metropolitan Tabernacle. The building was much larger than the City Temple, and the congregation was more than twice the size. Spurgeon's voice was much more expressive and moving and his oratory noticably superior. But they soon forgot all about the great building, the immense congregation, and the magnificent voice. They even overlooked their intention to compare the various features of the two preachers, and when the service was over they found themselves saying, 'What a wonderful Saviour is Jesus Christ!' (A.Dallimore, *Spurgeon*, p.216)

This was the hallmark of Spurgeon's ministry from first to last.

The Metropolitan Tabernacle chapel was more than just a huge preaching centre. It was open all week with a whole mass of activities associated with it. In one Annual General Meeting no less than sixty-six different activities were mentioned. Of these the Pastor's College was given pride of place. This had grown out of a single attempt to help support a man seeking to enter the ministry and was a great delight and inspiration to Spurgeon. Every Friday afternoon he went to the College to give a lecture on preaching. These were later published in his *Lectures to my Students*. These lectures contained practical aids for students coming to terms with the ministry, its demands and responsibilities. There was probably nowhere else where Spurgeon was more himself than when he was with his students. He often gave vent to his humour, causing the students to reel with laughter. His buoyant personality often shone through to cheer the aspiring preachers.

For someone endowed with such a lively spirit, Spurgeon experienced many severe bouts of depression. The enormous machinery he had built up around him weighed heavily upon him. He also suffered from the age of forty from rheumatic gout which gave him terrible pain. His wife had become a semi-invalid. For years, during the winter, he had to take his holidays – which were really forced retreats – alone and abroad. He often spent a lot of time in Mentone in the South of France where its warm climate helped to ease his pain.

On top of all this, between the years 1887 and 1889, he went through the most painful emotional time of his life, as he fought to maintain the purity of the gospel in what was termed the Downgrade Controversy. Due to his preaching exertions he was becoming prematurely old, but it was this controversy above all else which affected him most.

There was in the Baptist Union a growing shift of emphasis, by several of its leaders, away from the old gospel. Influenced by the upsurge of Darwin's *Origin of Species* and the influx of Germany's higher criticism, many preachers were being led astray into idle speculation. The inspiration of the Scriptures as the infallible word of God was increasingly being undermined. That is, true scriptural theology was on the 'downgrade'.

When Spurgeon became aware of this situation he was forced to take public action. He wrote to the Baptist Union asking them to adopt an Evangelical Statement of Faith, and this was rejected. He also claimed that there were some within the Union who no longer held to the evangelical faith. When he was asked to submit his evidence to back his claims, he refused. Not that he could not if he had so wished. He possessed all the hard facts, the names of several men who had jettisoned their belief for what was called the New Theology. Dr Booth, the General Secretary of the Union, had himself supplied him with names and details of several defectors. However, for some reason he refused to allow Spurgeon to use any of his letters, claiming that they were for personal use and not for public scrutiny. Spurgeon was too much of a gentleman to abuse this trust, even to clear his own name.

Eventually Spurgeon was forced to leave the Baptist Union because it failed to address the problem. To him, remaining in the Union meant collaborating with the enemy. These were not brethren, 'earnestly contending for the faith which was once delivered to the saints.' Rather they were those acting as a kind of fifth column undermining the faith. This long and drawn-out conflict had taken its toll. 'The strain', he could write, 'has nearly broken my heart already, and I have had all I can bear of bitterness.' After leaving the Baptist Union for conscientious reasons, he was asked to address a rally by the Evangelical Alliance, a gathering drawn from many denominations. Someone wrote:

> Never shall we forget the first meeting called by the Alliance for testimony to the fundamental truths of the Gospel, which was held in Exeter Hall. The reception given by the audience to Mr. Spurgeon when he rose to speak was overpowering in its fervour and heartiness. We occupied a seat on the platform near enough to witness the powerful emotions that agitated him, and the tears that streamed down his cheeks as he listened to the previous speakers; and though only a very few of his Baptist brethren were present, there was not wanting such a display of sympathy as must have cheered and comforted his heart. (A.Dallimore, *Spurgeon*, p.212)

As time progressed Spurgeon's ailments became worse. His last sermon preached in the Metropolitan Tabernacle was on 7 June 1891. A month before he was overcome with nerves and forced to leave the pulpit. Afterwards he persevered on through another month before being forced to retire. He was now seriously ill. The church met to pray morning, noon, and night.

When it seemed he was well enough to travel he set off for Mentone. He was never to return home again alive. After announcing the last hymn in a service in Mentone on 17 January 1892, Spurgeon deteriorated rapidly. For a while he drifted in and out of consciousness until he became totally unconscious on 28 January. He died three days later on Sunday, 31 January. His wife, who was by his side, knelt to pray. J.W.Harrald, Spurgeon's private secretary, recorded:

> We were touched beyond all expression . . . to hear the voice of the loved one, so sorely bereaved, thanking God for the many years that she had had the unspeakable joy of having such a precious husband lent to her . . . Seven months ago she gave her husband up to the Lord [during his extreme sickness in London] but the Lord lent him to her a little longer (A.Dallimore, *Spurgeon*, p.233)

When Spurgeon was finally brought home, several services were held because no place could be found large enough to accommodate all who wished to attend. When the coffin left the church, to be carried to the grave, people lined the five-mile journey between the church and Northwood cemetery. After all the criticism he had undergone from the secular and religious press Spurgeon still retained the love of the people. He was the best-loved preacher in London. For those who knew him intimately, he remained, Mr Great-heart.

29
Dwight L. Moody
(1837-99)

Along with C.H.Spurgeon, D.L.Moody was the most dynamic figure of the nineteenth century. He belonged to a rising generation of Christian lay preachers. Like Spurgeon he had a multiplicity of sides which could be examined. Everything he did seemed to prosper. Soon after his conversion he formed a strong attachment to the YMCA (Young Men's Christian Associatian), and was for several years its superintendent in Chicago. He established schools, founded the Chicago Evangelization Society, later to be known as the Moody Bible Institute, built churches and supported many other altruistic causes. The breadth of the man makes him a truly amazing figure. However, it is his fame as an evangelist that attracts our attention.

Strange as it may seem, it was his British missions which thrust him to the front of the American mind. Until then he was comparatively unknown except in Chicago, his adopted home. After his first British campaigns in 1873-5, he became a well-known name in America as his evangelistic activities captured their imagination.

Moody seemed to possess the stamina of three men. He never avoided a challenge, especially to his faith. When other workers became discouraged by difficulties, he simply rose above them. He trusted implicitly in a God who could overcome all obstacles. His most hated word was 'can't'. Whenever someone mentioned it he wanted to prove that it 'could'. He wanted to show that the 'can'ts' can become the 'cans' to the man of faith. This indomitable spirit was one of his great qualities. Even before his conversion it was there. Everything he did was done with enthusiasm. He was Chicago's best shoe salesman. While others waited for customers to come in, he was out in the street encouraging them to come in and try a pair of shoes. When he first came to Boston before going to Chicago his uncle was afraid to employ him because he thought that within a week he would be telling him how to run his business.

Like all truly great leaders Moody possessed the essential gifts to fulfil his task. He had that rare ability to motivate others, and his enthusiasm was contagious. Ira D.Sankey was to become Moody's chief assistant and make up the other side of the Moody-Sankey duo. Before they met Sankey was quite happy working as a civil servant. For several years Moody had been looking for a helper in his Chicago work; he wanted a good soloist to lead the singing. When he heard Sankey's deep baritone voice, he knew he had found his man. At first Sankey refused but was left to consider it. This was the beginning of a long-lasting and endearing partnership even though Sankey had to stand in the shadow of Moody.

Moody always considered Sankey's singing the ideal complement to his gospel preaching. This musical element was to become of immense importance to his ministry.

Moody was born at Northfield, Massachussetts, on 5 February 1837, the sixth child of Betsy and Edwin Moody. His father, who was a stonemason, was too attached to drink to be of any real use to the family. He died when Dwight was only four years old, leaving the family in serious financial difficulties. Except for the kindness of the local Unitarian minister their plight would have been far worse. He protected them from all the creditors who came knocking at their door demanding money.

At home he was taken to church. The children walked barefoot to church and then put on their shoes to enter the sacred building. However he hated to go; he could never understand why he had to work six days and then spend his only day off in church. When he did go he usually sat in the gallery where he could rest his head on the rail and go off to sleep. Later, after becoming a Christian, he was thankful he had gone to church as a boy, because it had formed an inflexible habit in him.

When Moody left home in Northfield, Massachusetts, he was seventeen years old. Originally he had gone to make his fortune. On his return he was rich in faith. After living in Boston for a while he moved to Chicago; but it was not the same Moody who went to Chicago who had gone to Boston.

One of the conditions of his employment in Boston was his regular attendance at Mount Vernon Congregational Church. Here his Sunday school teacher was amazed at his ignorance of the Bible.

When he was asked to read from John's Gospel, he began looking for it in the Old Testament. After listening to the story of Moses, he said, 'Say, Mr. Kimball, that man Moses must have been smart.'

Kimball was not put off by Moody's coarseness. He thought that the best way of dealing with him was to confront him directly with the gospel. He went to see Moody personally at work. As he approached the shop, he became nervous. Moody was in a backroom wrapping shoes. When he saw him Kimball caught hold of Moody by the shoulder and began explaining the gospel to him. The effect was dramatic as Moody immediately gave himself to Christ. It seems he was just ripe for the picking. God had already been at work in his heart and this additional prompt brought him through to salvation.

Though he was converted Moody did not fully understand the gospel. When he first applied for membership in Mount Vernon in May 1855, he was rejected because of his inadequate knowledge of doctrine. When asked, 'What has Christ done for you, and for us all, that especially entitles Him to our love and obedience?' he replied, 'I think He has done a great deal for us all, but I don't know of anything He has done in particular.' The following March he was accepted into full membership. Clearly, his biblical knowledge had vastly improved.

When he came to Chicago, Moody immediately joined a church. He had no intention of just sitting back and enjoying a free trip to heaven. His whole nature would have recoiled from the very idea. He was as enthusiastic as he was energetic and his enthusiasm became the outlet for his energy. He wanted to work in the church as well as wait in the pew. From then until his death Moody worked tirelessly for the extension of the gospel.

His first attempt at reaching the unsaved in Chicago was by renting four pews in the church, which he regularly filled. When he asked to become a Sunday school teacher, he was told he could become one only if he could gather a class. Within no time Moody had gathered a host of ragamuffins. He possessed a natural attraction for all the waifs and strays in Chicago. His Sunday school work grew so rapidly that he was forced to hire a special building for it, and eventually it numbered fifteen hundred children. Its growth was phenomenal. Discipline became a problem at times but this was outweighed by the benefits. Moody was reaching the untaught and

287

D. L. Moody

uncared-for street urchins of Chicago. He was always thinking of new ways of encouraging these children to the meetings and they loved him for it.

Though the work grew remarkably, nobody was converted. In fact, Moody never even thought of conversions, for he considered them to be the sacred domain of the church and its elders. Only through seeing a dying teacher embark on a private campaign to save his class did he realise the purpose of his work. He asked Moody to take him to visit every pupil in his class so that he could speak to them personally about salvation. Before he died they had all made a profession of faith. Once he saw the potential of his work Moody became zealous for conversions. He was so enthusiastic that people began calling him, 'Crazy Moody'.

Few preachers have known their Bibles like Moody. At first his knowledge was very scant. After his conversion he would pump anyone he thought could help him to a better understanding of the Bible. He would ask preachers about difficult passages and then file the information for future reference. His sermons, which were always topical, were constructed from little snippets of paper he had collected and kept in various envelopes. These contained the intelligence of many years, and from various sources, which he then structured into sermons. His inquisitiveness paid off, with interest, as his knowledge steadily increased.

Moody was sometimes very abrupt in his conversation. He was at times moved more by impulse than caution. When something needed to be said, he said it, whether it offended or not. In his London Campaign he felt that too many Christians were taking the best seats. As he began one service he said, 'It's time for Christians to stop coming here and crowding into the best seats. It's time for 'em to go out among these sailors and drunkards and bring them in and give them the best seats.' To Victorian England, with all its refinement and culture, Moody must have appeared an uncouth American. He was coarse and abrasive and in desperate need of refining.

· His first visit to England before his great Campaigns in the early 1870s was in 1867. This was due to his wife's asthmatic condition when her doctor advised her to take a long sea voyage. While in England he was asked to speak at a special anniversary meeting in London. It was the custom at this meeting for the invited speaker to propose a resolution. He was to 'move a vote of thanks to the noble Earl' (Shaftesbury) who had presided over the meeting. He was introduced as their 'American cousin, the Rev. Mr Moody of Chicago.' With a sudden abruptness, all his own, he stood up and addressed the meeting:

> The chairman has made two mistakes. To begin with, I'm not the 'Reverend' Moody at all. I'm plain Dwight L. Moody, a Sabbath-school worker. And then I'm not your 'American cousin'! By the grace of God I'm your brother, who is interested with you in our Father's work for His children. And about this vote of thanks to 'the noble Earl' for being our chairman this evening. I don't see why we should thank him, any more than he should thank us. When at any time they offered to thank our Mr Lincoln for presiding over a meeting in Illinois, he stopped it. He said he'd tried to do his duty, and they'd tried to do theirs. He thought it was an even thing all round. (W.R.Moody, *The Life of Dwight L. Moody*, p.120)

289

The 'noble Earl' was too magnanimous to take offence at this unconventional prelude. When Moody returned to England in the 1870s Shaftesbury often went to hear him preach. Moody was exceptionally quick-witted. He had a marvellous ability to turn the most common statements into humour. When he met Gladstone in London, Gladstone looked at him and said, 'I wish I had your shoulders.' Moody replied, 'I wish I had your head on them!'

However he was more than a mere humourist. He also saw the serious side of life and death. Eternal realities were of the greatest importance to him. They had such an effect on him that they sobered him, especially when he remembered the lost. The famed Congregational minister, Dr Dale of Birmingham, said of him, 'He could never speak of a lost soul without tears in his eyes.' In his preaching he always aimed at an immediate response. To delay trusting in Jesus was to endanger the soul.

In his earlier preaching, he had never pressed for decisions but left people to consider what he had said. After the great Chicago fire in 1871, his position altered. It appears this was more the result of circumstance and of what he experienced than the result of any theological study on his part. At the time he was preaching a series on Bible characters in Chicago. When he came to the life of Christ he felt that the only way he could do justice to the theme was by devoting six Sundays to it. After preaching his fifth sermon on 'What then shall I do with Jesus which is called Christ?' he told them they would come to Calvary next Sunday and then they could make up their minds. 'What a mistake, what a mistake!' he often cried afterwards. 'I have never dared to give an audience a week to think of their salvation since.' The fire, when it began, spread so rapidly through Chicago that many of that evening's congregation died in it. Moody always regretted what he had done and determined never again to allow a congregation to leave without pressing for an immediate decision.

In many of his campaigns Moody witnessed true revival. His first experience of it came in 1857, when revival spread across America and into Ireland, Wales, Scotland and certain parts of England. At the time he was involved in the wonderful prayer sessions held in Chicago. His campaigns were remarkable for the crowds they attracted and the many conversions.

One of the most extraordinary meetings he ever held was in London in 1872. He was asked to preach by a minister who had met him at a prayer meeting. After the morning service he felt it had been a complete waste of time. Needless to say, he was not looking forward to the evening service. What happened in the evening was a complete reversal of the morning. A strange hush came over the congregation. Suddenly they became aware that God was there. When Moody asked for those who wished to become Christians to stand for prayer, it seemed as if the whole congregation rose to its feet. At first he thought they had misunderstood him. He then told those who wanted to become Christians to go into the inquiry room. To his surprise the room was packed and within ten days four hundred people were added to the church.

What had caused this dramatic event? Moody later found out that there were two sisters in the church, one of whom was bedridden. She felt that because of her condition the only thing she could do for the church was to pray. So she prayed day and night for God's blessing to come. When she read about Moody she prayed that God would send him to revive her dying church. After that morning's service her sister came home and asked her, 'Who do you think preached this morning?' When she heard that it was Moody she knew God had heard her prayer and was about to bless the church.

From the beginning of his Christian life Moody was an innovator. Like his Sunday school work he was always thinking of new ways of reaching the unconverted. Preaching remained central but his approach to different situations changed according to particular needs. He employed soloists, duets, quartets and choirs. He asked people to stand up and own Christ, come to the front or go to the inquiry room. He would put Christians in a kind of witness box and interrogate them. Whatever he thought was legitimate, he used.

His sermons were characterized by brevity. As far as he was concerned, tedium was the unforgivable sin of preachers. To send a congregation off to sleep through sheer boredom was inexcusable. If he saw anyone dropping off to sleep, he would ask for the windows to be opened. He knew a sleeping congregation could not benefit from his message. His sermons were often full of illustrations to maintain his congregation's attention. He never aimed to impress in his preaching. He always considered himself more of a speaker than a preacher, and because of this some felt he lowered the tone of the pulpit by his simple style. But he sought to gain their ear and if anyone thought he was too common, it never worried him. As long as people heard the message and were converted he remained unrepentant.

He also knew how to get the best out of his helpers. His natural simplicity attracted many supporters. They saw his openness and felt his genuineness. He was never high-minded or acted the part of the orator or philosopher. He was a simple man speaking to simple people in a simple way, and it won him friends. As his workers increased he was like a general directing them. Each helper was given a specific task. After giving a broad outline of what he wanted he left the details for others to sort out. He was expert at marshalling his forces and strategically placing them. Without this, most of his evangelistic campaigns would have failed because their organization was immense.

One of his keenest supporters in Scotland was Andrew Bonar, Robert Murray McCheyne's biographer. He was attracted to Moody because he recognised in him a gospel preacher. When Moody came to Scotland he became instrumental in reviving many of its churches. Bonar wrote of this time:

> There have been not a few awakened of late and the interest is deepening. The ministers of all denominations take part most cordially. Men are coming from great distances to ask the way of life, awakened to this concern by no directly human means, but evidently by the Holy Spirit, who is breathing over the land. It is such a time as we have never had in Scotland before. The same old Gospel as aforetime is preached to all men: Christ who was made sin for us, Christ the substitute, Christ's blood, Christ's righteousness, Christ crucified: the power of God and the wisdom of God unto salvation; but now the gospel is preached 'with the Holy Ghost sent down from heaven,' and amid all this the enemy is restrained. (W.R.Moody, *Life of Dwight L. Moody,* p.178)

Moody's Scottish Campaign in late 1873 and 1874 met with tremendous success. People were reminded of the days of Whitefield and the huge congregations he attracted. Moody soon became the most popular preacher in Scotland since Thomas Chalmers.

His last meeting in Scotland was held in the Botanical Gardens, Glasgow. The crush of people was so dense that Sankey found it difficult to get into the building. By the time Moody arrived it was impossible. Apart from the near seven thousand within there was an estimated number of nearly thirty thousand outside. When he realised the impossibility of the task he stood on the coachman's box and preached for an hour on 'Immediate Salvation'. Afterwards, he told those interested in salvation to go to the inquiry meeting, which was quickly congested. When he asked them to stand if they wanted to be saved, two thousand stood for prayer.

After this triumphant series of campaigns in Britain he returned to the United States and undertook evangelistic campaigns in Brooklyn, Philadelphia and New York, moving on to Chicago, Boston, Baltimore, St Louis, Cleveland and San Fransisco. During his lifetime it has been estimated that he travelled more than a million miles and addressed more than a hundred million people.

Moody could never boast of his meagre education, yet he became a true people's champion. They saw him as an example of what a layman could do without any specific preparation for the ministry. Some were offended at this and maintained the necessity of an educated ministry. However, Moody always regretted his lack of a good education. He considered it vitally important for ministers to be well-taught. He also acknowledged that there were other preachers who were much superior to himself. Even his success remained a mystery to him. 'I know perfectly well', he said, 'that wherever I go and preach, there are many better preachers known and heard than I am; all that I can say about it is that the Lord uses me.'

He was never worried about repeating sermons if they were good. As an itinerant evangelist he used them often, but what concerned him was the frequency with which the press used them. He feared that everyone would have read his sermons in print before they had heard him in person. This meant that they would drastically reduce his stock of sermons.

He never let an opportunity pass without speaking of salvation to the lost. Once on a train, a paper-boy came through the carriages shouting 'Here you are, Ingersoll on Hell! Ingersoll on Hell!' (Ingersoll was an agnostic who had turned his back on Christianity). Moody had a famous sermon on 'Heaven'. He called the boy over and gave him a copy and told him to offer that also. As he carried on through the train he shouted, 'Ingersoll on Hell, Moody on Heaven, Ingersoll on Hell, Moody on Heaven.'

One of his main areas of activity was fund raising. The kind of missions he conducted needed large sums of money to support them. He soon became an adroit beggar. He seemed to know intuitively the best way to make an appeal and was usually successful. His appeals were not confined to his mission work but went far beyond it. He was instrumental in raising funds for other projects such as the first YMCA built in Chicago. This was also true of the second after the first was burnt down in Chicago's great fire.

His fund raising extended both to spiritual and philanthropic causes. During a meeting in Scranton, Pennsylvania, he became concerned for the young people of the town and suggested building a centre for the YMCA at a cost of $75,000. An appeal was made and a meeting held which brought in $25,000. When Moody was told that a very rich old man was absent from the meeting, a man they had hoped would have contributed a large sum, he set off to see him. But the man was as mean as he was rich. When Moody met him he said, 'We need a Moses to lead the way for the young men of Scranton. The Association is out on the street nearly all the time begging for its living, when it ought to be trying to save the ten thousand young men of the city. We want you to give $20,000 to lead the way for the building.' The old man was staggered and did not know quite what to say. When he regained his composure, he said he could not possibly give. Moody pleaded with him again, this time for $10,000, but still without success. Finally, he said, 'You will be at the meeting tonight?' 'Yes,' he replied. 'Well, I want you to take a seat on the platform,' said Moody. As the meeting was about to start, Moody went up to him and asked, 'How much is it – ten, ten?' 'Oh no,' was the reply, 'just the half, just the half.' Moody's tenacity finally paid off.

Moody had such a winsome way about him that few could refuse his appeals. He went to see a very generous man about a worthy cause to which he thought he might like to contribute. After putting his case before him he was turned down on the grounds that he had just given $700,000 to several other causes. He told Moody, 'Why don't you go to those who don't give anything instead of coming to us who give?' Moody replied, 'If you wanted a good pail of milk, would you go to a cow which was milked regularly or to one which was only milked once in a long time?' Shortly after he received a cheque for $5,000 from him. When Moody met William Thaw of Pittsburg he was impressed by his generosity. Because of the need for finance for a new school he went and asked him to help. Thaw told him he had changed his method of giving. He now gave lesser amounts but more frequently. In Moody's case, he said, he would make an exception and offered him $5,000. Moody replied, 'I am a very busy man, Mr Thaw, and I hardly see how I can find the time to come and see you once a month or so to get the other $5,000 in the smaller instalments.' Thaw was so amused by his reply that he gave him the other $5,000.

Moody's appeals for money were never for himself. This is why they rarely met with a refusal. People knew the stature of the man and responded accordingly. If he had wanted, he could have been a very wealthy man. The royalties on his hymn book, *Sacred Songs and Solos*, alone amounted to over $1,250,000 by the time of his death, yet he never received a cent of it. All royalties were dispersed through several administrators to different causes.

Moody was a man of gigantic proportions, a man of faith, zeal, courage and above all, humility. When he died on 22 December 1899, in the midst of his last evangelistic campaign in Kansas City, he left behind a glowing legacy to his work in Northfield. But his greatest attribute was his ability to inspire others. He was so hot himself he inevitably set others ablaze.

30
Aiden Wilson Tozer
(1897-1963)

Tozer, as he is best known, has become famous through his books which have been read and translated into many languages. Their growing popularity reveals something of the appeal of his message as opposed to any interest drawn to himself. Tozer would have hated being anything like a personality cult figure. His aim throughout life was to magnify and exalt God before men. It was God first, second, third and last. God was everything and the sooner man became familiar with him the better.

His last book, *The Knowledge of the Holy,* was a fitting climax to his life. It is a presentation of God in which his attributes are stated and defined. His whole reason for writing it was because he felt the twentieth-century Church had lost its sense of God. He was no longer the transcendent God far above everything else but an utilitarian God to be used, or worse, abused by men. The modern view was to see God as a kind of giant pharmacist to whom you hand in your spiritual prescription. The idea of man being overawed by God had become alien. In Tozer's preface he states that his intention is to bring Christians back to a true worship of God, a spiritual worship, which is the natural result of knowing what God is like. It is impossible for man to worship God effectively if his true character is unknown. God must be known and appreciated for who he is before the heart bows in adoration before him.

> We have lost our spirit of worship and our ability to withdraw inwardly to meet with God in adoring silence. Modern Christianity is simply not producing the kind of Christian who can appreciate or experience the life in the Spirit. The words, 'Be still, and know that I am God' mean next to nothing to the self-confident, bustling worshipper in this middle period of the twentieth century. *(The Knowledge of the Holy*, p.6)

It was this intense inwardness of worship which was the hallmark of Tozer's ministry. He loved reading 'so-called' Christian Mystics, people who were never content to just paddle on the shore but felt compelled to launch out in search of the deep things of God. These have the tendency to draw a person away from the world of sense and into the inner world of communion with God. It was this intense longing for estrangement from the world that caused Tozer's biographer to describe him as a 'married monk'. He desired to live totally dead to the world but alive to God, even if at times he appeared extreme. 'He owned neither car nor real estate, wanted no bank account, turned his back on ventures that offered financial rewards and sometimes even refused an increase in salary. Wife and children often were deprived of his company as he went off on preaching engagements'. For Tozer everything had to give way to this one, all-consuming passion for God.

A.W.Tozer was born on 21 April 1897, in Newburg, Pennsylvania. He was the third of six children and brought up on a farm, and only received a basic education. He was needed too much on the farm, especially after his brother moved to Akron to work in a rubber factory, to allow him to spend his time at school. His grandfather was an English immigrant who emigrated to America in the mid-nineteenth century. His grandmother was extremely superstitious and kept a dream book which she consulted every morning to know what her dreams meant. Tozer once said: 'If dreams meant anything, long since I would have been in a padded cell.'

Tozer was a warm and sensitive boy who kept pets. His favourites were a pig and lamb which he had helped to rear. He had adopted these because one was under-nourished and the other was openly rejected by its mother. There was also a mischievous side to him. While out playing with his sister he climbed into a tree and started to sing as he pranced about the branches, 'Is there any room in heaven for a little lad like me?' Suddenly he was startled when a voice from behind the bushes said, 'If there's going to be any room for you in heaven you'll have to mend your ways!'

In 1912 the family moved to Akron to be nearer his brother. Tozer, his father and sister and brother, all began to work in the same rubber factory. When he enrolled for cartoon lessons his wit became only too apparent. But something far more significant happened to him in Akron. For the first time ever he was able to attend church. He started going to the Sunday school though it was not until he was almost eighteen years old that he was converted.

While walking down a street he heard an open-air preacher on a busy corner say, 'If you don't know how to be saved, just call on God, saying, "Lord, be merciful to me a sinner"' He went home that day and in his attic sanctuary he prayed that God would save him. When he came down from the attic he had left the world's side for ever. A new determination took hold of him. He was now set on separating himself from the world and consecrating himself to God. Afterwards he joined Grace Methodist Church but found it unbearable because of their opposition to his street and lay preaching. Unprepared to give way to their pressure to desist he took his membership to Locust Street Church where the spiritual climate was far more conducive to his spiritual progress.

Tozer was also somewhat unorthodox in his approach to prayer groups. He marched in where angels feared to tread. He would arrive on someone's doorstep, ring the bell and request a prayer meeting. Perhaps the sudden surge of new life and enthusiasm manifested in him was more than most could cope with. Because of his unusual behaviour it is not surprising that some lost sympathy with his preaching endeavours.

However, like many before him, Tozer's conversion awoke his intellectual faculty. Prior to this it had been almost dormant. Stirred by the Holy Spirit his mind opened to a completely new perspective. He now had a thirst for knowledge hitherto unknown. One of his greatest aids in realising his new desire was his mother-in-law. Tozer had married Ada Pfautz whose mother had prayed that God would give her a godly son-in-law. When Tozer appeared on the scene she encouraged him to read much and gave him several books on loan.

Not long after his marriage Tozer was called up. He joined the army towards the end of the First World War. When he returned to civilian life he resumed his church work. In February 1919 he was appointed pastor of the Alliance Church in Nutter Fort, West Virginia. Although he had no college training it was obvious to all that God's hand was upon him. His gifts testified to his calling and the need of a formal preparation in his case seemed pointless. This appointment was no rash or hasty decision by the church. His ordination was postponed until 18 August 1920, a year and a half after his induction. This may have been due to a trial period he underwent. Whatever the reason for the delay his ministry was immediately appreciated.

His ordination was the most serious thing that ever happened to him. After the official recognition in the church he went aside to pray. Alone, in the solitude of God, he prayed:

> Lord Jesus, I come to Thee for spiritual preparation. Lay Thy hand upon me. Anoint me with the oil of the New Testament prophet. Forbid that I should become a religious scribe and thus lose my prophetic calling. Save me from the curse that lies dark across the face of the modern clergy, the curse of compromise, of imitation, of professionalism. Save me from the error of judging a church by its size, its popularity or the amount of its yearly offering. Help me to remember that I am a prophet; not a promoter, not a religious manager – but a prophet. Let me never become a slave to crowds. Heal my soul of carnal ambitions and deliver me from the itch of publicity. Save me from bondage to things. Let me not waste my days puttering around the house. Lay Thy terror upon me, O God, and drive me to the place of prayer where I may wrestle with principalities and powers and the rulers of the darkness of this world. Deliver me from overeating and late sleeping. Teach me self-discipline that I may be a good soldier of Jesus Christ. (David J. Fant Jr, *A.W.Tozer: A Twentieth-Century Prophet,* p.18)

The idea of a New Testament prophet was one which remained with Tozer throughout life. He often used to describe himself as a 'minor prophet'. But his idea of a prophet is far removed from that in current vogue. Its emphasis lay not in inspiration but illumination. God has nothing more to reveal. Everything he wants us to know has already been given in the Bible, his full and final revelation. No additional revelation, whether of a primary or secondary nature, was considered necessary. For Tozer the modern prophet possesses insight not foresight.

It was this feature in his ministry that made his preaching so relevant. He addressed the problems of today with a pertinence almost unparalleled by any other American preacher. He addressed the immediate decline and low spiritual attainments of the twentieth-century Church. He was like a voice crying in the wilderness for the Church to return to its Creator God.

The first few years of his ministry saw him go through several short pastorates in rapid succession. It was not until 1928 that he began his long and famous ministry in Southside Alliance Church, Chicago. He continued there almost to the end of his life. In 1959 he resigned and moved to Toronto, Canada.

Geographically, his position in Southside could not have been more favourable. With the Moody Bible Institute so near he had plenty of opportunity of speaking to the students. He considered it a great privilege to be able to influence a rising generation of godly young people. One of his main delights was in preaching at Young People's Conventions. He often travelled throughout the country to address them. His popularity and attraction to young people can be seen by an incident which happened in Chicago. A preaching service was arranged for 6:30 a.m. where well over six hundred youngsters turned up. These had come specifically to hear him preach. He had nothing else to offer them but the Word of God.

By some people's standard Tozer was no pastor. He had no time for ordinary chit-chat. Others were appointed in the church as counsellors and visitors so that he could confine himself to preaching. A story is told, which may have been fabricated by one of his more jovial members, about the pastor's reluctance to visit people. An elder of the church was sick and Tozer, who just happened to be in the neighbourhood, decided to visit him. When he saw Tozer at the door he said, 'Dear Lord! I'm not that sick, am I?' Probably the story is not true, but it does illustrate the infrequency of his visits.

In 1941 a new church was built to house the growing congregation in Southside. This became Tozer's pride and joy. Everything was new. The whole fabric of the building was designed to meet their immediate circumstances. After its dedication he went around the building praying and consecrating every part to the Lord. To him it was the Lord's house, erected for his worship and intended for his glory.

One of the blights of our modern day evangelical ministry is incessant committee meetings. Tozer refused all overtures to get him involved in any committee. His only exception was a seat on the Board of Managers of the Christian and Missionary Alliance. This was due primarily to his concern and high regard for missionary work. He believed that a church which was not missionary-minded

300

was destined to failure. He often praised and applauded missionaries as the frontier troopers of God's mighty army. They carried his banner, fought the good fight and led the field of all Christian advancement. His stint on the Board lasted from 1941 to 1950. When they intimated their intention of making him President, he resigned.

In 1950 two significant things happened. He was awarded an honorary doctorate by Wheaton College, thus becoming Dr Tozer. However, more important to him was his appointment as editor of *The Alliance Weekly*, a Christian magazine, which helped him to develop his literary style. His articles were always topical and current. He wanted to deal with living issues. These were often a broadside on modern tendencies within the Church and were as relevant as his preaching. They also challenged the shallow thinking of today's Christianity. To him much of what went under the banner of evangelicalism was nothing more than opportunism. In an effort to gain adherents the standard of godliness was permitted to deteriorate. The main aim of some preachers was to create a following for themselves and not to produce followers of Jesus. The age of the personality cult was dawning. To Tozer preachers are not entertainers but heaven-sent messengers. He wrote:

> I have done everything I can to keep 'performers' out of my pulpit. We do not think we are called to recognize 'performers'. We are confident that our Lord never meant for the Christian church to provide a kind of religious stage where performers proudly take their bows, seeking human recognition for themselves. *(Tragedy in the Church, p.11)*

When men begin to rob God of his glory and take it to themselves the Church comes dangerously close to extinction. It is then no longer the world that is trying to destroy her, but herself. Tragically she sometimes sows the seeds of self-destruction within herself.

> In this day, when shimmering personalities carry on the Lord's work after the methods of the entertainment world, it is refreshing to associate with the sincere, humble man who keeps his own personality out of sight and places the emphasis upon the inworking of God. It is my belief that the evangelical movement will continue to drift farther and farther from the New Testament position unless its leadership passes from the modern religious star to the self-effacing saint who asks for no praise and seeks

no place, happy only when the glory is attributed to God and himself forgotten. (David Fant Jr, *A.W.Tozer: A Twentieth-Century Prophet*, p.74)

Tozer's main assault was against the rampant superficiality of Christians which he saw getting more prevalent in the Church. The spiritual giants of former years seemed so far removed from anything and everything around him that it made for a very sad picture. The possibility of regaining what was lost seemed almost impossible, as if the cause had drifted so far from its moorings that it was now irredeemable. Instead of succumbing to despair Tozer came out with all guns blazing. He unmasked its hypocrisy and insincerity. He highlighted its hollowness and sounded its shallowness. It lacked depth as well as moral fibre. These anaemic Christians failed to realise that true faith is not only a belief but a moral dynamic which affects a person's whole life. If there is no moral improvement there can be no real faith.

But what irked Tozer most about the modern Church was its perception (or lack of it) regarding God himself. It had lost the vision of God's majesty and greatness. Tozer realised there was a fundamental flaw in all the Church's reasoning. Christians tended to believe that God was not to be wondered at but worked upon. He was to be manipulated to get what you want out of life. This was the parent of our present day 'health and wealth' teaching, the idea of an utilitarian God. It begins with man and his needs and looks to God to meet them. Instead of glorifying him they want him to gratify them. It is a futile attempt by man to strike a bargain with God – they will render worship to him just so long as he supplies their wants.

The gulf between this and Tozer's view of Christianity was enormous. Their whole aim in life was self-gratification not self-renunciation. They sought to reassert their ego, not destroy it. The idea of a person humbled by his sin was anathama to them. Sermons were patronising and titillating, almost a plea for people to pity God. Tozer saw God's sovereignty despised:

> In this quasi-Christian scheme of things, God has become the Aladdin lamp who does the bidding of everyone that will accept His Son and sign a card. The total obligation of the sinner is discharged when he accepts Christ. After that he has but to come with his basket and receive the

religious equivalent of everything the world offers and enjoy it to the limit . . . This concept of Christianity is in radical error, and because it touches the souls of men it is dangerous, even deadly, error. At bottom it is little more than a weak humanism allied with Christianity . . . Invariably it begins with man and his needs and then looks around for God. True Christianity reveals God as searching for man to deliver him from his ambitions. Always and always God must be first. The gospel in its scriptural context puts the glory of God first and the salvation of man second. (*A Twentieth-Century Prophet*, p.77)

How he deplored sensational preachers and sermons which took the headlines for their topics. He believed that the preacher's message should unfold from the Scriptures. Interpreting providence is often difficult and fraught with danger. But God's voice is heard distinctly in the Bible. Tozer used to tell the story of a young preacher who was advised by his college professor only to preach the Word. After a cyclone had struck his town he preached on 'Why God Sent The Cyclone To Centerville.' Unlike most Sundays the church was packed. Confused by the situation he went to see his professor to ask if he should continue to preach in a more sensational way? The old man replied, 'If you preach the Word you will always have a text; but if you wait for cyclones you won't have enough to go around.'

When Wilber M. Smith accepted a call to Fuller Theological Seminary it left a vacuum in the local radio's Saturday morning broadcast, run by the Moody Bible Institute. They invited Tozer to take his place, which he accepted. The name was changed from 'Chats from a Pastor's Library' to 'Talks from a Pastor's Study.' This half-hour slot became one of the radio's most popular programmes. Many ministers often listened in to hear the Pastor of Southside. They found his messages always helpful, relevant and to the point.

If he agreed with radio broadcasts as a means of evangelism and instruction he was not open to every form of approach. Religious movies he detested. He believed that 'the religious movie was out of harmony with the whole spirit of the Scriptures and contrary to the mood of true godliness; this type of movie has a harmful effect upon everyone associated with it.' Acting he considered was completely out of keeping with Christian experience. How could anyone act their way through conversion, repentance and faith? It was impossible!

However it was his preaching that always remained central. Opportunities came which allowed him to exercise his gifts. Through these his ministry blossomed and flourished. His years of experience and insight only added weight to his addresses. They were the distilled thought of hours of waiting in the presence of God. He loved the gathering of God's people for divine service and collective worship, but he stressed that the programme of service was not as important as the presence of God. To Tozer, this was paramount. 'There were times in Tozer's preaching', wrote his biographer, 'when his hearers felt as if they were standing on the holy mount, witnessing the Saviour transfigured before them and, like Peter, never wanting to leave.'

In his books Tozer continues to speak to our generation. Some men's writings are destined to oblivion. But Tozer's books have a timeless relevance about them. There is a freshness about them which make you think that you are sitting, listening to him preach. His voice cannot be silent as he summons us back to a closer walk with God. One of his friends, Dr William Culbertson, who wrote the introduction to his book, *The Divine Conquest*, said of him: 'The author is a prophet, a man of God; his life as well as his sermons attest that fact. Here he speaks; no, he preaches; no, he thunders the message of God for those of us who are dreadfully poverty-stricken, though we think we are rich and have need of nothing.'

The ageing prophet himself recorded, 'I have found God cordial and generous and in every way easy to live with.' Tozer was an experienced veteran who knew something of the sweetness of God. On Sunday 12 May 1963 Tozer suffered a sudden heart attack. He was rushed to hospital where he lingered on until just after midnight when he left this world to become an inhabitant of another.

31
D. Martyn Lloyd-Jones
(1899-1981)

The Doctor, as he was affectionately known, has influenced the course of Evangelicalism in Britain this century more than any other twentieth century Christian leader. Like the Apostle Paul, he possessed a brilliant mind. It was logical, even clinical, and yet charged with the fire of a true Welsh Calvinistic Methodist. For him, Christianity affected the whole man, his mind, his heart, his life.

Though he lived most of his life in England, the Doctor's heart remained in Wales. He was a Welshman through and through. Early on he showed symptoms of what the Welsh call *hiraeth,* a deep, inexpressible yearning for home. On 20 December 1899 David Martyn Lloyd-Jones was born in Cardiff. He had two brothers, Harold and Vincent. In 1906, the family moved to West Wales, to Llangeitho, the heart of Welsh evangelicalism in the eighteenth century under Daniel Rowland. Here, his father bought the local greengrocer's shop. The only religion he knew was nominal.

His father, Henry Lloyd-Jones, was a keen Liberal who saw the need for social change through education and politics. He preferred the moderate Liberalism of Asquith to the more radical politics of Lloyd George. Untouched by the spiritual powers of almost two hundred years before, Martyn preferred football to religion. Neither was there anything of that enthusiasm for reading which was to characterize his later life. As a boy he lived a carefree life, sheltered from the harsh realities of this world.

This happy state continued until a fire destroyed the family home and shop when Martyn barely escaped with his life. This tragic event materially affected the family's fortunes and his own outlook on life. Life now took on a new form. Suddenly, everything had become serious and study essential. He also began to feel a strong sense of destiny, that he had been spared for some specific purpose.

His father never fully recovered from this disaster and finally went bankrupt. Afterwards, in 1914, as Henry pondered the family's future, the best possibilities seemed to lay in Canada, where he went for a short time. However, things there were just as bad as in the old country, and he was forced to return. With Martyn, and without money, he went to London looking for work, and finally found a small milk round for sale at a reasonable price. He managed to borrow some money and bought the business. After being separated for several months, the family were again reunited and settled in their new home at 7 Regency Street, London. Martyn had to leave Tregaron Grammar School. Now with their prospects improved he found himself resuming his studies at Marylebone Grammar School. Here his academic potential blossomed. If he had been stirred to study by the events of that fire, four years before, its fruit was now beginning to show. Later he went to St Bartholomew's Hospital to train as a medical doctor.

During his time at Bart's, and being so close to the Houses of Parliament in Westminster, he often went to hear the great Welsh orator and politician, Lloyd George. He also attended the Welsh chapel on Charing Cross Road. This meant skirting around Westminster Chapel, where his great London ministry was to be carried out. It was after his future success as a doctor was assured that God began ruffling his feathers. He came to see the futility of wealth and honour: that people could have both and still be very unhappy. He was also made to realize the precarious nature of life when his elder brother Harold died in 1918. It was a tremendous blow.

Apart from these circumstances there was also a growing awareness within of his own sinfulness. Though he maintained the veneer of respectability, he was conscious that deep down he had a major problem, a sinful heart. 'He [God] brought me to see that the real cause of all my troubles and ills, and that of all men, was an evil and fallen nature which hated God and loved sin. My trouble was not only that I did things that were wrong, but that I myself was wrong at the very centre of my being.'

The precise time of his conversion remains uncertain. There was no one major critical event, but there were a whole train of events leading up to it. What is clear is that after experiencing this change of heart his view of life and death dramatically changed.

For the next few years, Lloyd-Jones struggled to decide whether

Dr D. Martyn Lloyd-Jones, aged 32

or not to enter the ministry. It was a major decision and one not to be taken lightly. Humanly speaking, his future in medicine was secure but a nagging conviction haunted him. He felt sure that God wanted him to preach. Some suggested that he should carry on in medicine and preach occasionally as opportunities presented themselves. At first, this compromise seemed to solve the problem. However, as his conviction intensified, it soon became clear that it was an unsatisfactory solution.

One major problem he faced was that of overcoming his strong attachment to medicine. He knew that he could be of very real service to the sick and infirm. Yet he soon came to see that it was far better to heal a man's soul than his body: that man needed to be reconciled with heaven more than being restored back to health.

In 1969, when he delivered a series of lectures to the students at Westminster Theological Seminary in Pennsylvania, he alluded to his call to preach:

> I would say that the only man who is called to preach is the man who cannot do anything else, in the sense that he is not satisfied with anything

307

else. This call to preach is so put upon him, and such pressure comes to bear upon him that he says, 'I can do nothing else, I must preach.'

Or let me put it like this – and I am speaking from personal experience. You are certain of the call when you are unable to keep it back and to resist it. You try your utmost to do so. You say, 'No, I shall go on with what I am doing; I am able to do it and it is a good work.' You do your utmost to push back and to rid yourself of this disturbance in your spirit which comes in these various ways. But you reach the point when you cannot do so any longer. It almost becomes an obsession, and so overwhelming that at the end you say, 'I can do nothing else, I cannot resist any longer.' (D.Martyn Lloyd-Jones, *Preaching and Preachers*, pp.105-06)

With such a strong sense of calling, the young doctor began planning his next move and how best to proceed. As he considered his future he felt it was not to be in England, but in his own beloved Wales. Neither did he see it in a large established church, but in a poor needy area. With this in mind Dr Lloyd-Jones applied to the Forward Movement in Wales for a post. This was the evangelistic arm of the Presbyterian Church of Wales (formerly the Welsh Calvinistic Methodists).

His first invitation to preach in Wales came from a large church in Newport for 11 November 1926, but he felt no inclination to join them. It was too well-established and too prosperous for what he had in mind. Three weeks later he preached in a struggling cause in Bethlehem, Sandfields, Aberavon. It was small and in desperate need. As soon as he saw it he felt it was exactly what he was looking for. After preaching there for the day he asked them if they would have him. This was the start of an amazing ministry for the next eleven years in this little town in South Wales.

His decision to come to Sandfields caused a huge commotion. It was so unusual that the national newspapers were full of it. It was unheard-of for a Harley Street doctor to turn local preacher, to leave such a prestigious position for the backwaters of South Wales. Some viewed it with suspicion, others with curiosity. Some even thought it was a ploy to win the town back to Liberalism from Socialism! However his motive was not social but spiritual. He was more concerned for their spiritual welfare than their material good. Even in the deprived area of Aberavon he had no intention of propagating any social gospel, but longed for the church to return to its former glory, where gospel truth was made vital by the Holy Spirit's power.

Early in 1926 Dr Lloyd-Jones came with his young bride, Bethan, to Sandfields. It was the beginning of a ministry that was to alter a church and have a marked effect further afield in Wales. His preaching was quite different from that of other Welsh preachers. It was devoid of all philosophical allusions or sentimental stories. In one fell swoop he attacked both an arid intellectualism and a weak emotionalism. He believed that Wales needed to be restored to its historic Calvinistic Methodist tradition. He surveyed history to find an antidote to the spiritual decline in Wales. It was clear that Wales needed another great spiritual revival, similar to that witnessed by Rowland and Harris in the eighteenth century.

What surprised people most about Dr Lloyd-Jones's early ministry was its fervour. He was intensely earnest. These early years were to mark him out as an outstanding evangelist. Today, we think of him as the great expository preacher; this was not the case in his early days. He was almost in his mid-thirties before his ministry took on the shape for which it became famous.

Later he was led to examine the apostle Paul's writings more thoroughly after being introduced to B.B. Warfield's ten volume set. Before this he had concentrated more on the Gospels and the Acts of the Apostles than on the Epistles. However after reading Warfield he found himself increasingly attracted to Paul's letters. Though he never lost sight of his evangelistic thrust, which he maintained throughout his ministry, he became more exact in his exegesis. One reporter who went to hear him soon after his arrival in Aberavon wrote:

> Mine was a human failing of curiosity on visiting the Bethlehem Forward Movement Church, Aberavon, last Sunday. Curiosity soon vanished, however. The presence of the young doctor in the pulpit, the tremendous zeal revealed in his preaching, the air of great faith and certainty that he carried, all combined to sweep it away. I remained to wonder and respect . . . My versions of the sermons are but a weak picture of the originals, but I dare to hope that the reader will get a faint conception of the tremendous impetus behind the preacher. (Iain Murray, *The First Forty Years*, p.144)

With a gentle strength, Dr Lloyd-Jones began dismantling much of the church's superstructure. He wanted to restore it to the basics

309

and not be weighed down by trivialities. His ministry consisted of two main things, prayer and preaching. 'No one will ever understand my husband until they realise that he is first of all a man of prayer, and then an evangelist.' As far as he was concerned everything else could go. If he emptied the church of its stage he soon filled it with people. What happened in those first few years was nothing short of a mini-revival. It did not affect the rest of Wales, but all the essential ingredients were there. There was prayer and the felt presence of God. Souls were saved and the church increased in an unprecedented way. There was a new love and warmth among the people. Some of the most ungodly characters were dramatically converted. There were problems, but nothing that could not be overcome. Soon Dr Lloyd-Jones was more than just the talk of the town.

Dr Lloyd-Jones never conformed to the Welsh pattern of preaching. Instead, his whole approach was different. He himself acknowledged:

> I am not and have never been a typical Welsh preacher. I felt that in preaching the first thing that you had to do was to demonstrate to the people that what you were going to do was very relevant and urgently important. The Welsh style of preaching started with a verse and the preacher then told you the connection and analysed the words, but the man of the world did not know what he was talking about and was not interested. I started with the man whom I wanted to listen, the patient. It was a medical approach really – here is a patient, a person in trouble, an ignorant man who has been to quacks, and so I deal with all that in the introduction. I wanted to get the listener and *then* come to my exposition. They started with their exposition and ended with a bit of application. (Iain Murray, *The First Forty Years,* pp 146-47)

As he travelled throughout the Principality preaching, huge congregations gathered to hear him. It was common for the people to tramp to church long before the service began, to secure a seat. While many had to stand, others were turned away. His preaching had an enduring appeal. The people knew there was something special about his ministry.

In 1932 Dr Lloyd-Jones was invited to preach in Toronto. This was a yearly pilgrimage for the better known British preachers, who stood in for their counterparts in Canada during their summer vacations. Though he was the least known of this preaching contingent, he made the greatest impression. Richard Roberts, the pastor of the church where he preached wrote, 'It is no exaggeration to say that Dr Lloyd-Jones has taken the city by storm. On the last two or three Sundays large numbers of people have failed to get into the church. He is pre-eminently an evangelistic preacher with a mighty passion for souls.'

Throughout his time in Sandfields Dr Lloyd-Jones's influence continued to grow. He was invited to preach in America in 1937. The most significant thing to happen to him there was his meeting with Campbell Morgan in Philadelphia. This unexpected event was to culminate in his coming to Westminster Chapel, London. Though almost two years were to pass before this came about, Morgan's decision was virtually made by then.

The following year, 1938, he resigned from Sandfields, much to the distress of the people. They had grown to love and respect him for his preaching ministry, but he was now totally exhausted and in need of a rest. Prior to this he had already turned down an offer of a church in London. No sooner had he announced his resignation that another invitation came. This time, it was from Campbell Morgan, asking him to come and assist him in Westminister Chapel for six months. As his future remained uncertain, Lloyd-Jones accepted the invitation. As far as he was concerned it was only a temporary arrangement. He was, at the time, waiting to hear if he would be offered a post in the Presbyterian College in Bala, North Wales. However, religious politics were soon to sink this idea and so Dr Lloyd-Jones was lost to Wales for ever.

When it became clear that he was not to be offered a position in Bala, he accepted a call to Westminster Chapel, a call which he had strenuously resisted before. This new situation was to open up a world-wide ministry. He attracted people from around the globe. Those who were visiting or studying in London often wended their way to the Chapel. The contrast between the two men's preaching was immediately apparent. Yet, instead of conflicting with each other, their dual ministry complemented one another. There was no internal squabbling about Arminianism and Calvinism. Rather, the two lived in complete harmony.

When the war started in 1939, the huge pre-war congregation was virtually decimated. When the war ended the congregation had to be completely rebuilt. When Campbell Morgan resigned in July 1943, Dr Lloyd-Jones took complete charge of the church, though not without a tussle with some who opposed him. However the relationship between the two men was always warm and cordial. Morgan wrote of Lloyd-Jones, 'I mean to keep on as long as I can and am able. I am greatly comforted and helped by my colleague . . . He is a remarkable preacher and a delightful personality.' Again he wrote, 'I cannot tell you with what pleasure I listen to him . . . It is mighty preaching, most appropriate for these days.'

The following years was to see Dr Lloyd-Jones exert a growing influence within Evangelicalism. Through him several major activities were to be put into operation which would profoundly affect and mould an ever increasing band of evangelical preachers. He was involved in the Inter-Varsity Fellowship. He helped to found the London Bible College and the Evangelical Library. He led the Westminster Fellowship for ministers, who regularly met to discuss points in relation to the ministry. He was connected with the establishment of the Banner of Truth Trust. The annual Puritan Conference (later the Westminster Conference) was created in the Chapel. All this was to give Evangelicalism in general, and Calvinism in particular, a renewed impetus.

Throughout his time in Westminster Chapel, Dr Lloyd-Jones maintained a close link with other evangelical churches throughout Britain. During the early part of the week he often travelled around the country preaching, using this as an opportunity for evangelism. Through this he was able to assess the spiritual climate of the land. Though his workload was immense he continued this itinerant ministry.

Summer vacations were also times of activity, this time in other countries. His ministry in Westminster Chapel had made him an international figure and invitations came from all around the world to speak at various conferences. With the formation of the World Council of Churches in 1948, and its ecumenical emphasis, evangelicals were put under considerable pressure within their denominations to become involved. While the line of demarcation was clearly defined, with the ecumenicals on the one side and the evangelicals on the other, there seemed little chance of them ever co-operating. The gospel's distinctiveness seemed sufficient to keep them apart.

However, time was gradually eroding that distinctiveness and blurring the issues. With his unique understanding of the spiritual climate, Dr Lloyd-Jones sensed a shifting away of some evangelicals from a hard-line conservatism to a more conciliatory position. The main cause of this switch of emphasis he traced to the rise of mass evangelism. The Harringay Campaign of 1954 by Billy Graham had confused the issue. With their policy of allowing non-evangelicals to participate with them in the programme they undermined the distinctive features of the gospel. Here were evangelicals working alongside non-evangelicals, co-operating in an evangelistic campaign intended to further the gospel. If such an action could be accommodated here, why not on a national or even an international level? Why not seek to unite the Church under the minimum theological common denominator, and not even enforced at that?

For Dr Lloyd-Jones, this was impossible. He had for years been in dialogue with ecumenicals, but their discussions had floundered on the fundamentals of the gospel. No doctrinal agreement could be reached, and therefore their continuation had become futile. It was not that he was adverse to dialogue. Rather, he knew that it was impossible for the two sides to amalgamate when the doctrinal foundations were not in place. To him, it was clear: doctrine was the first thing to sort out before there could be any question of unity. The ecumenicals held to a fundamentally different gospel, another gospel, which was no gospel at all. The essence of the argument lay in their different approach to doctrine. 'Here is the great divide', he said, 'the ecumenical people put fellowship before doctrine. We, as evangelicals, put doctrine before fellowship.' To him, fellowship on any grounds other than doctrine was a sham. The whole basis of our fellowship stems from our doctrine, what we believe.

This critical situation was fast developing into a head-on collision. Some evangelicals were now openly co-operating with non-evangelicals in their denominations. The seriousness of the situation could not be overlooked.

In October 1966, Dr Lloyd-Jones issued a call for evangelicals to leave their mixed denominations and unite together as evangelicals. Not as another denomination but in inter-church activities. A conference arranged under the auspices of the Evangelical Alliance was to be held on 18 October, where Dr Lloyd-Jones was asked to state his views publicly in an opening address. It was an impassioned plea.

I am a believer in ecumenicity, evangelical ecumenicity . . . My dear friends, we are living in tremendous times. We are living in one of the great turning points in history. I have said already, and I say it again; there has been nothing like this since the sixteenth century. It is a day of glorious opportunity, unexampled opportunity, if only we could see it, and rise up and take it. We may be small in numbers, and that seems to deter some people. Since when has the doctrine of the remnant been forgotten among evangelicals? It is one of the most glorious doctrines in the whole of the Bible. As a well known American put it last century, 'One with God is a majority.' Evangelicals are not interested in numbers. We are interested in truth, and in the living God. If God be for us, who can be against us? Go home and read the story of Gideon again . . . We shall need great grace. We shall need to be filled with the Spirit. We shall all need to be humble. Who knows but that the ecumenical movement may be something for which, in years to come, we shall thank God, because it made us face our problems on the Church level, instead of on the level of movements, and really brought us together as a fellowship or an association of evangelical churches. May God speed the day. (Iain Murray, *D. Martyn Lloyd-Jones: The Fight of Faith 1939-1981,* pp.524-25)

For Dr Lloyd-Jones there was no turning back. Though it drove a huge wedge between those wanting to fish within and those prepared to opt out, the point had to be made. The Church issue now became the central issue. There was no question of schism. For how can you divide with those in a denomination who were not real Christians anyway? It was only with truly evangelical Christians that schism could take place. To bring oneself alongside evangelicals while breaking with a defective denomination could not be considered schism. Instead, it was adhering to the biblical concept of Christ's mystical body (those who have been born again and attached to Christ through the indwelling of the Holy Spirit and hold to the distinctive doctrines of the gospel).

Soon after this historic event, Dr Lloyd-Jones was to retire from Westminster Chapel. Though his congregation supported him wholeheartedly in his stand and joined the Fellowship of Independent Evangelical Churches, he was no longer a young man. On 7 March 1968 he was admitted to hospital to undergo major surgery for an obstruction in the colon, brought about by cancer. After recuperating for several months, Dr Lloyd-Jones made up his mind to retire. It was now forty-one years since he had entered the ministry, thirty of which had been spent in Westminster Chapel.

In a sense it was the end of an era and yet it was the dawning of another. For years publishers had pleaded with him for material, but his time was too restricted to allow him the freedom to devote to manuscripts and editing. He had kept himself strictly to preaching, and writing was of secondary importance to him. After his retirement volume upon volume have poured off the presses, and there seems to be very little let up in the demand for his printed sermons and lectures. His doctrinal and practical sermons came out in his books on Romans and Ephesians. His diagnostic ability is apparent in his *Spiritual Depression*. While his lectures to the students at Westminster Theological Seminary, published in *Preaching and Preachers*, will continue to be a standard work for all would-be preachers.

For those who heard him and now read his sermons, his distinctive voice still resounds in their ears. It is as if he is standing there, with all the gravity of an Old Testament prophet, beckoning to saint and sinner alike to trust in God and in the glorious gospel of his Son. His ministry was not ended but expanded in those latter years of his life.

He was also convinced of the need for a new Bible College to train men called to the ministry. This was to culminate in the establishing of the London Theological Seminary, which opened on 6 October 1977.

In 1979 he was again taken ill. He resumed preaching in early 1980, but before the end of the year he was forced into permanent retirement. After being treated for cancer with chemotherapy, he knew the end was in view. Towards the end of February he lost his voice through a weakened constitution, but he remained cheerful throughout. 'Don't pray for healing,' he wrote to his family, 'Don't try to hold me back from the glory.' On 1 March 1981, St David's Day, the great Welsh preacher breathed his last.

Perhaps one last personal note can be offered on Dr Lloyd-Jones's preaching, and in many ways on that of all the other great preachers mentioned in this book. Not long after my conversion, Dr Lloyd-Jones was to preach one of his annual sermons in Gorseinon, South Wales, to commemorate the last major Welsh revival in 1904.

When I was asked if I was going to hear him preach, I was surprised, as I thought that all the great preachers were historical figures, not living men, but it was the finest thing I ever heard. If anything gave me an understanding of what is called 'seraphic preaching', it was this. The pulpit seemed to be aglow with an inexpressible aura. The preacher was so animated with his message that there was life in his very words. This was preaching at its very best, and preaching which I can never forget.

INDEX

Companion volume to *Christian Preachers*

Christian Hymn-writers

Fifty Chapters on great Hymn-writers through the ages

First published in 1982 and now in its fourth reprint, this 288 page large paperback by Elsie Houghton has proved to be very popular. It includes biographies of well-known hymn-writers from Martin Luther and earlier to Frank Houghton in this century. It also includes over 60 illustrations and a valuable index.

'So often the life story of the hymn-writer, or some incident from it, finds expression in the form of a hymn that then becomes a means of blessing to many thousands of people . . . Elsie Houghton has put the Christian world in her debt. She has sketched in some of these remarkable details of their lives that can help us to appreciate at a new deeper level words that we have sung and loved for years. To have done so in a manner that always keeps our interest and is so easy to read should guarantee that this book will be welcomed wherever great hymns are appreciated.'

Graham Harrison
Joint Editor of *Christian Hymns*

SOME PRESS COMMENTS

'This book is a gem . . . It will inform the mind and warm the heart' – *Evangelical Times*

'A remarkably complete and useful account of the writers of our hymns' – *Methodist Recorder*

'The best available introduction of its kind to this important aspect of the work of the Christian church . . . Mrs Houghton tells her story with verve and delight, combining anecdote and contemplation . . . This little book has true devotional value' – Dr Bobi Jones in *Book News From Wales*

ABOUT THE AUTHOR

Elsie Houghton, lately deceased, was the wife of the late Mr S. M. Houghton, well-known in Christian circles for his editorial work for the Banner of Truth and as one time editor of the *Bible League Quarterly*. She herself had been Secretary of the Bible League, besides having been engaged in various forms of Christian service until her last declining years in Abingdon.

Evangelical Press of Wales, Bryntirion, Bridgend
Mid Glamorgan, CF31 4DX, UK. Tel: 0656-655886; Fax: 0656-656095